Color as Field

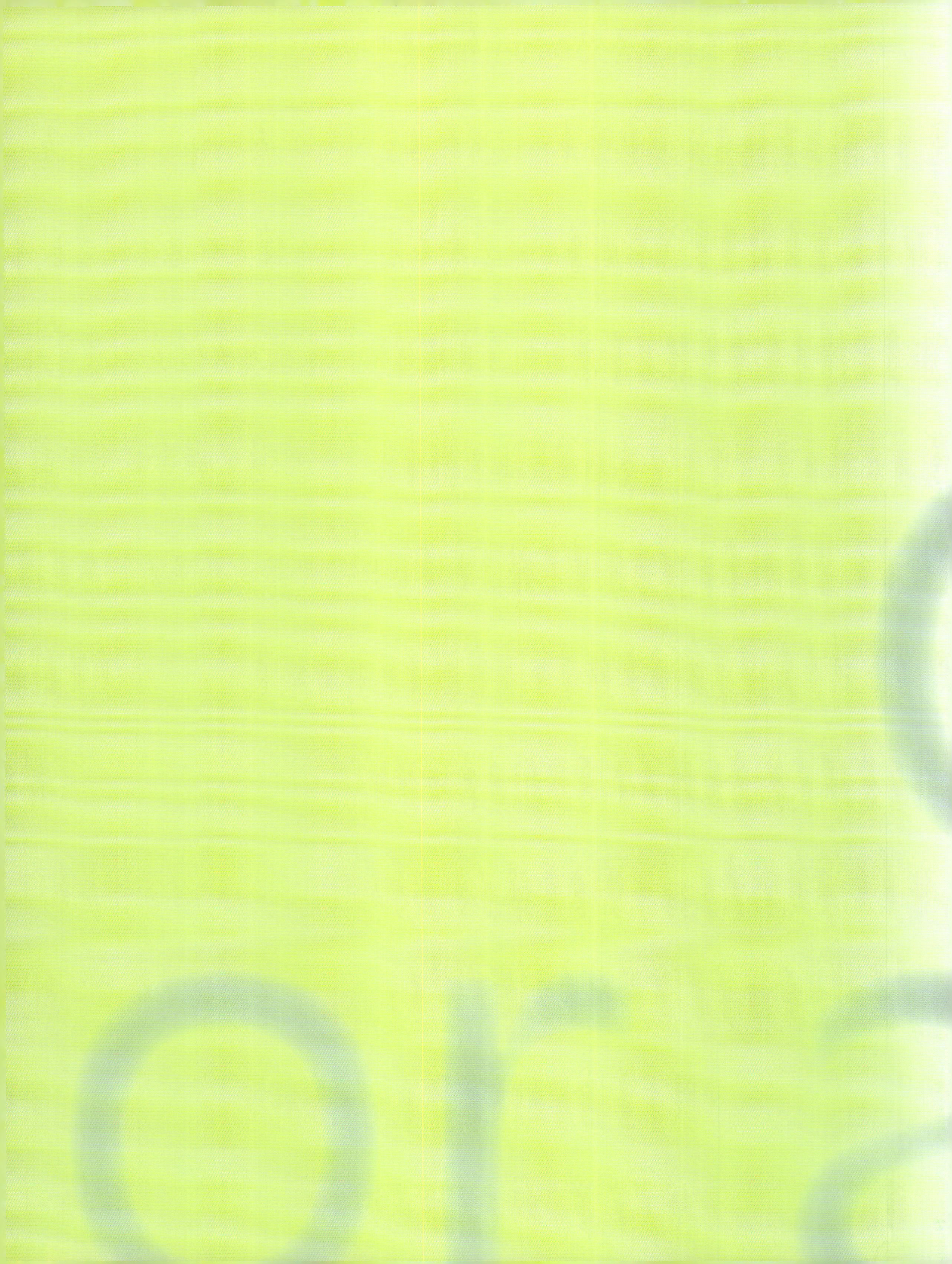

Color as Field
American Painting 1950–1975

Karen Wilkin
With an essay by Carl Belz

American Federation of Arts in association with
Yale University Press, New Haven and London

This catalogue is published in conjunction with *Color as Field: American Painting, 1950–1975*, an exhibition organized by the American Federation of Arts and made possible, in part, by grants from the Henry Luce Foundation and the National Endowment for the Arts as part of American Masterpieces: Three Centuries of Artistic Genius.

The AFA is a nonprofit institution that organizes art exhibitions for presentation in museums around the world, publishes exhibition catalogues, and develops education programs.

Guest Curator: Karen Wilkin
Coordinating Curator: Yvette Y. Lee
Publication Director: Michaelyn Mitchell
Design: Barbara Glauber, Hilary Greenbaum, and Emily Lessard, Heavy Meta
Editor: Stephanie Salomon
Indexer: Laura Ogar

Published in 2007 by the American Federation of Arts in association with Yale University Press, New Haven and London.

American Federation of Arts
305 East 47th Street, 10th Floor
New York, NY 10017
www.afaweb.org

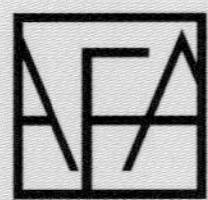

Yale University Press
P.O. Box 209040
302 Temple Street
New Haven, CT 06520-9040
www.yalebooks.com

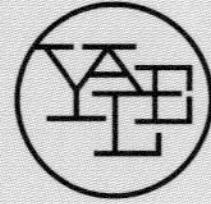

Printed and bound in China

EXHIBITION DATES
Denver Art Museum
November 9, 2007–February 3, 2008

Smithsonian American Art Museum
Washington, D.C.
February 29–May 26, 2008

Frist Center for the Visual Arts
Nashville, Tennessee
June 20–September 21, 2008

LIBRARY OF CONGRESS CATALOGING-IN-PUBLICATION DATA
Wilkin, Karen, 1940–
Color as field : American painting, 1950–1975 / Karen Wilkin ; with an essay by Carl Belz.
p. cm.
Published in conjunction with the exhibition held at the Denver Art Museum Nov. 9, 2007–Feb. 3, 2008, Smithsonian American Art Museum, Washington, D.C., Feb. 29–May 26, 2008, and Frist Center for the Visual Arts, Nashville, Tenn., June 20–Sept. 21, 2008.
Includes bibliographical references and index.
ISBN 978-1-885444-36-3 (pbk. : alk. paper)
ISBN 978-0-300-12023-3 (hardcover : alk. paper)
1. Color-field painting—United States—Exhibitions.
2. Painting, American—20th century—Exhibitions.
I. Belz, Carl. II. Denver Art Museum. III. Smithsonian American Art Museum. IV. Frist Center for the Visual Arts (Nashville, Tenn.) V. American Federation of Arts. VI. Title.

ND212.5.C6W55 2007
759.13'0904507473—dc22

2007021054

Acknowledgments

The great Color Field paintings of the 1950s, '60s, and early '70s display an exquisite beauty and vitality, and the AFA is delighted to be presenting this overdue reassessment of one of the crowning achievements of postwar American abstract art. *Color as Field: American Painting, 1950–1975*, presents a remarkable opportunity to fully comprehend the aims of the core Color Field artists and to experience the visual magnetism of their pictorial handling of expansive space and color.

Thanks go first and foremost to Guest Curator Karen Wilkin for the guiding expertise she has lent this project. We also appreciate the contributions of Carl Belz, who has written a lively and insightful essay, and Hrag Vartanian, who has compiled the artist biographies.

The entire AFA staff has come together to make this exhibition a reality. Yvette Y. Lee, Curator of Exhibitions, skillfully guided every aspect of the exhibition with the assistance of Curatorial Assistant Theo Walther and former Curatorial Assistant Julia Perratore. The publication came together under the leadership of Michaelyn Mitchell, Director of Publications and Design, with assistance from Editorial Assistant Sarah Ingber. Kathleen Flynn, Director of Exhibition Administration, adeptly handled countless organizational issues. Anna Hayes, Head Registrar, and Sirena Maxfield and Dottie Canady, Registrars, worked diligently to coordinate the tour of traveling works, ensuring appropriate installation and care of the art. I would also like to recognize Janet Landay, former Director of Exhibitions and Programs; Suzanne Burke, Director of Education; Geoffrey Glick, Director of External Affairs; and Karen Chen, Grant Writer, as well as Thomas Padon, former Deputy Director of Exhibitions, who was instrumental in developing the project and overseeing it in its early stages.

We are very grateful to Barbara Glauber and Emily Lessard of Heavy Meta for the design of this handsome catalogue and to Stephanie Salomon, who edited the texts. We are delighted to be continuing our partnership with Yale University Press and wish to acknowledge Patricia Fidler, Publisher of art and architecture titles at Yale, in particular, for her support of the project.

We are of course grateful to the lenders, whose generous participation made this project possible.

Special thanks go to the Henry Luce Foundation and the National Endowment for the Arts for their generous support. It is especially exciting that *Color as Field* has been made part of the NEA program American Masterpieces: Three Centuries of Artistic Genius. We are honored to be associated with this nationwide initiative to present America's best creative legacy to a broad public throughout the United States.

Finally, we express our deepest appreciation to the museums presenting the exhibition—the Denver Art Museum, the Smithsonian American Art Museum, and the Frist Center for the Visual Arts—for partnering with us to make *Color as Field* fully accessible to wide audiences in diverse regions.

JULIA BROWN
DIRECTOR
AMERICAN FEDERATION OF ARTS

Acknowledgments

I am grateful to all the lenders to this exhibition for making their valued works available to a wider audience and to Carl Belz for contributing his expertise and insight to this catalogue. Special thanks are due David Mirvish, Diane Vanderlip, Lewis Cabot, and James Yohe for their invaluable advice and good counsel. I am indebted, too, to my colleagues William C. Agee and David Anfam for their grace and friendship.

Many ideas in the essay "Notes on Color Field Painting" were first explored in the catalogue of the 2004 exhibition *Color Field Revisted: Paintings from the Albright-Knox Art Gallery*, at the Haggerty Museum, Marquette University, Milwaukee. I would like to thank the Haggerty Museum for the opportunity to begin consolidating my ideas about the evolution of Color Field painting and the American Federation of Arts for the occasion to develop them further.

KAREN WILKIN

Notes on Color Field Painting

Karen Wilkin

ALMOST A CENTURY AGO, IN *PRINCIPLES OF ART HISTORY*, THE GREAT Swiss art historian Heinrich Wölfflin (1864–1945) distinguished between what he termed "linear" painting—exemplified by the crisply delineated, lucidly organized pictures of Renaissance Florence—and "painterly" painting—embodied by the turbulent, broadly brushed, theatrically lit images of the Baroque. Wölfflin posited, too, a continuing alternation between these extremes throughout the history of art. Just as the painterly extravagances of the Baroque succeeded the linear order of the Renaissance, disciplined, linear Neo-Classicism supplanted the sensual, painterly Baroque, while Neo-Classicism was in turn challenged by the painterly dramas of the Romantic period. And so it went.

Wölfflin's notions can seem prescient. It is not only possible, as an intellectual exercise, but also useful, as a way of negotiating the complexities of art history, to adopt Wölfflin's terms in distinguishing between, say, Analytic Cubism's geometric rigor and Synthetic Cubism's exuberance. Closer to our own day, these categories can provide interesting models for describing both the salient characteristics and the course of American postwar modernist art, from Abstract Expressionism's painterly gestures to the clean-limbed clarity of the work that followed. Clement Greenberg (1909–1994), arguably the most perceptive and articulate critic of mid-twentieth-century American modernism, cited his Swiss predecessor in describing the work of the Abstract Expressionists. In a 1962 article, Greenberg wrote, "If the label 'Abstract Expressionism' means anything, it means painterliness: loose, rapid handling, or the look of it; masses that blotted and fused instead of shapes that stayed distinct; large and conspicuous rhythms; broken color; uneven saturations or densities of paint, exhibited brush, knife, or finger marks—in short, a constellation of qualities like those defined by Wölfflin when he extracted his notion of Malerische from Baroque art."[1] Two years later, in 1964, Greenberg again invoked Wölfflin, this time in a catalogue essay for a seminal museum exhibition, which he helped to curate, celebrating a group of vital, mostly young artists who rejected painterliness—here defined as "the blurred, broken, loose definition of color and contour"[2]—in favor of a new emphasis on what Greenberg called "openness and clarity."[3] In homage to Wölfflin, Greenberg titled the show *Post Painterly Abstraction*.[4]

Greenberg plainly subscribed to Wölfflin's notion of the alternation of styles. In his essay "After Abstract Expressionism," from which the first passage is drawn, he listed the characteristics of 1950s gestural abstraction, not only to describe them but also to underline how this approach differed from the crisp geometric efforts of the American "non-objective" artists of the 1930s and the lean, color-based compositions of the paint-

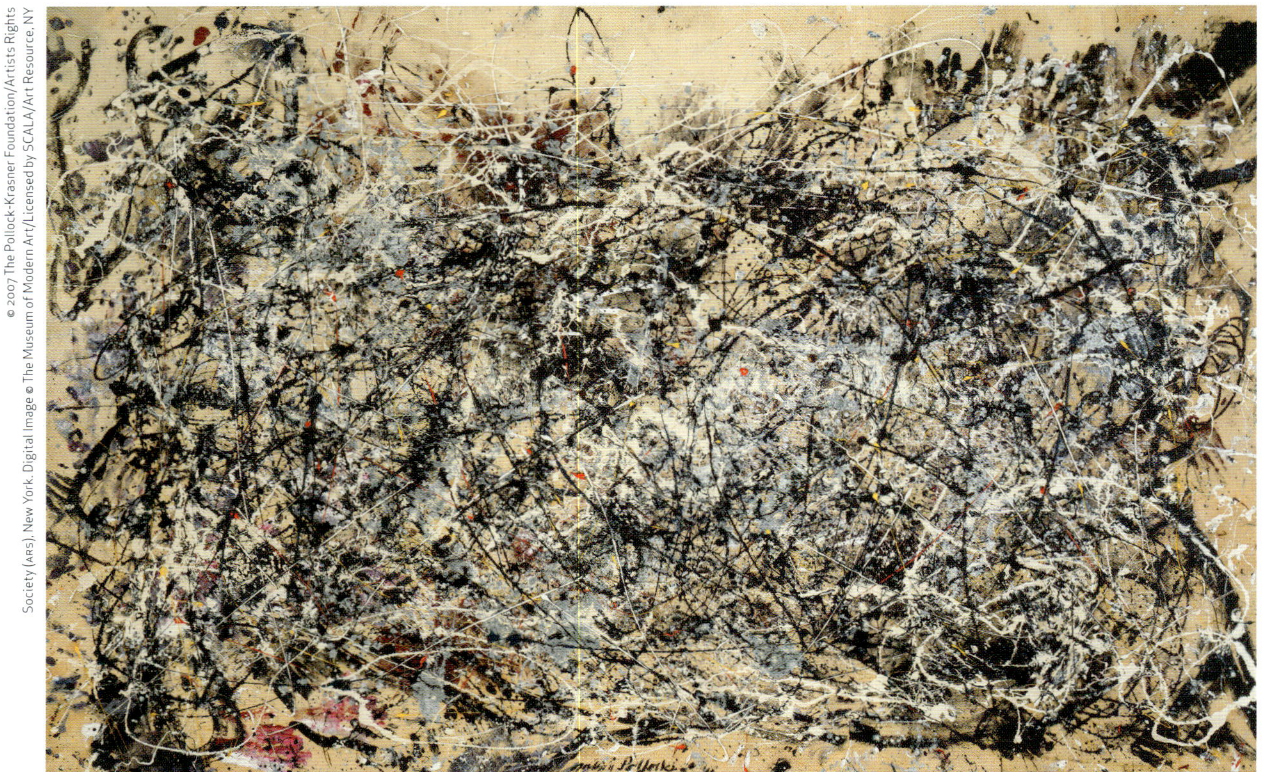

Jackson Pollock, *Number 1A, 1948*, 1948
Oil and enamel on unprimed canvas, 68 x 104 inches. The Museum of Modern Art; purchase (77.1950)

ers who rose to prominence in the 1960s—a tidy sequence that would seem to fit Wolfflin's model precisely. Yet the history of art is messier and more haphazard than most theories allow. (The distinguished art historian Eugene Goossen (1921–1997) used to maintain that he had no interest in movements, "only artists.") Greenberg himself pointed out that even if painterliness were the first thing "the label 'Abstract Expressionism'" brought to mind, "the dividing line between the painterly and the linear is by no means a hard and fast one."[5] Painterly painting was not universal even among the first generation of Abstract Expressionists. If the Malerische (the "painterly") was exemplified by Willem de Kooning's layered, wet-into-wet, gesture paintings, its opposite was embodied, in various ways, by Jackson Pollock's flickering snarls and skeins, Mark Rothko's and Barnett Newman's sheets of uninflected color, Clyfford Still's glaciers of viscous paint, and Robert Motherwell's and Adolph Gottlieb's bold, graphic configurations, to name only a few examples.

The painterly and nonpainterly Abstract Expressionists were united by their shared belief in the necessity of abstractness and their common certainty that the source of art was the unconscious; they shared, too, the conviction that an "authentic" painting was infused with every aspect of its author's personality and that the history of a painting's evolution was an important part of its meaning. But for the painterly Abstract Expressionists, assertive gestures were both declarations of individuality and carriers of emotion; layering was essential to "authenticity" as a visible indication of the painting's previous and future states, and by implication, a sign of the artist's anxiety and the existential instability of the moment. For the anti-Malerische Abstract Expressionists—Rothko and Pollock, for example—overt gesture was largely expendable. A sense of expansiveness and "all-overness" was more crucial than evidence of past and future change. All-overness announced that the painting was a continuous surface of a particular dimension, inscribed with a record of the artist's willed and unwilled intentions; at the same time, all-overness implied that this self-sufficient entity was also a fragment of a larger continuum. For the anti-Malerische artists, expansiveness and all-overness suggested boundlessness and endless possibility. If the layered gestures of painterly abstraction evoked the agonized indecisions of the present moment, openness, clarity, and all-overness were signs of a desire for the infinite, even the eternal.

Yet such distinctions are neither absolute nor exclusive. It is possible, for example, to describe Pollock's pours and drips or Still's repetitive strokes as gestures. (In his later work, in fact, Pollock returned to a rather conventional kind of gesture drawing.) But in nonpainterly abstract painting, such "gestures" were all but subsumed by the expanses of color they cumulatively produced. In painterly abstraction, tonality usually subsumed hue. Dragging sweeps of pigment over underlying layers or overlapping them onto nearby zones created an appearance of spontaneity and endless mutability, but it often muddied or modulated chroma. Such dragging and muddying is conspicuously absent in the pulsing tangles of Pollock's poured paintings, just as it is absent in the thinly painted, economical canvases of Rothko and Newman, and, in different ways, in the work of Still, Motherwell, and Gottlieb. Here, other concerns, perhaps most notably, color relationships, take precedence over the overt semblance of emotional turmoil. It could be argued that the work of these artists, far from demonstrating that painterliness was the defining characteristic of abstract painting in the 1950s and early 1960s, suggested wholly new ideas about what abstract pictures could be.

Rothko's best-known canvases, with their hovering rectangles, appear to be dispassionate and introspective, in contrast to the emotionally unbuttoned work of so many of his fellow Abstract Expressionists. The paintings Rothko made depend not on bravura gestures and roiling accumulations, but on minimally inflected, scrubbed-in sheets of paint. They seem to possess color but not substance, to assert a literal surface and simultaneously establish a kind of ambiguous space. We experience Rothko's floating rectangles, some intense and glowing, others like spent coals, as coherent but disembodied blocks, but we also feel that we can see into them, as if mentally entering zones of, say, redness or blueness whose limits are defined only by the radiance of hue. Rothko's color is neither symbolic nor structural. Instead, it functions as an equivalent for space or atmosphere, for place, emotional temperature, or state of mind, detached from description or identification but freighted with myriad, evocative associations.[6]

Newman's most audacious, drastically simplified canvases announce an even more extreme desire for economy and universality, expressed in terms of minimal divisions and pared-down color relationships. This reduction of painting to its essential nature as pigment on a surface seems to echo Greenberg's much discussed view of the trajectory of modernism as the history of each discipline's jettisoning of what was not integral to its medium.[7] Greenberg frequently pointed out that this formulation was not imposed or preconceived, but rather, deduced from his experience of the art he encountered in his tours of studios and exhibitions—which included Newman's paintings. Newman's mature works, with their flat expanses, especially the assertive vertical Zips, simultaneously speak to the irreducible nature of

CONTINUED ON PAGE 16

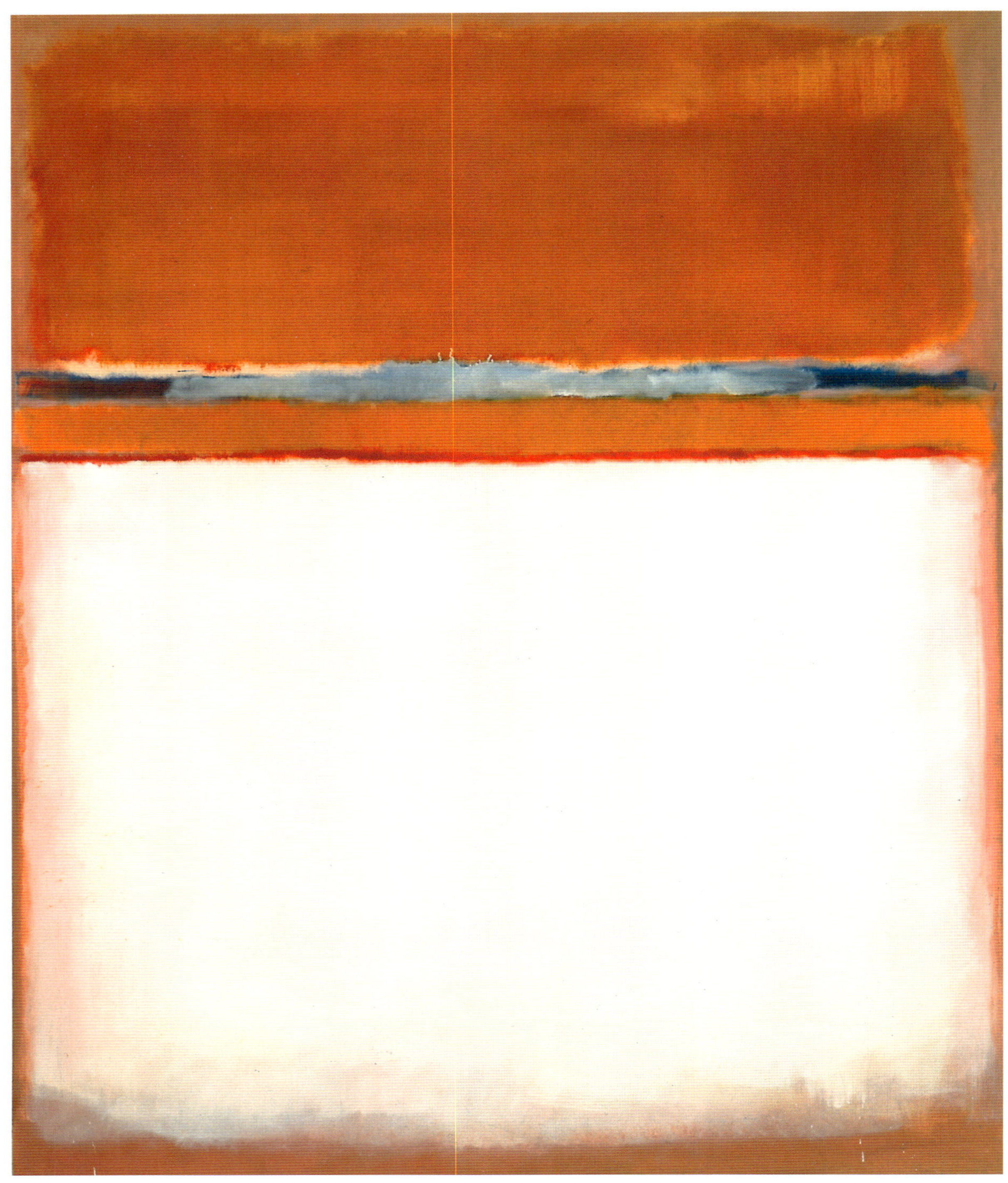

PLATE 1

MARK ROTHKO

Number 18, 1951
Oil on canvas
81 ½ x 69 ⅞ inches
Munson-Williams-Proctor Arts Institute,
Museum of Art, Utica, NY (53.216)

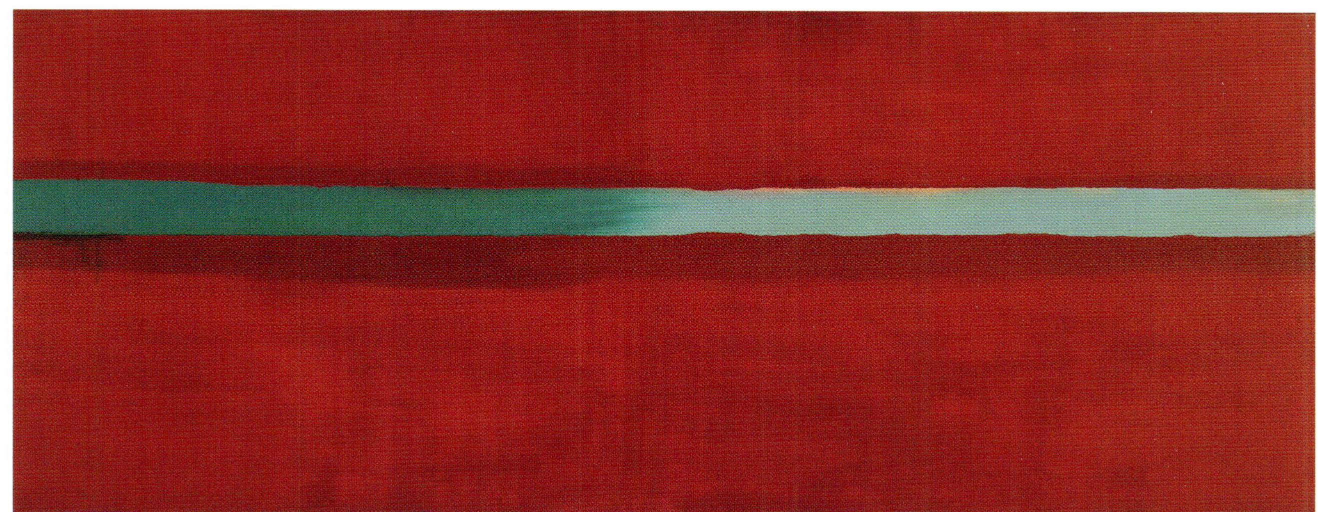

PLATE 2

BARNETT NEWMAN

Horizon Light, 1949
Oil on canvas
30 ½ x 72 ½ inches
Sheldon Memorial Art Gallery, University of Nebraska-Lincoln, UNL; Gift of Mr. and Mrs. Thomas Sills (1974.U-1184)

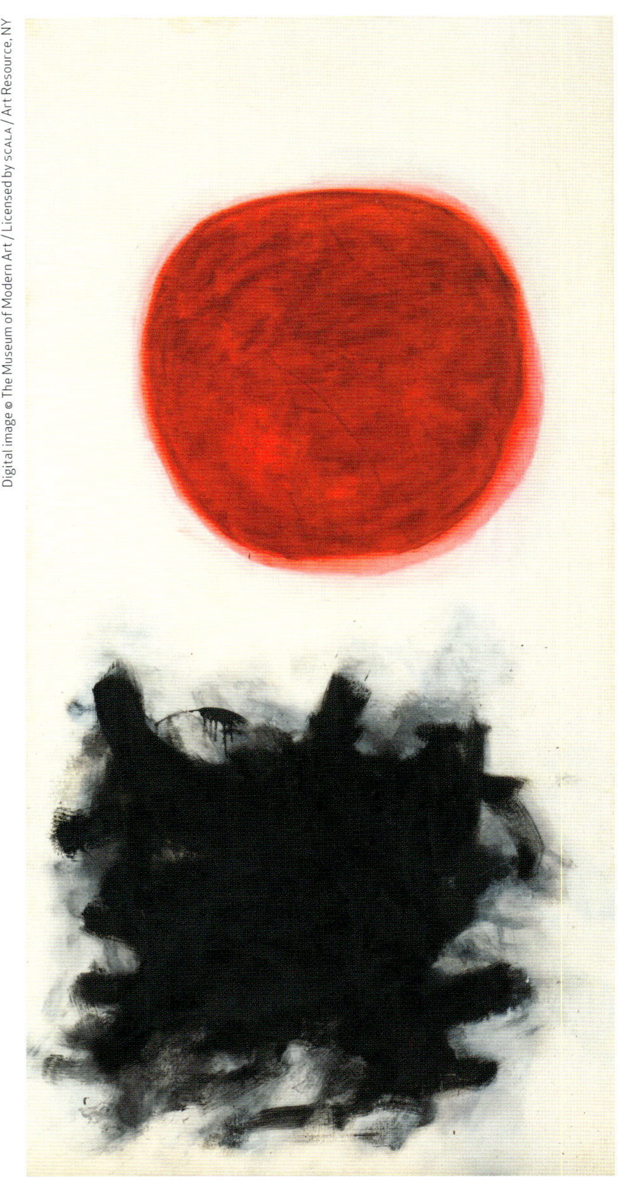

Adolph Gottlieb, *Blast 1*, 1957
Oil on canvas, 7½ feet x 45⅛ inches
The Museum of Modern Art: Phillip Johnson Fund (6.1958)

painting, in Greenbergian terms, and the yearning to invent an image that evokes the infinite with the greatest simplicity of means. Still's confrontational, aggressively physical paintings probably spring from similar motivations, but in them, the sobriety of Newman's canvases has been replaced by undercurrents of brooding romanticism, so much so that Still's largest paintings have often been discussed in relation to the tradition of the American sublime. With their ragged contours and often abrupt contrasts of tone and color, Still's abstractions have frequently been compared to those vast views of spectacular wilderness scenery that mesmerized nineteenth-century audiences. Still's slow, cumulative repetitive strokes, like Pollock's rapid drips and pours, may be read as gestures; yet far from seeming driven by emotion, these deliberate marks appear to celebrate the act of spreading paint as an end in itself. They bear witness to labor expended, to the sheer effort of covering a large surface with small increments of paint.

Gottlieb's and Motherwell's paintings of the 1950s suggest still other possibilities. Both artists were master draftsmen capable of eliciting maximum expression from line, whether disciplined or explosive. Gottlieb's first major series of abstract paintings, the Pictographs of the 1940s, were essentially rows of mysterious drawn "glyphs" arranged on loosely defined grids, enlivened and heightened by unexpected combinations of hues. As the series evolved and Gottlieb became increasingly daring, large areas of thinly brushed color began to dominate, no longer simply as backgrounds for the "glyphs" but rather, as key elements in establishing mood and emotional climate. There are subtle echoes of Joan Miró's eloquent canvases, with their monochrome fields and exquisite floating drawing, but Gottlieb's ambiguous imagery and moody palette are wholly his own.

Hans Hofmann, although a generation older than the artists associated with Abstract Expressionism, nevertheless played an important role in defining their aesthetic aims, through the example of his work and his teaching. Greenberg often spoke of how important hearing Hofmann's lectures was to the formation of his approach to works of art, during his early years as a critic, in the late 1930s. In the 1940s and 1950s, Hofmann was said to be more respected than admired by many of

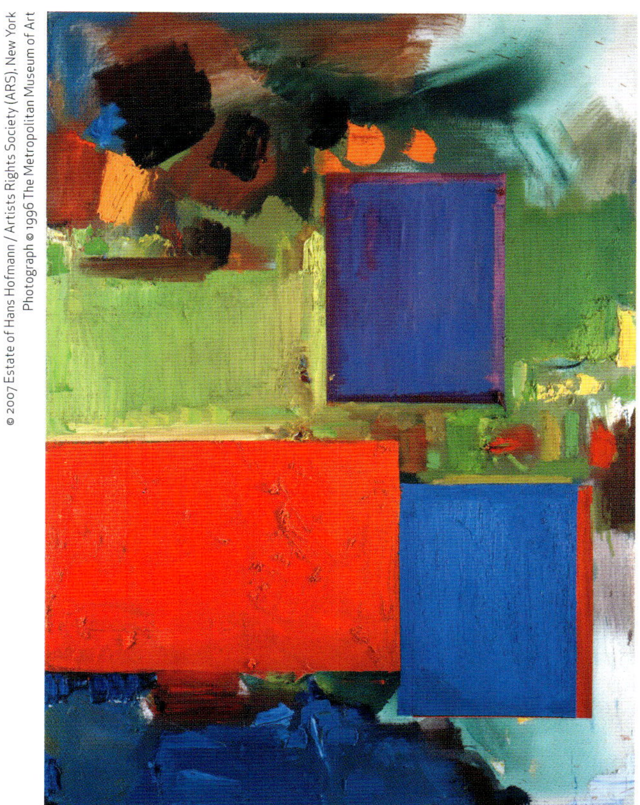

Hans Hofmann, *Rhapsody*, 1965
Oil on canvas, 84¼ x 60½ inches. The Metropolitan Museum of Art; gift of Renate Hofmann, 1975

his fellow painters, but for those who paid attention, his work announced original ways of creating dynamic structure through color and placement. Hofmann's love of richly articulated surfaces, from transparent washes to clots of pigment, may have allied him, on some levels, with the painterly painters, but his clear-headed structures and all-stops-out, mouth-puckering colors were notably at odds with the loose fluctuations and modulated hues of gestural Abstract Expressionism.

The works of these painters dramatically enlarge the meaning of the label "Abstract Expressionism," but through the clarifying lens of hindsight, they also seem to prefigure ideas explored by some of the most inventive American artists of the next generation: the loosely associated, aesthetically and chronologically diverse group who came to be categorized under the rubric "Color Field." These were the painters—among them, Helen Frankenthaler, Morris Louis, Kenneth Noland, and Jules Olitski—whose work was included in the exhibition *Post Painterly Abstraction*. Their art can be read as departing from the possibilities suggested by Rothko's poised rectangles: the primacy of color, frontality, spatial and emotional ambiguity, and a paradoxical "signature" anonymity, with the deployment of surprising hues made to assume the burden of associative meaning. Yet, in many ways, these paintings are more distinguished by their "cool"—in Marshall McLuhan's sense of the word—than by any obvious relation to Abstract Expressionism. Louis's, Noland's, Olitski's, and, to a degree, Frankenthaler's otherwise diverse paintings, with their insubstantial surfaces and deliberately suppressed "handwriting," all appear strikingly reticent, not only physically but also psychologically. As their younger colleague Frank Stella famously remarked, "What you see is what you see."[8]

Stella's frequently quoted assertion did not mean, however, that his work or that of his older peers was empty or devoid of feeling. While scrupulously avoiding anything resembling psychological symbolism, the "post-painterly" conception of "cool" included the belief that a painting, no matter how apparently restrained, could address the viewer's whole being—emotions, intellect, and all—through the eye, just as music did through the ear. (It was assumed that any work of art worthy of the designation was loaded with the artist's baggage, and that viewers would view any work of art through the filter of their own prejudices and associations.) What sets the best Color Field paintings apart is the extraordinary economy of means with which they manage not only to engage our feelings but also to ravish the eye. At times, it can seem as if the artist's goal was to see how stripped-down a

CONTINUED ON PAGE 22

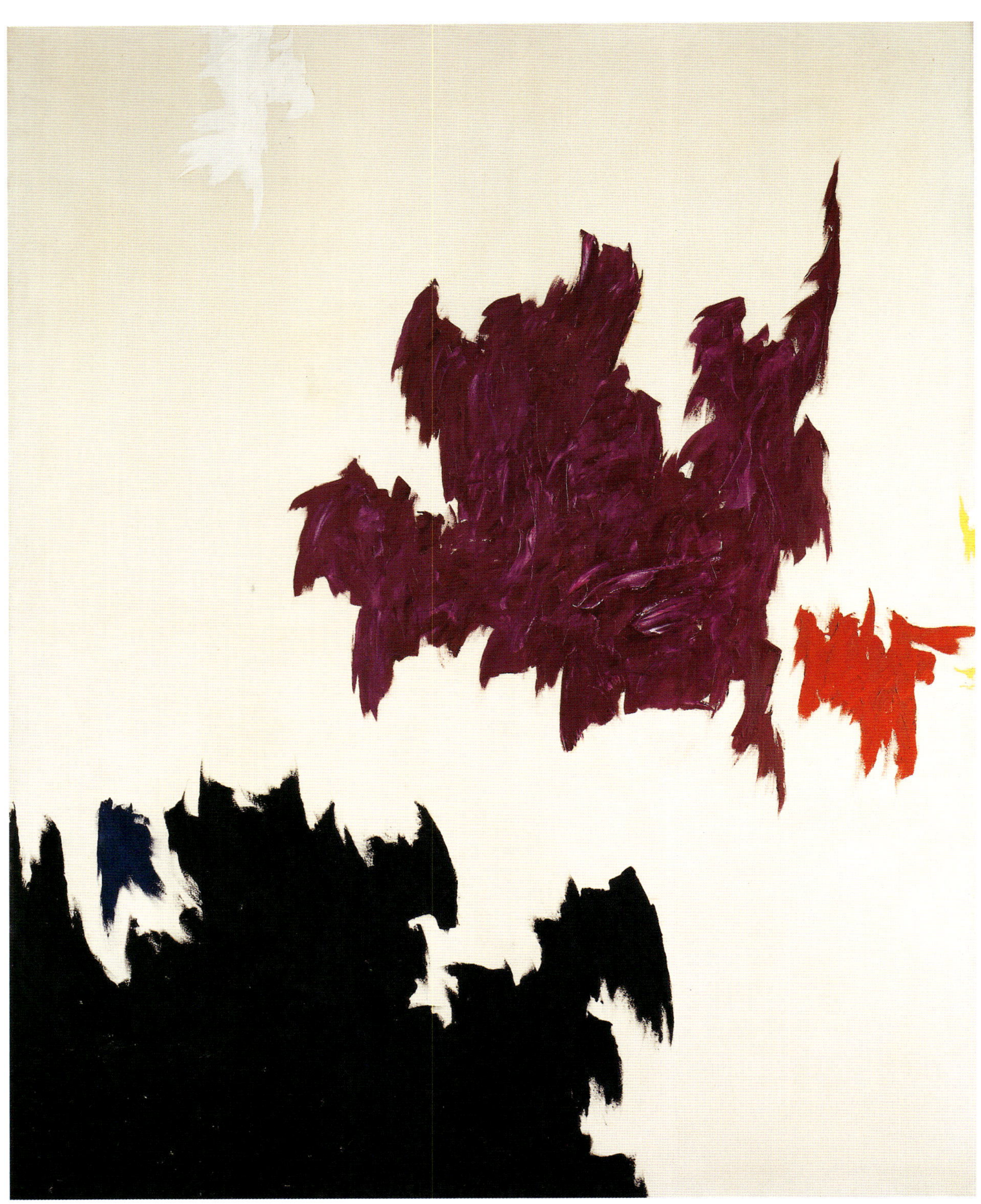

PLATE 3

CLYFFORD STILL

Untitled, 1965
Oil on canvas
111¾ x 89 inches
Private collection, Denver

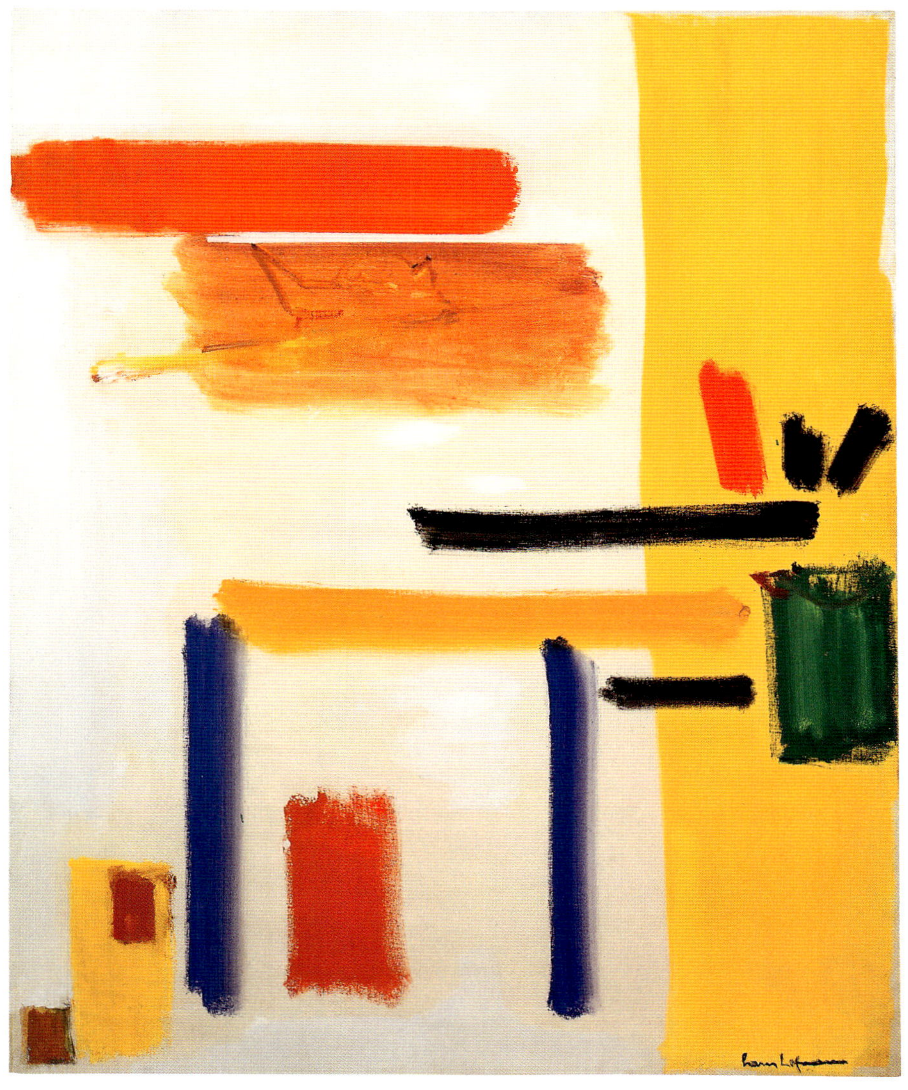

PLATE 4

HANS HOFMANN

Yellow Hymn, 1954
Oil on canvas
50 x 40 inches
The Renate, Hans and Maria Hofmann Trust; courtesy
Ameringer & Yohe Fine Art, New York

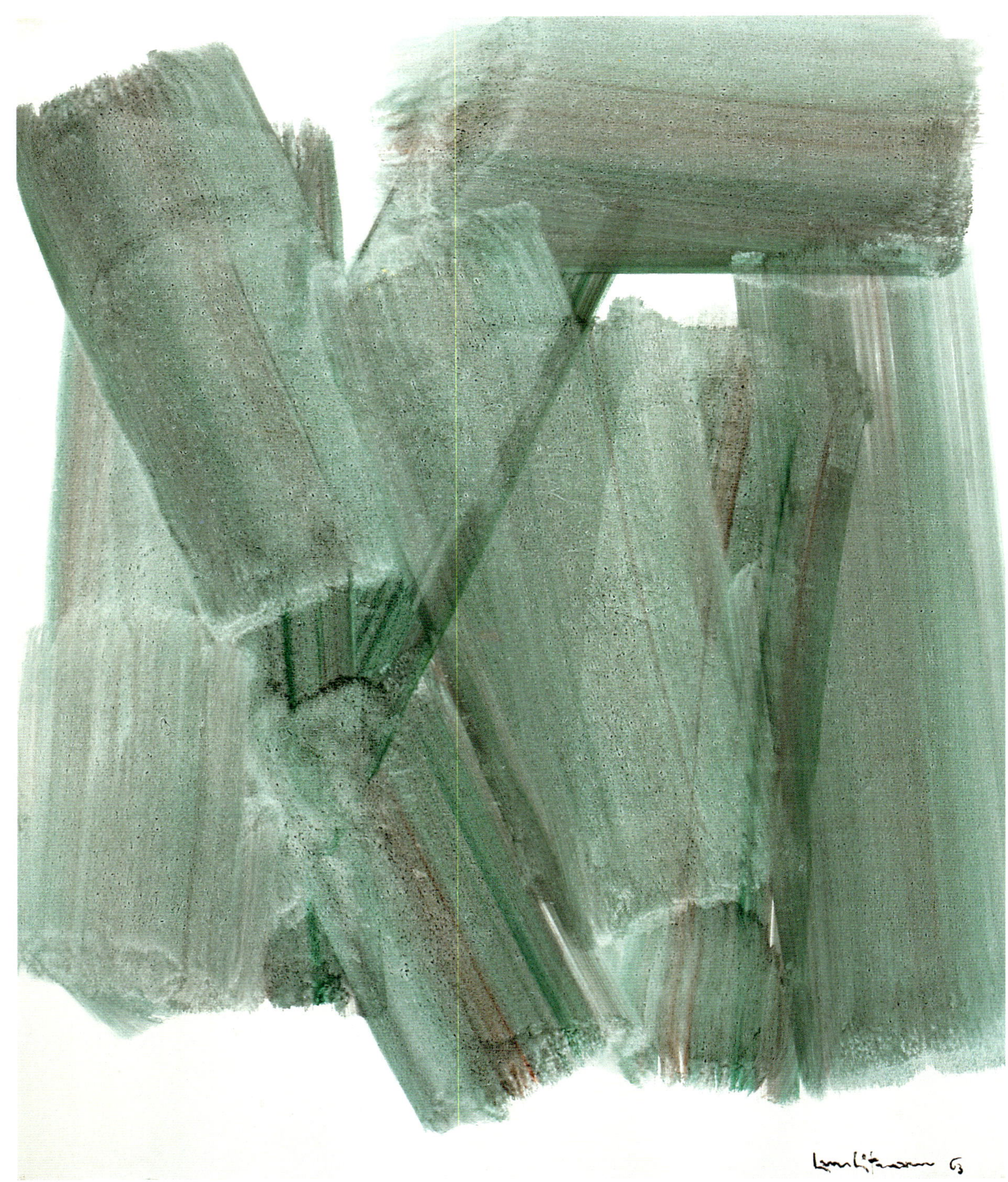

PLATE 5

HANS HOFMANN

Gray Monolith, 1963
Oil on canvas
72 x 60 inches
The Renate, Hans and Maria Hofmann Trust; courtesy
Ameringer & Yohe Fine Art, New York

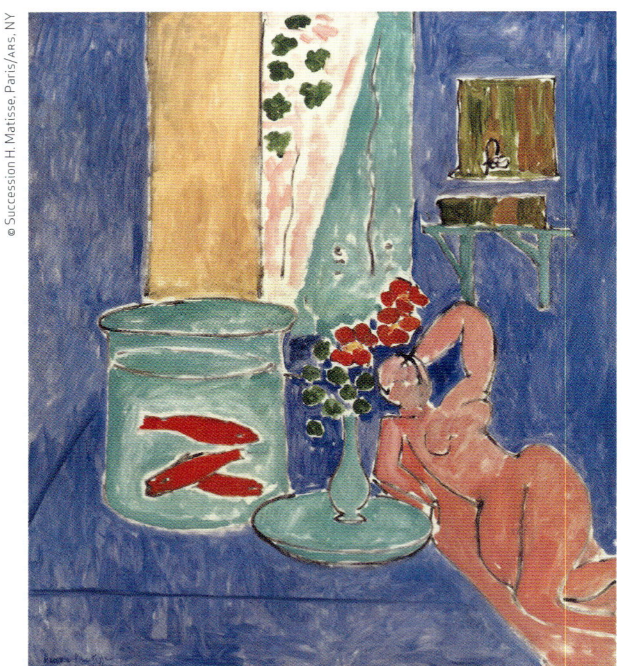

Henri Matisse, *Goldfish and Sculpture*, 1912
Oil on canvas, 46 x 39⅝ inches. The Museum of Modern Art; gift of Mr. and Mrs. John Hay Whitney (199.1955)

picture could be before it ceased to be interesting to look at. Discrete shapes, dynamic imbalances, cursive drawing, and even the most elliptical, implicit suggestions of narrative were all jettisoned, in various combinations and sometimes all at once. The single indispensable element proved to be color—in generous amounts—which, paradoxically, both emphasized the painting's presence as an object and suggested vast, ambiguous spaces that one saw into but could not, even metaphorically, enter. "Size," Greenberg wrote, "guarantees the purity as well as the intensity needed to suggest indeterminate space: more blue simply being bluer than less blue."[9]

This emphasis on color was usually allied with a strenuous avoidance of the materiality so crucial to gestural Abstract Expressionism. Touch could be so reduced that paint application in Color Field abstractions can seem, depending on our sympathies, either inexplicably magical or almost mechanical. Color can appear to have been breathed onto the surface or, when thinned down and soaked into the canvas, to have fused with it, the way dye fuses with fabric. The result is an ineffable, seemingly weightless expanse. Even though essentially all we are left to contemplate are the physical materials of painting (refined as they are), the result is an exquisitely rarefied type of abstraction in which material means are almost completely subservient to the visual. Any lingering vestiges of the painting's long history as depiction disappear, and we are faced with pure, eloquent, wordless seeing.

Again, such observations are subject to qualification. Affinities can be found, for example, between Abstract Expressionist gesture and Frankenthaler's "wristy" (as she calls it) placement of washes whose boundaries create expressive shapes, while, as Michael Fried, one of the most perceptive critics of the Color Field generation, has pointed out, the superimposed floods of Louis's Veils create a kind of gestural, internal drawing, detached from the hand but crucial to the mood and emotional range of the picture. Yet compared to the work of young artists who remained fascinated by gestural abstraction and appeared to make painterliness an end in itself, the transformed traces of the Malerische in Frankenthaler's or Louis's paintings are inconsequential. Some of their contemporaries so zealously imitated de Kooning's wet-into-wet, frayed-off paint handling that what had once been a formal and emotional imperative became, at best, the arbitrary sign of a style, and at worst, a full-blown cliché, a signal of slavish adherence to a set of dogmatic beliefs; Greenberg dismissively called this version of gestural abstraction "the Tenth Street touch."

What the Color Field painters shared most importantly with the Abstract Expressionists was the conviction that the role of art was not to report on the visible, but to reveal the unknown. They shared, too, the belief that paintings that resembled nothing preexisting could have the presence, authority, and associative richness of other real things in the world. Perhaps because of these shared assumptions, close ties existed among some first-generation Abstract Expressionists and the Color Field painters. A number of older artists who had initially provided models for the "post-painterly" abstract painters found themselves on the same path as their younger colleagues, sometimes, it seems, even following their lead. Gottlieb, Motherwell, and Hofmann, in particular, became part of a complex, intergenerational conversation with the young practitioners of post-painterly abstraction.

Beginning in the late 1960s, Motherwell embarked on a series of rigorously pared-down paintings known as Opens, whose drawn images, while far from literal, seemed to derive from his experience of the studio, with its robust easel and stacked canvases. In their restatement of the geometry of the canvas as elegant drawing against a sheet of color, the Opens seem equally indebted to Newman's Zips and to Henri Matisse's 1914 ventures into near-abstraction, but they also appear to be responses to the "cool" abstraction signaled by the work of the younger generation. Since Motherwell and Frankenthaler were married from 1958 to 1971, it is not surprising that there are provocative connections between their paintings of these years, but Motherwell's work also shows evidence of wider cross-fertilization. From the mid-1960s on, Gottlieb, like Motherwell, gave freer rein to his powerful gifts as a colorist, in contrast to the more disciplined palette—often red, black, white, and earth tones—of the signature Bursts that cemented his reputation. As he had in his seminal Pictographs of the 1940s and early 1950s, but without sacrificing the graphic intensity of the Bursts, Gottlieb once again made hue as crucial as placement in determining the emotional key of the picture. Hofmann, who in 1958 at age seventy-eight had finally closed his school to paint

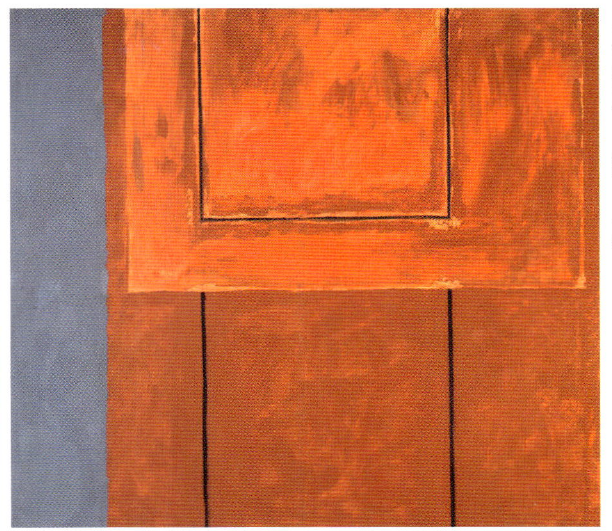

Photo © 2006 Museum Associates/LACMA

Robert Motherwell, *Open #104 (The Brown Easel)*, 1969
Acrylic on canvas, 54 x 60 inches. Los Angeles County Museum of Art; purchased with funds provided by Daisy and Daniel Belin, Alice and Nahum Lainer, Leona Palmer, Marvel and Robert Kirby, Barbara and Buzz McCoy, Sandra and Jacob Terner, Anita and Julius L. Zelman, Patricia and Michael Forman, and Mr. and Mrs. William A. Mingst through the 1995 Collectors Committee and gift of the Dedalus Foundation

full-time, began to produce some of the most exuberant, assured work of his long life, including many of the firmly constructed arrangements of intensely colored "slabs" with which he is most closely associated. Occasionally, though, he explored ideas of all-overness and transparency that appear to have been suggested by the work of younger artists, including Frankenthaler—who had very briefly been his student, at the beginning of her career, and had become a friend and summer neighbor, in the artists' enclave of Provincetown, on Massachusetts' Cape Cod. Frankenthaler describes this implied dialogue across generations, with her characteristic wry humor, as Hofmann's way of saying "OK kids, this is how you do it."

It is worth noting that for the Color Field painters, as for so many of their predecessors throughout the history of Western art, technical developments were inextricably linked with aesthetic ones. Just as the widespread use of oil

CONTINUED ON PAGE 30

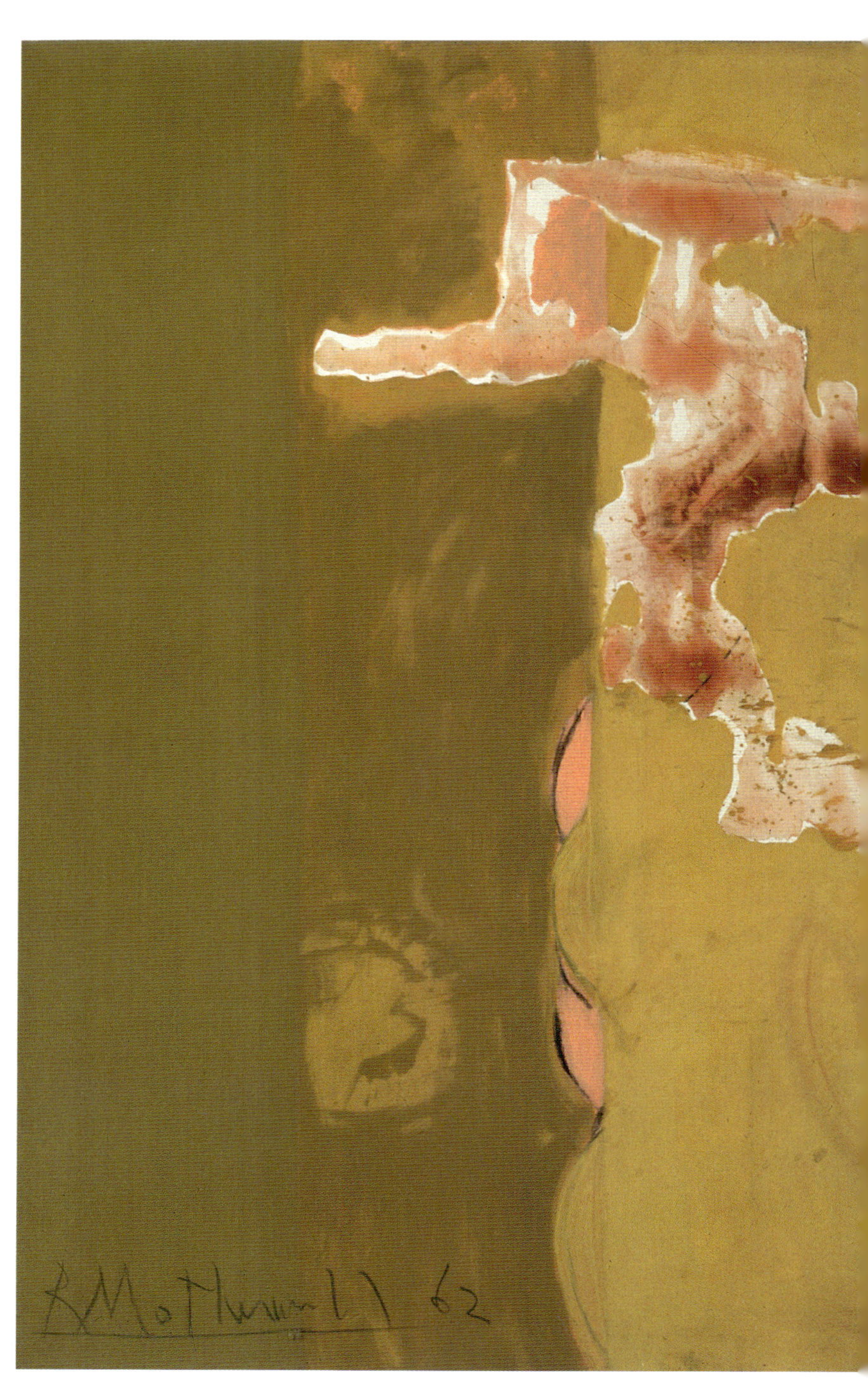

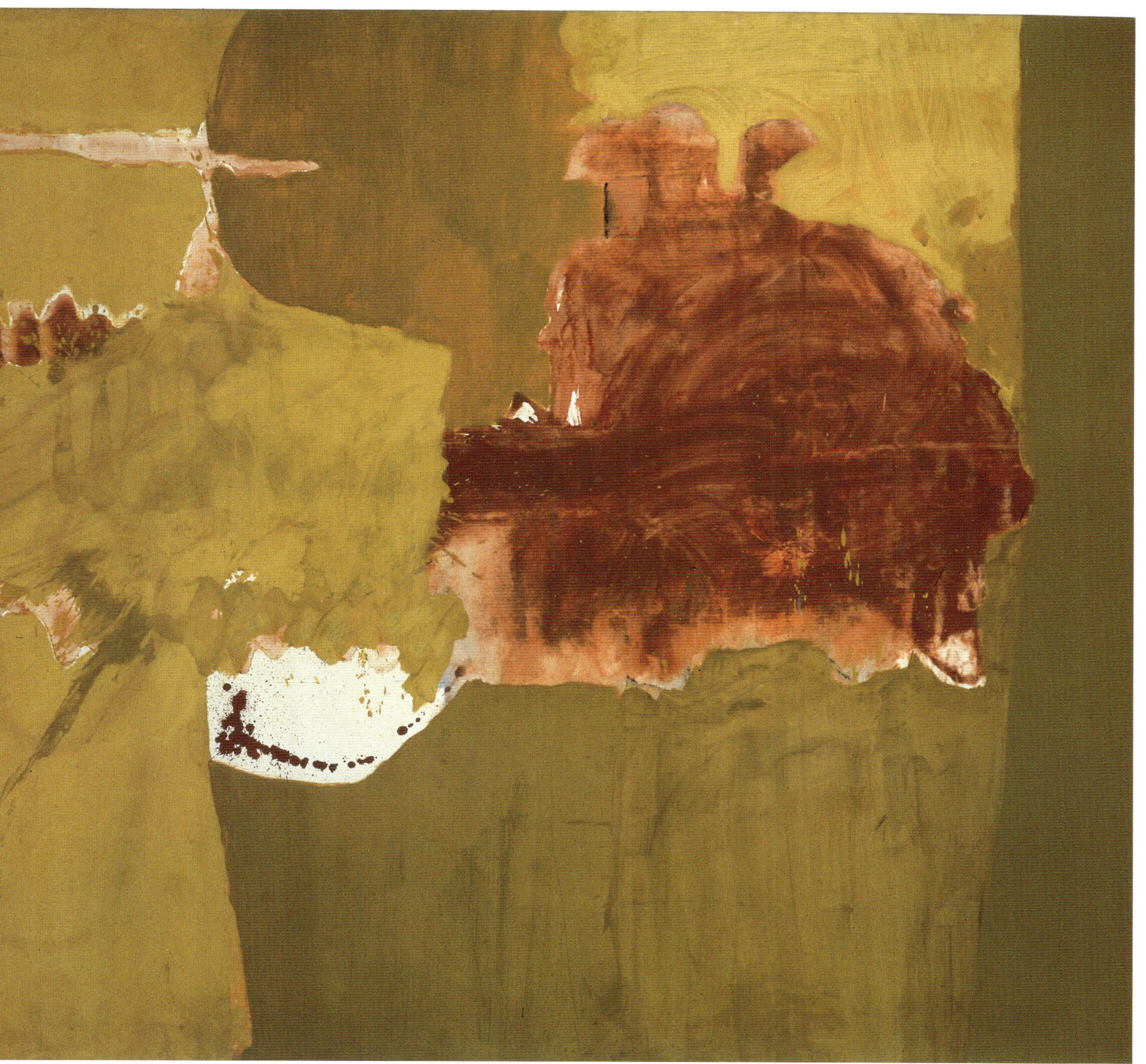

PLATE 6

ROBERT MOTHERWELL

Chi Ama, Crede, 1962
Oil on canvas
82 x 141 inches
The Phillips Collection, Washington, D.C.; purchased by The Phillips Collection through funds donated by The Judith Rothschild Foundation, Mr. and Mrs. Gifford Phillips, The Chisholm Foundation, The Whitehead Foundation, Mr. and Mrs. Laughlin Phillips, Mr. and Mrs. Marc E. Leland, and the Honorable Ann Winkelman Brown and Donald Brown, 1998

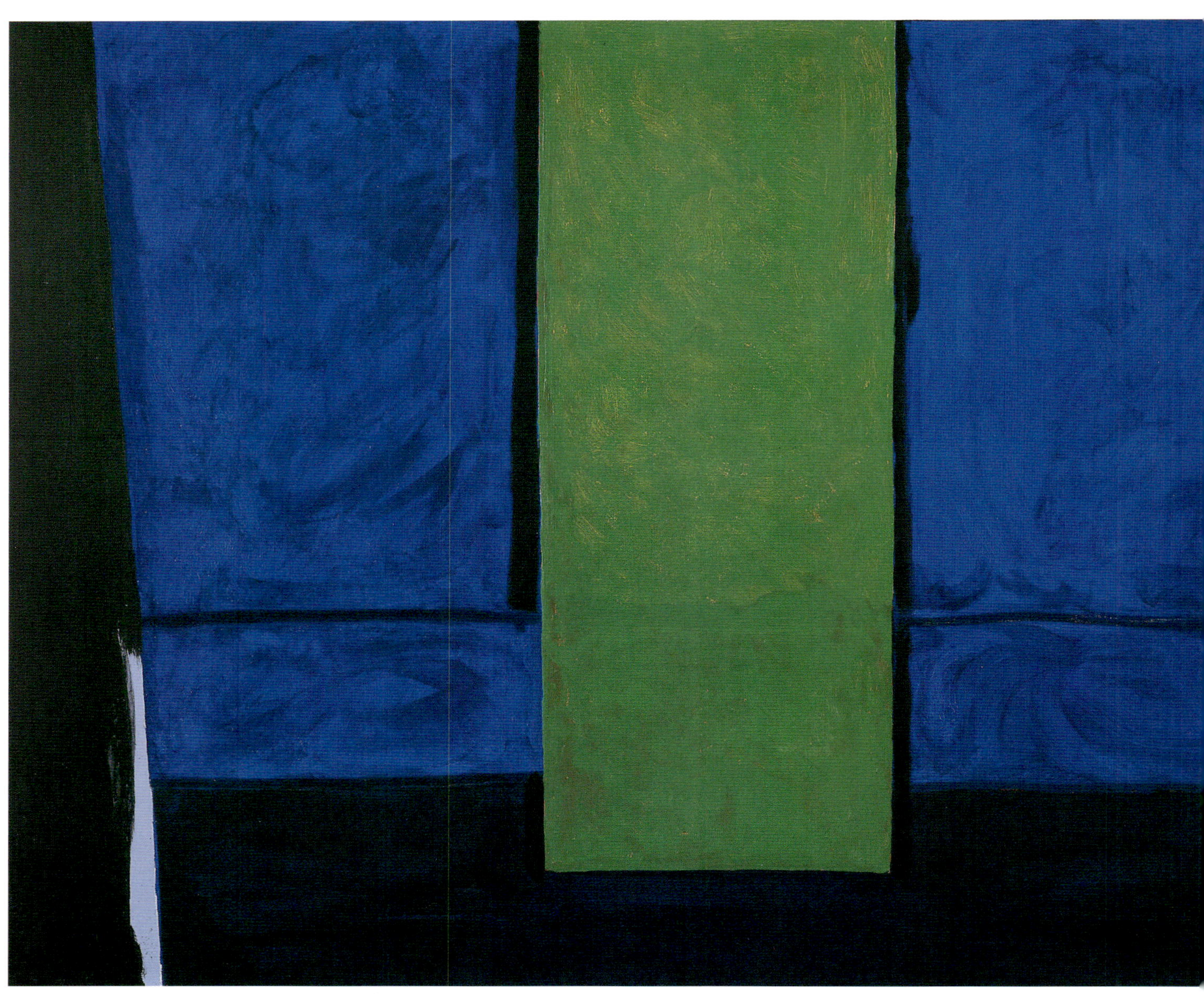

PLATE 7

ROBERT MOTHERWELL

Open 165, 1970
Acrylic on canvas
53½ x 108 inches
Collection Mr. and Mrs. David Mirvish, Toronto

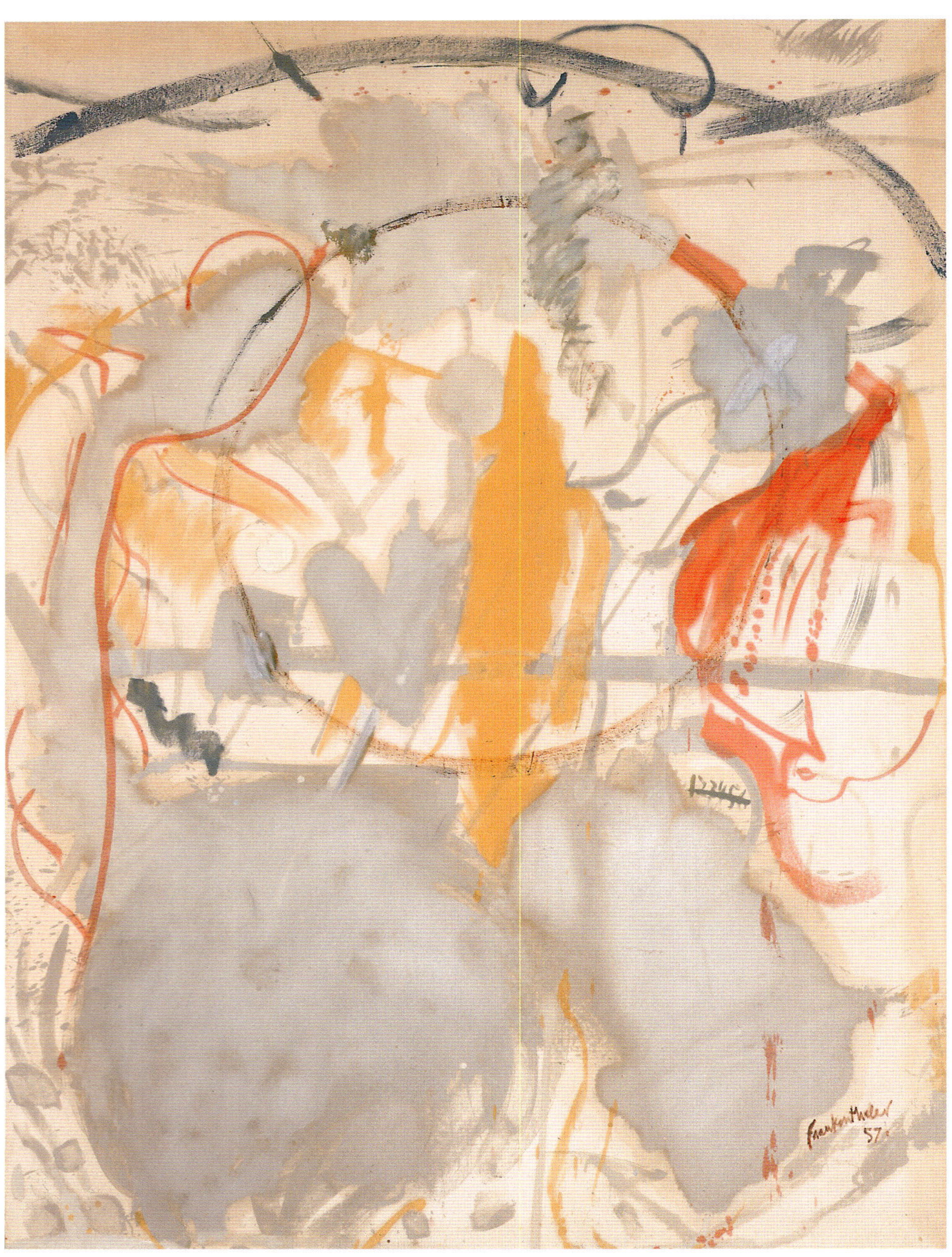

PLATE 8

HELEN FRANKENTHALER

Seven Types of Ambiguity, 1957
Oil on canvas
95 1/2 x 70 1/8 inches
Private collection

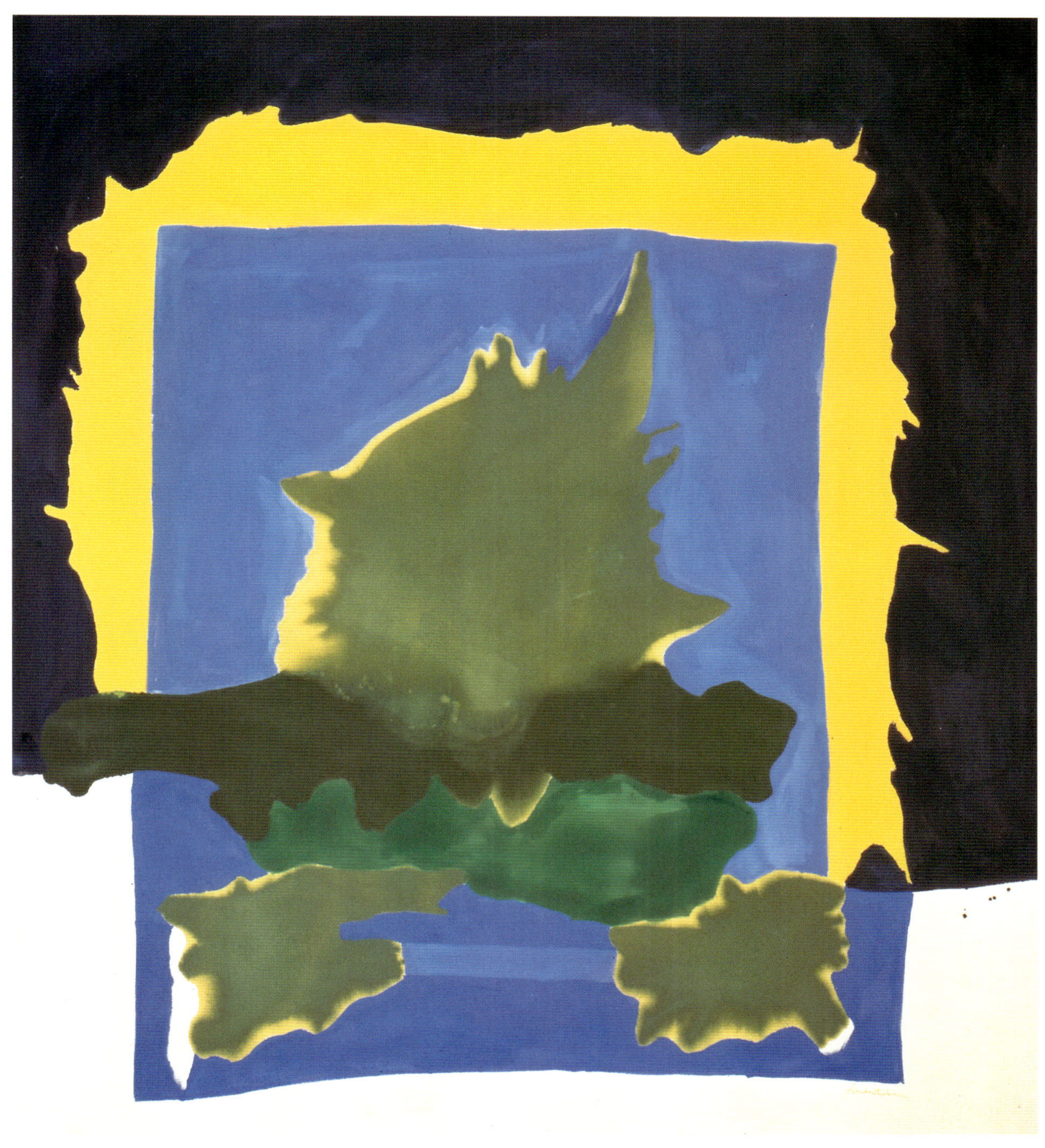

PLATE 9

HELEN FRANKENTHALER

Interior Landscape, 1964
Acrylic on canvas
$104\frac{7}{8}$ x $92\frac{7}{8}$ inches
San Francisco Museum of Modern Art; gift of the Women's Board (68.52)

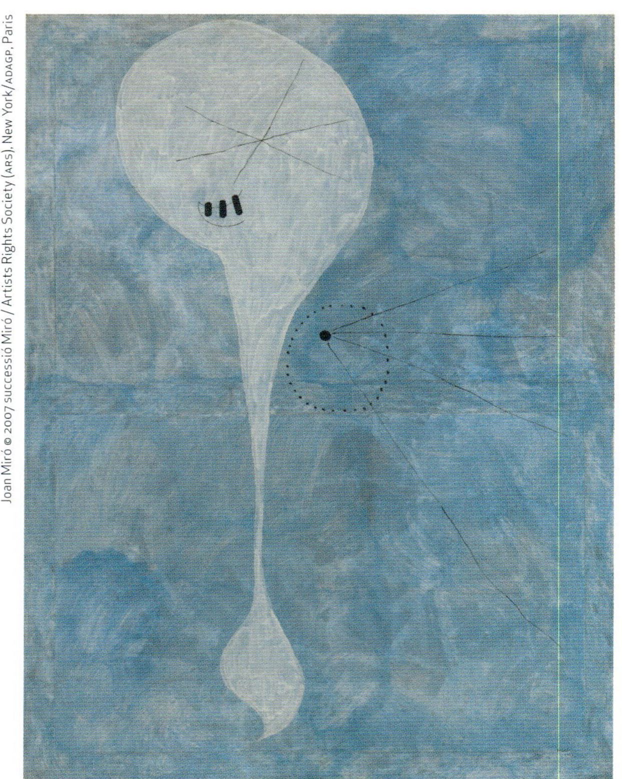

Joan Miró, *Personage*, summer 1925
Oil and egg tempera on canvas, 51¼ x 37⅞ inches
Solomon R. Guggenheim Museum, New York (48.1172.504)

paint paralleled the quest for subtle illusionistic modeling and the availability of commercially prepared, brilliant oil paint in easily portable tubes corresponded to the advent of plein-air painting and, eventually, Impressionism, there is a synergy between the invention of acrylic paint and the Color Field painters' exploration of the possibilities of large expanses of intense, relatively unmodulated color, applied with a neutral touch. While the earliest Color Field paintings, like those of the "anti-gestural" Abstract Expressionists, were made with oil paint, thinned with turpentine, their authors soon began to experiment with the new water-soluble pigments, originally intended for commercial use, that appeared on the market in the 1960s. Unlike oils, acrylics remained bright even when diluted and could be spread easily and smoothly over large areas. Unlike oils, they dried quickly. Also unlike oils, they could be both thin and opaque. It is impossible to determine which came first: the painters' desire to cover large surfaces with thin, saturated, evenhanded color or the existence of paint that made this possible. The development of the language of color-based abstraction was closely entwined with the changing capabilities of acrylic paint, which followed the rapid development of plastics technology in the 1960s. Younger painters associated with the Color Field movement, especially, took full advantage of what new technology made possible, as acrylic paint and its additives evolved, using it to expand conceptions of what an abstract painting could be.

If the Color Field painters' emphasis on the expressive possibilities of extended passages of radiant, minimally modulated hues would seem to confirm their descent from Rothko, other artists prove to have been even more significant ancestors, perhaps most notably, Matisse. The post-painterly abstract painters' admiration for Matisse, in fact, sets them apart from the generation immediately preceding theirs, for whom Picasso retained the greatest authority. Among the first-generation Abstract Expressionists, Motherwell was unusual in his abiding interest in Matisse; and Hofmann, remarkably, emphasized the importance of this master colorist throughout his teaching career, instilling the virtues of using color to structure a painting in the young artists who studied with him. From Matisse, the Color Field painters learned how to build pictures by setting brilliant, unmodulated hues side by side, how to evoke emotional and visual experience by adjusting weights and amounts of color, and how to clarify exuberant chroma by a judicious use of neutrals. Another potent example of the expressive and pictorial possibilities of large areas of color was provided by the work of Miró, which like Matisse's, was exhibited regularly in New York, and whose biomorphic imagery was crucial to the evolution of postwar New York abstraction. Yet, in the end, Pollock, a painter usually more admired for his ability to extract drama from pulsating, tonal expanses rather than for his command of chromatic color, may have been the Color Field painter's most authoritative precursor. In describing her early formation, as a precocious New York artist in the early 1950s, Frankenthaler has said,

...I looked at and was influenced by both Pollock and de Kooning and eventually felt there were more possibilities for me out of the Pollock vocabulary. De Kooning made enclosed linear shapes and "applied" the brush. Pollock used shoulder and ropes and ignored the edges and corners. I felt I could stretch more in the Pollock framework... You could become a de Kooning disciple or satellite or mirror, but you could depart *from Pollock.*[10]

Willem de Kooning, *Easter Monday*, 1955–66
Oil and newspaper transfer on canvas, 96 x 74 inches
The Metropolitan Museum of Art; Rogers Fund, 1956 (56.205.2)

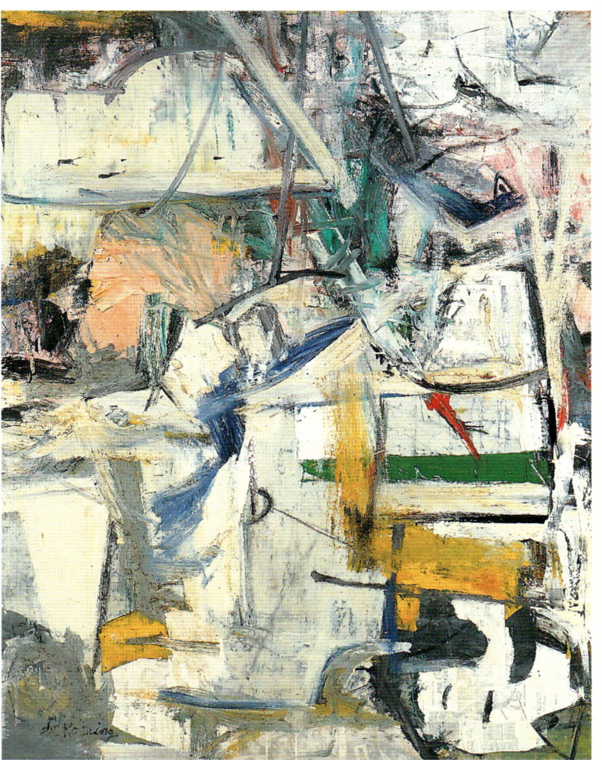

Frankenthaler adopted Pollock's practice of pouring thinned-out pigment onto unprimed canvas, but departed from him by creating, instead of skeins and tangles, broad, fluid lines and spreading pools of pale color. Soaked into the canvas, like stains, they fused painting and drawing without resorting to conventional painting techniques or gestural drawing marks. Frankenthaler's generously scaled canvases, with their vigorous, but ambiguous drawing, their almost intangible surfaces, and their expanses of white canvas, were as direct, spontaneous, and transparent as watercolors, but they had the presence, authority, and visual weight of large-scale canvases. The elusive images and luminous hues of Frankenthaler's fresh, uninhibited pictures of her early years rapidly established her as a painter to be reckoned with.

That Frankenthaler's stain method suggested a fruitful direction for some of her older colleagues has become the stuff of art historical legend. In 1953, Noland and Louis, who taught at the same art school in Washington, D.C., traveled to New York to see galleries and studios and to visit Clement Greenberg, whom Noland had met in 1950 at the legendary Black Mountain College and continued to see frequently. Noland introduced Louis to the exacting critic, who arranged for them to see the new work of the young, virtually unknown Frankenthaler, in her absence. The now famous encounter with her iconic *Mountains and Sea* (1952) proved decisive. Following Frankenthaler's example, the two painters began to experiment with staining on their return to Washington. Louis developed ways of "veiling" with broad pours of color, flooding the canvas with repeated layers, tempering superheated hues with cool, transparent darks to create confrontational "curtains" of mysterious color. Noland, after exploring a variety of formats, became fascinated by the possibilities of concentric bands generated by acknowledging the center of a square canvas, a flexible format that

CONTINUED ON PAGE 40

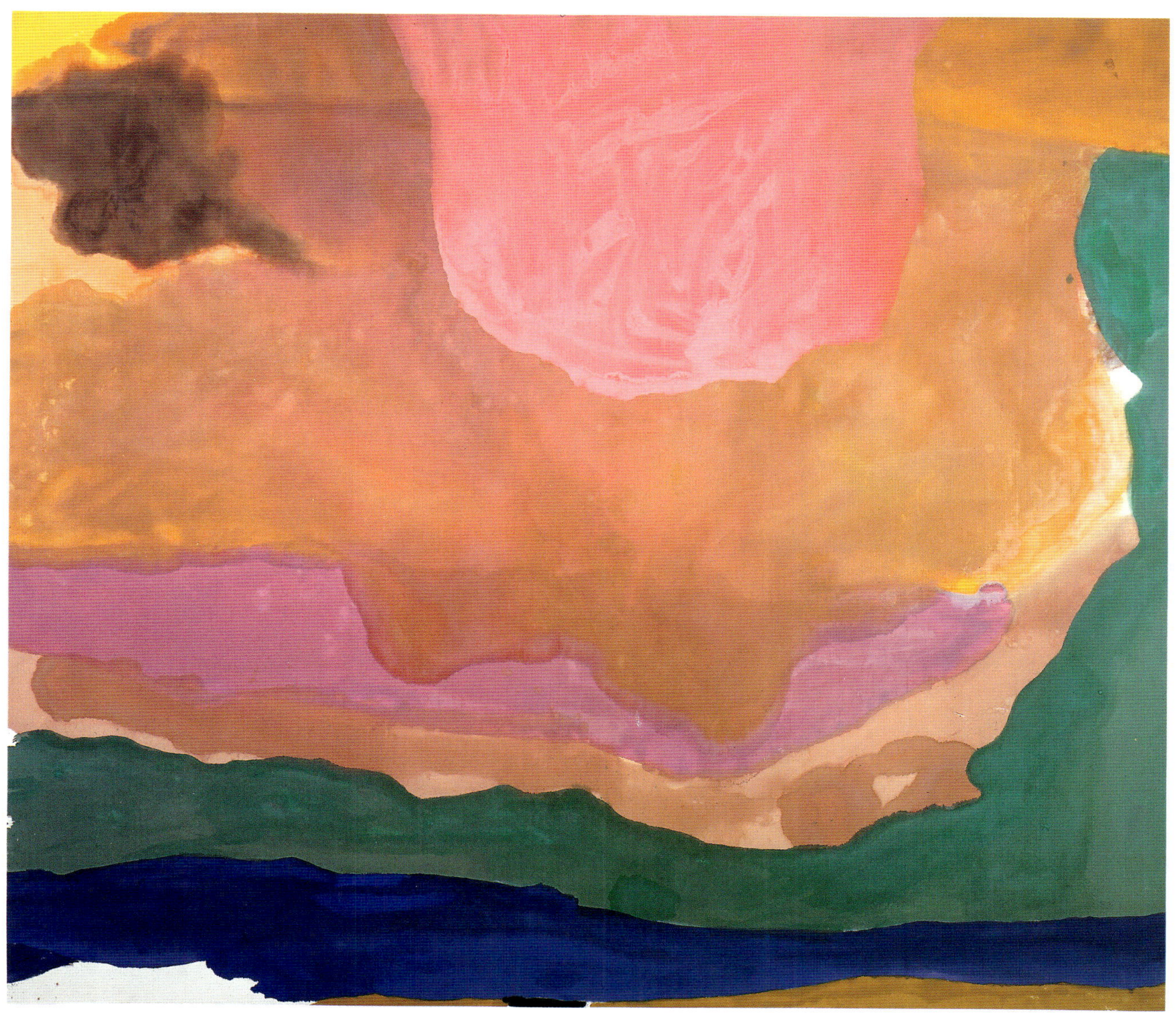

PLATE 10

HELEN FRANKENTHALER

Flood, 1967
Synthetic polymer on canvas
124 x 140 inches
Whitney Museum of American Art, New York;
purchase, with funds from the Friends of the Whitney
Museum of American Art (68.12)

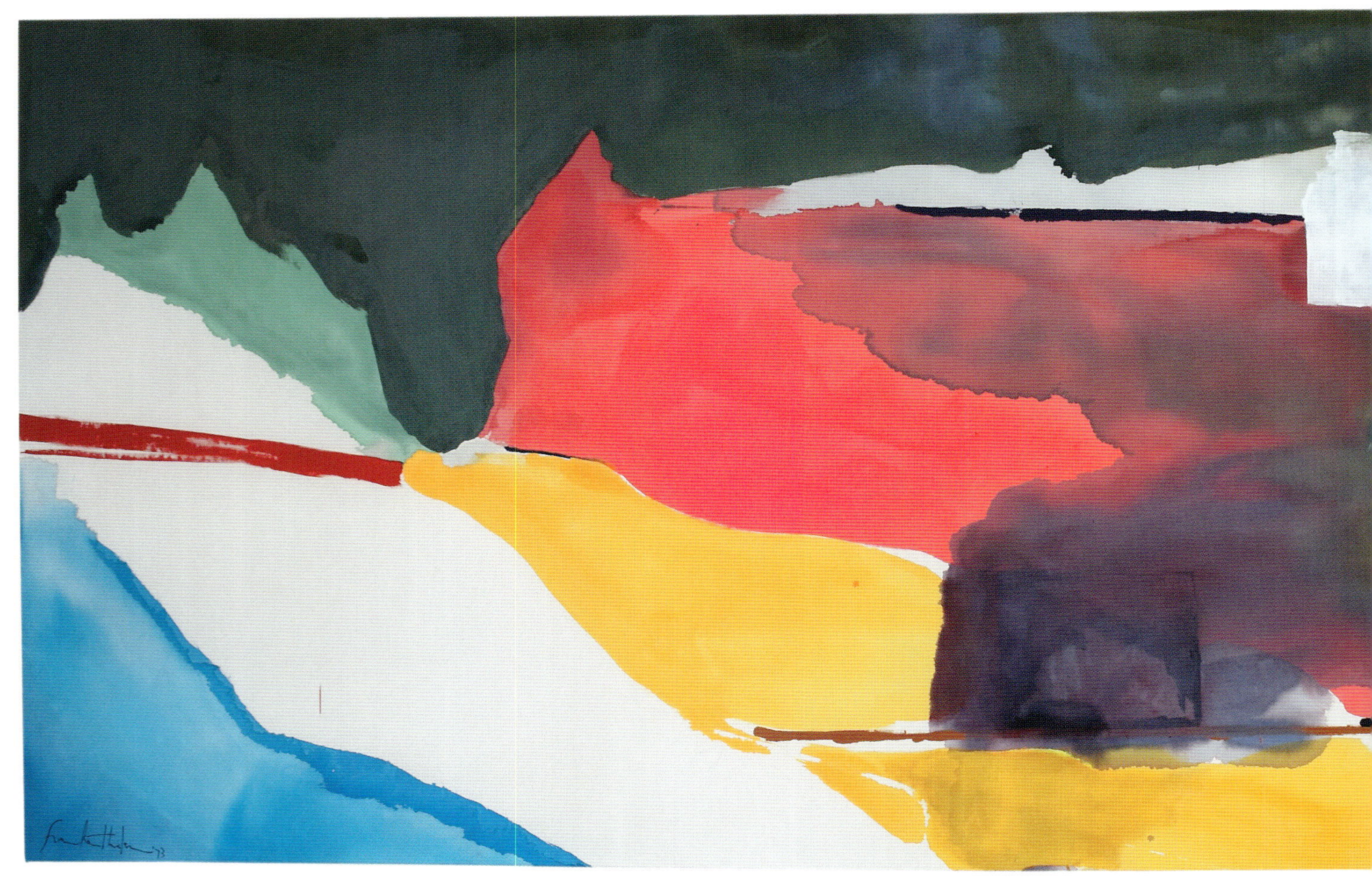

PLATE 11

HELEN FRANKENTHALER

Off White Square, 1973
Acrylic on canvas
79 1/2 x 235 inches
Greenberg Van Doren Gallery, New York;
Bernard Jacobson Gallery,
London; Leslie Feely Fine Art, New York

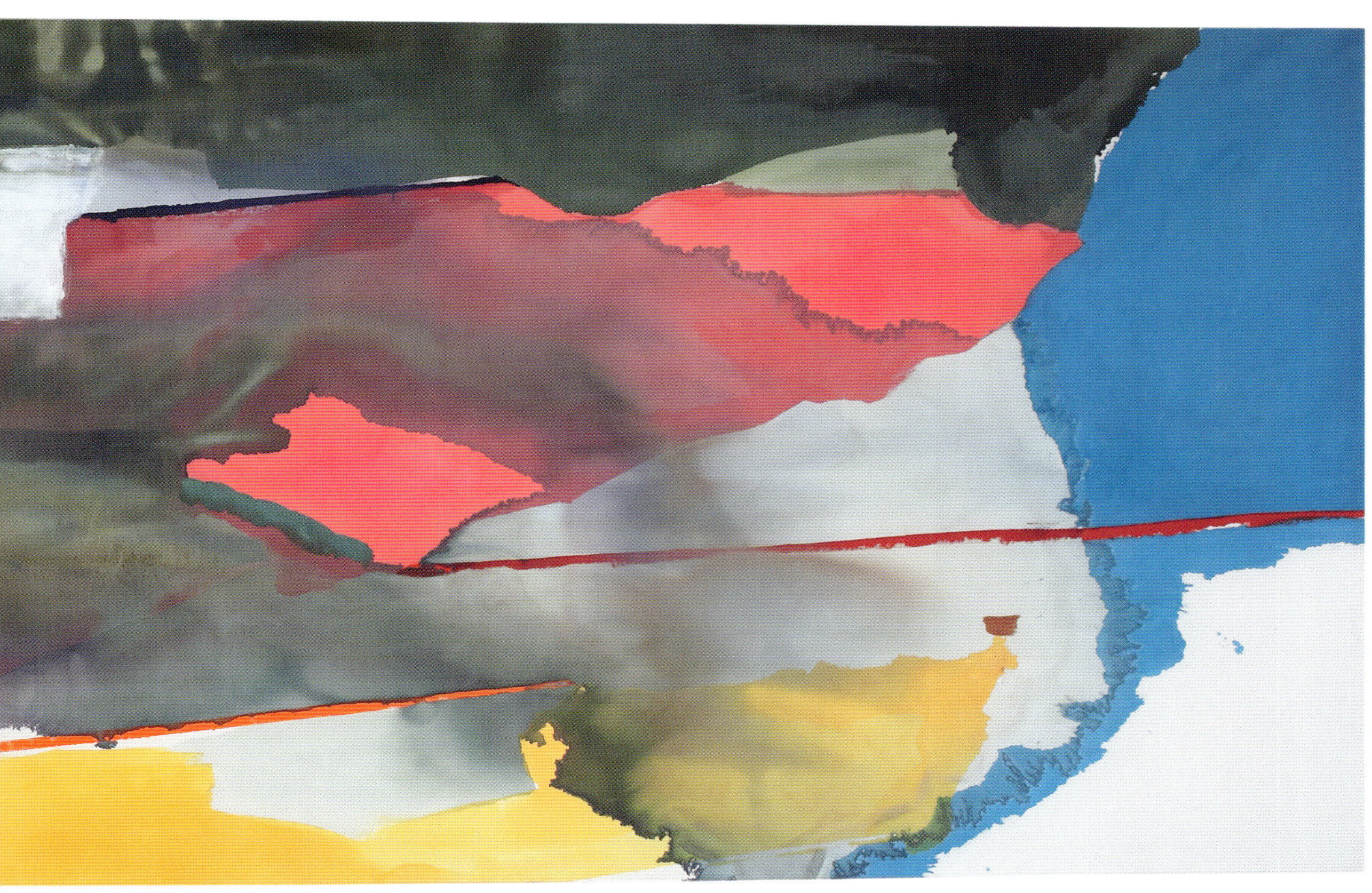

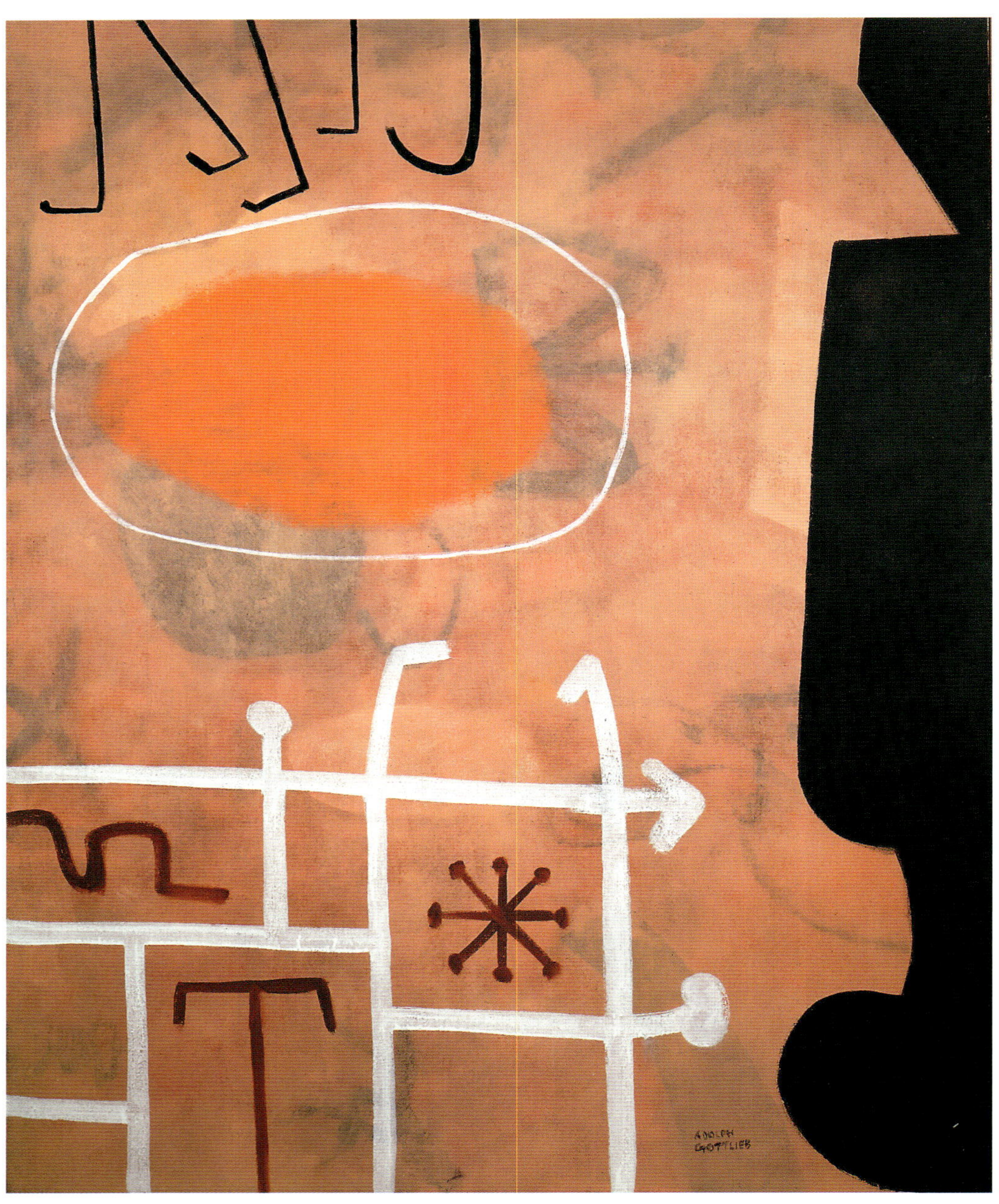

PLATE 12

ADOLPH GOTTLIEB

Sentinel, 1951
Oil on linen
60 x 48 inches
Adolph and Esther Gottlieb Foundation,
New York

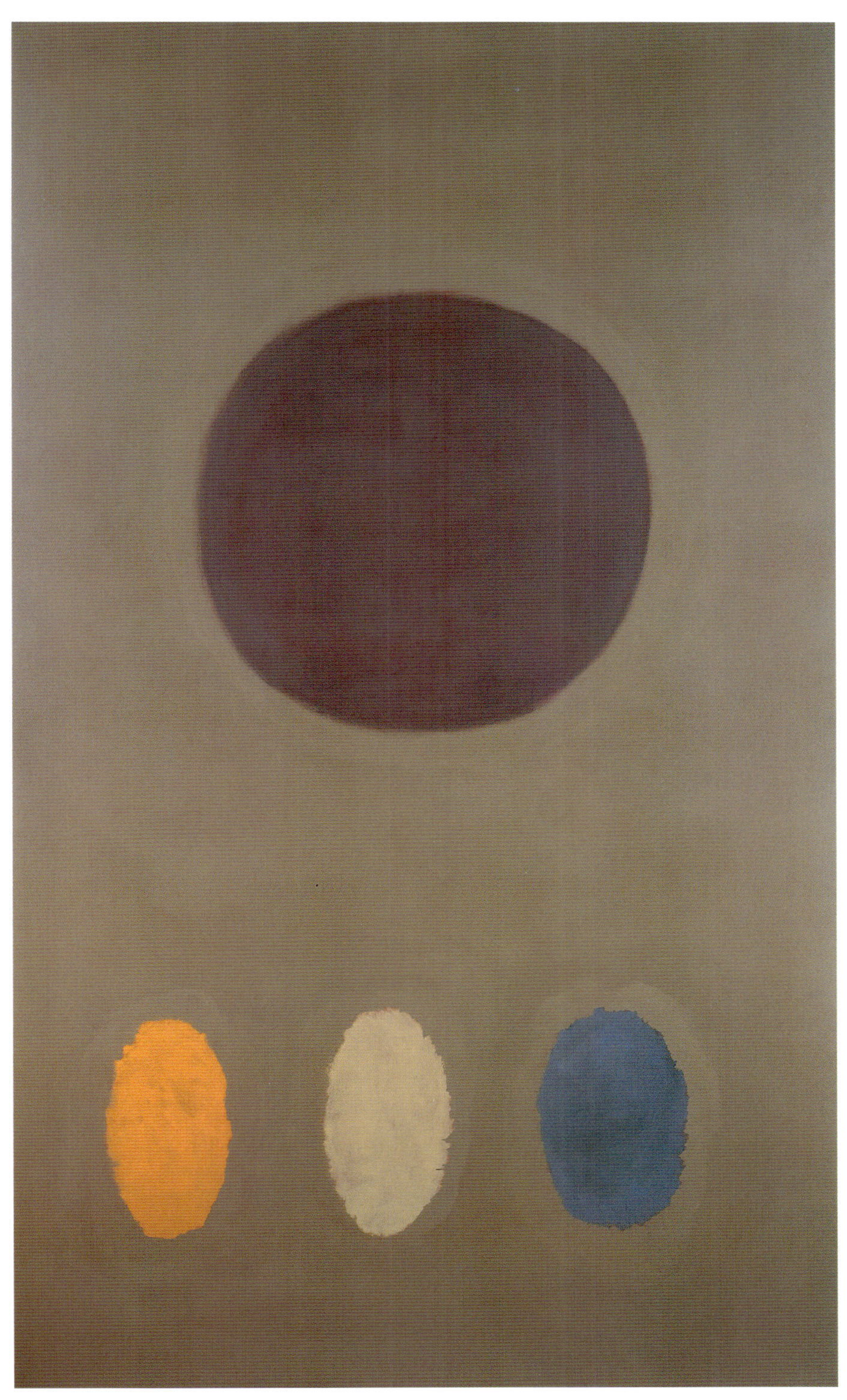

PLATE 13

ADOLPH GOTTLIEB

One, Two, Three, 1964
Oil on canvas
132 x 78 inches
Adolph and Esther Gottlieb Foundation,
New York

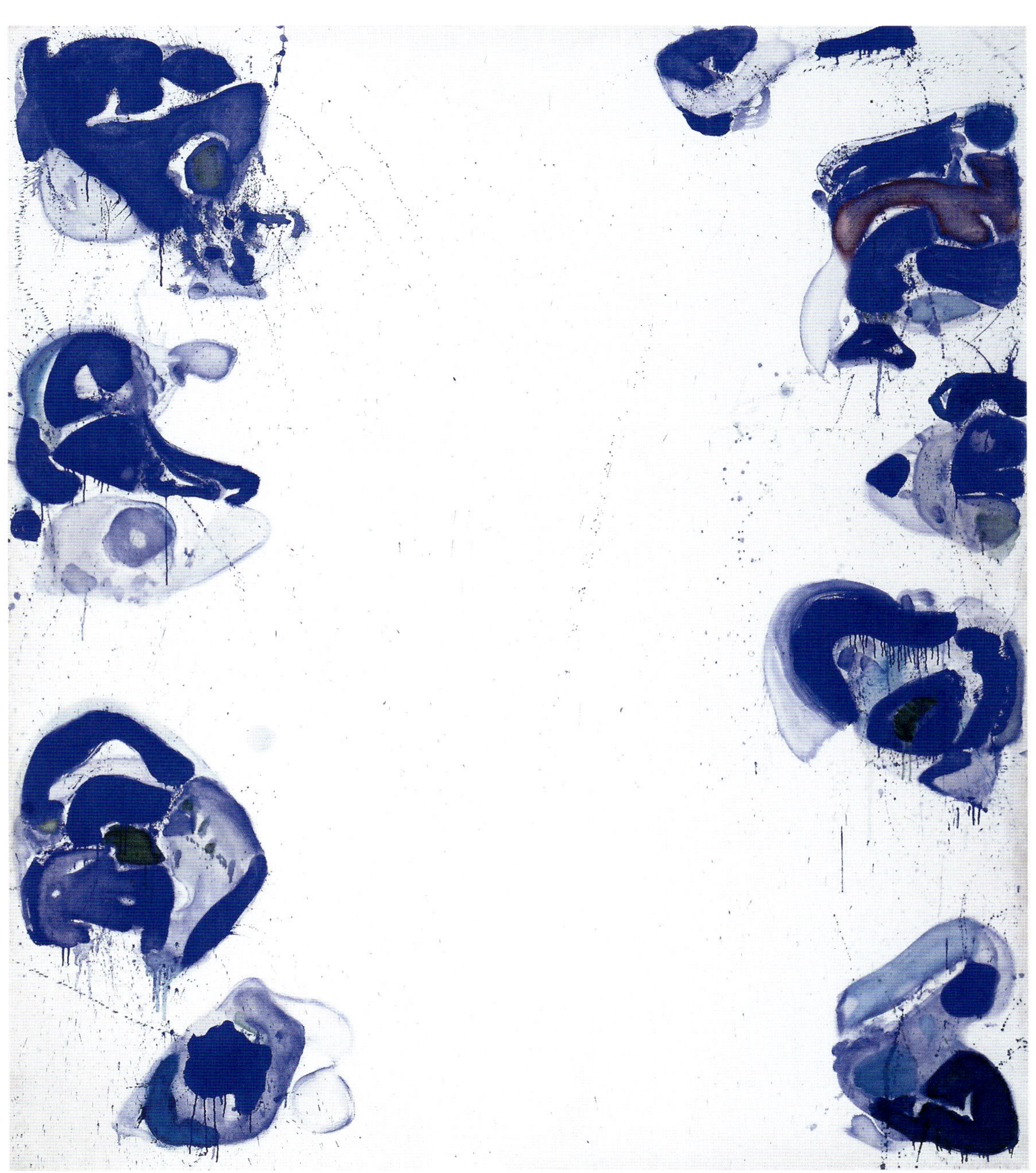

PLATE 14

SAM FRANCIS

Blue Balls, 1960
Oil on canvas
90 5/8 x 79 1/8 inches
Smithsonian American Art Museum; gift of S. C. Johnson & Son, Inc. (1968.52.17)

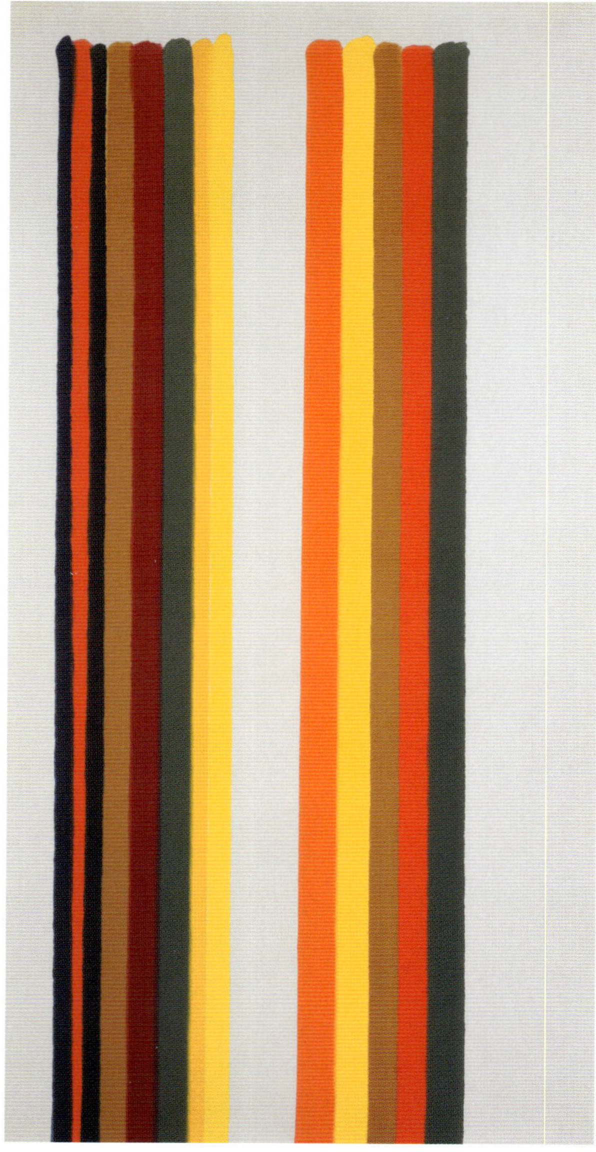

Morris Louis, *No. 1–68*, 1962
Acrylic resin on canvas, 83¾ x 42 inches
Solomon R. Guggenheim Museum, New York (67.1846)

preoccupied him for many years. "I knew what a circle could do," Noland has said. "Both eyes focus on it. It stamps itself out like a dot. This, in turn, causes one's vision to spread, as in Tantric art."[11]

Having arrived at layouts they found provocative and accommodating, both Louis and Noland continued to work in series, since they discovered that adopting largely predetermined formats as starting points was liberating. Instead of concentrating on composition, they could focus on intuitive adjustments of edge, density, and placement, on the width of bands or pours, on how far they were from other bands or pours, or from the center or the edge of the canvas, and above all, on nuances of color. Infinite variations seemed possible. Having devised the resonant, monolithic Veils, Louis blew the image apart in the Florals, with their explosive, radiating clouds of color. He then turned the looming mass of the Veils inside out, in the Unfurleds, in which rivulets of clear hues cascade from opposite sides of wide canvases, to delineate empty but charged zones of space whose defining characteristic is absence. Similarly, Noland, after a number of years of ringing changes on concentric circles—reveling in the associative differences between clean edges and loose ones, broad bands and narrow lines, pale, luminous hues and saturated chroma—began to explore more precise, symmetrical, geometric arrangements in the Chevrons. In these, he diagrammed the forces of his preceding series, literally connecting the center of the canvas to its edges with bars of unnamable color; at the same time, he began to place new emphasis on shape, sometimes turning square supports into diamonds or compressing them into narrow lozenges, to pose absorbing questions about the autonomy of the painted surface.

The next step for Noland was to test the limits of horizontality in paintings based on groupings of parallel stripes. As in his Circles, his principal concerns were interval, proportion, and the play of astonishing hue against astonishing hue, but the horizontal formats of the Stripes allowed him to investigate, as well, such questions as just how long (or narrow) a picture could be without escaping our field of vision or how assortments of differently sized colored bands might be placed to provoke different responses. (Louis's last series of paintings, the Columns, also depended on parallel bands, although they were very different from Noland's. Louis's bars of colors were narrow streams that usually ran vertically against generous amounts of unpainted canvas, rather like compressed Unfurleds, trued and faired, as confrontational as the monumental Veils, although more intimate.) The permutations of Noland's Stripes seemed virtually inexhaustible, to judge by his range of arresting variations of the motif, yet in the early 1970s, he became interested in the energy generated by crossed bands and initiated a series known as Plaids. At first, these were tall verticals, in contrast to the extended Stripes, but the chromatic crescendos where bands intersected led Noland to a renewed investigation of shape, in response to the internal dynamics of the picture. These explorations were always dictated by intuitive choices, not by systems. Noland, a deeply knowledgeable music lover with special expertise in jazz, approaches picture-making rather like a musician—he speaks of a painting's being "keyed off" a particular color—employing chromatic harmonies and assonances as much for their emotive power as for formal reasons.

Frankenthaler never shared Louis's and Noland's affection for even loosely predetermined formats. Family resemblances exist among groups of her pictures, evidence of recurring preoccupations or of what she calls "worrying an idea until I have exhausted it,"[12] but unpremeditated drawing, informed by her concerns of the moment and her instincts about color, is always the generating force of her pictures. During the 1960s and 1970s, in part because of her adoption of acrylic paint, the delicate dramas of her earlier works gave way to more muscular orchestrations of larger pools of frankly gorgeous color. But Frankenthaler's images, however abstract or evocative, remained improvised or discovered, never deduced from a set of givens. Often, the zones of surprising, luminous color in her paintings appear to have found their own shapes, because of the way paint flows, at the same time that they seem willed into place by a powerful personality. As always, Frankenthaler's multivalent images seem to distill the large phenomena of the natural world—sea and sky, night and day, and changing weather—into subtle, richly modulated relationships of hue.

As the list of artists included in the exhibition *Post Painterly Abstraction* reveals, during the early 1960s, a significant number of painters had begun to investigate alternatives to "the Tenth Street touch," some in response to Frankenthaler's stain painting and the work of her colleagues, others arriving by independent paths. Although it now appears that some artists included were working out of different conceptions than the "core" group of Color Field painters (or later evolved in different directions), the selection, a joint effort by Greenberg and James Elliott, the curator at the Los Angeles County Museum of Art who initiated the exhibition, still holds as a fine cross section of some of the most inventive, original painters of the period. It also indicates the wide reach of color-based abstraction, by the early 1960s. Artists from New York, Washington, D.C., the West Coast, and Canada, were represented, among them—along with such founding members of the Color Field school as Frankenthaler, Noland, and Louis—Walter Darby Bannard, Jack Bush, Gene Davis, Friedel Dzubas, Sam Francis, Jules Olitski, Larry Poons, and Frank Stella, all of whom were reveling in the expressive possibilities of what Greenberg had called "openness and clarity," using broad areas of unmodulated color in a great variety of manners. Other equally serious, ambitious painters on the east and west coasts, such as Ronald Davis and Sam Gilliam, were not included in the exhibition but were exploring similar ideas in original ways. Some members of the group were roughly Frankenthaler or Noland's age,[13] many were five or ten years younger, and a few were considerably older, but their concerns

CONTINUED ON PAGE 48

PLATE 15

MORRIS LOUIS

Loam, 1958
Acrylic on canvas
90 ¾ x 148 inches
The Museum of Fine Arts, Houston; museum purchase with funds provided by the Brown Foundation Accessions Endowment Fund (76.319)

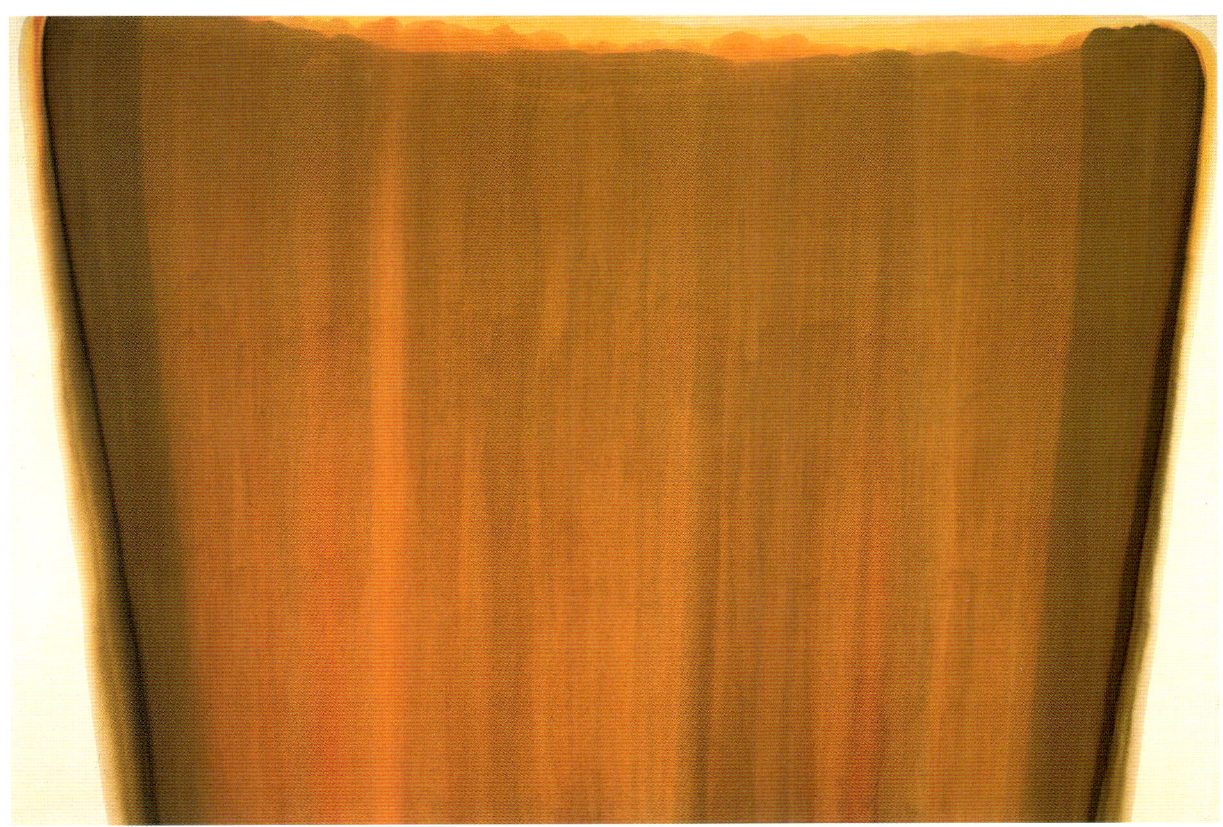

PLATE 16

MORRIS LOUIS

Mem, 1959
Acrylic on canvas
97 x 140 inches
Collection Virginia and Bagley Wright, Seattle

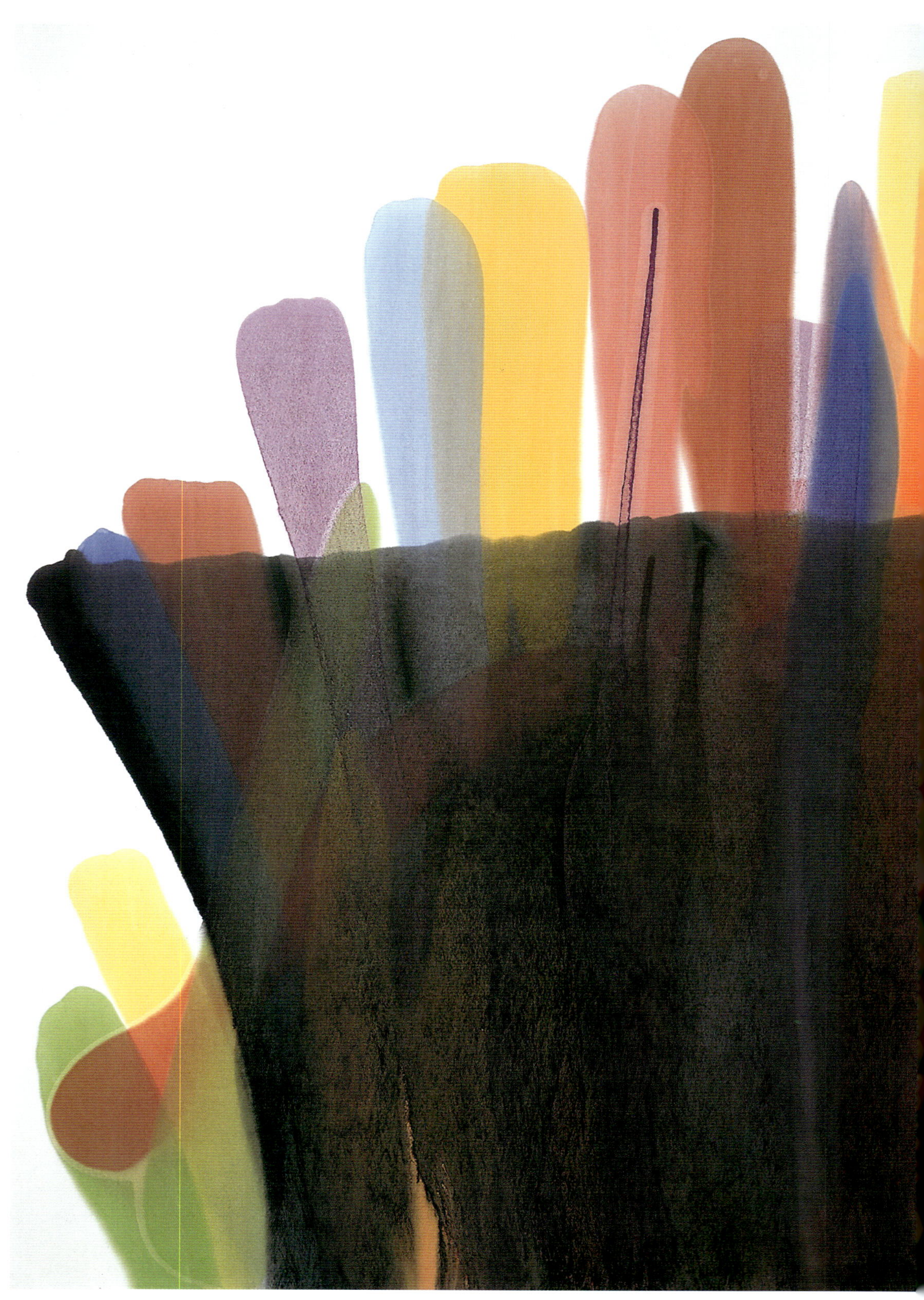

PLATE 17

MORRIS LOUIS

Floral V, 1959–60
Acrylic and magna on canvas
98 3/8 x 137 13/16 inches
Private collection, Denver

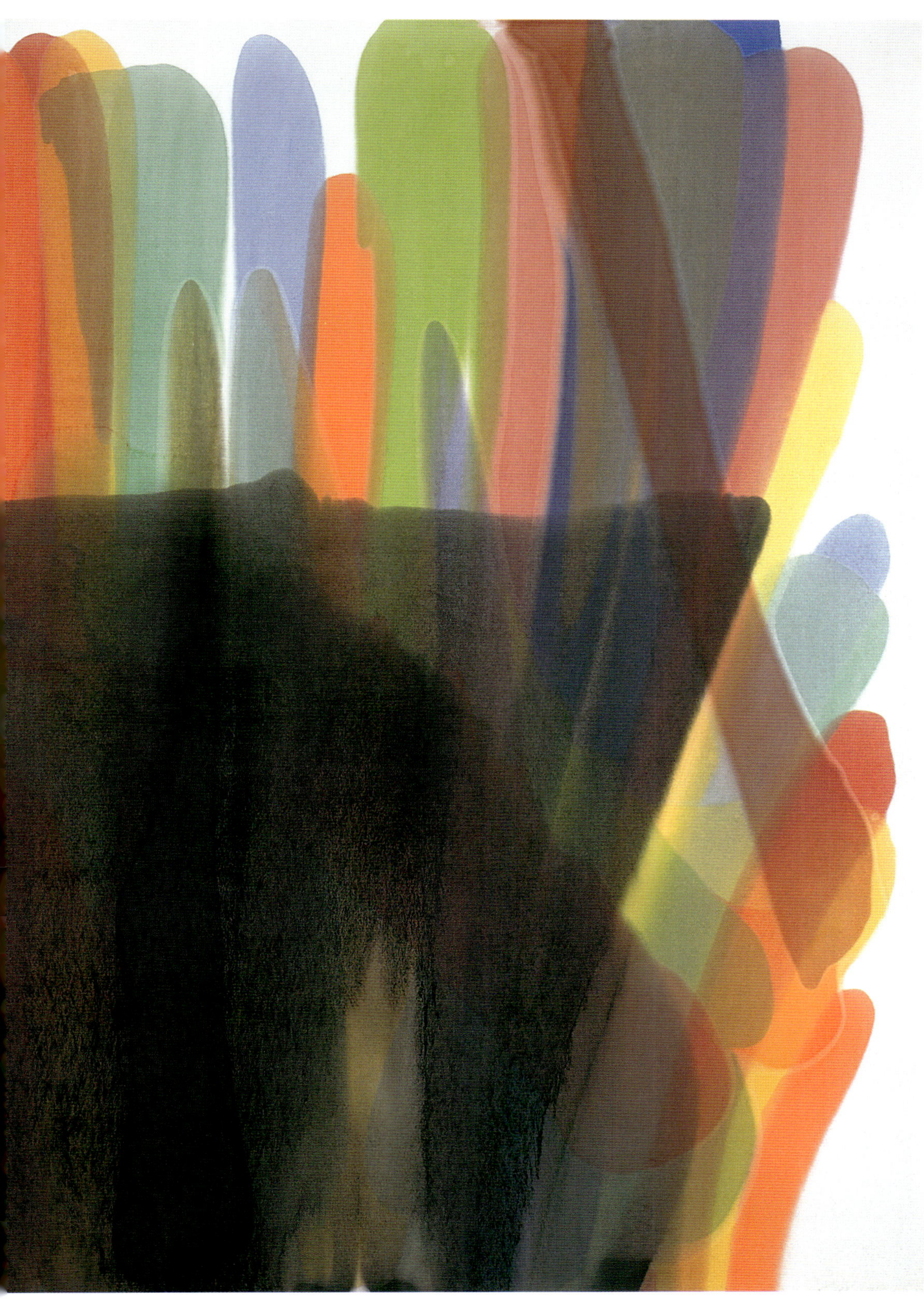

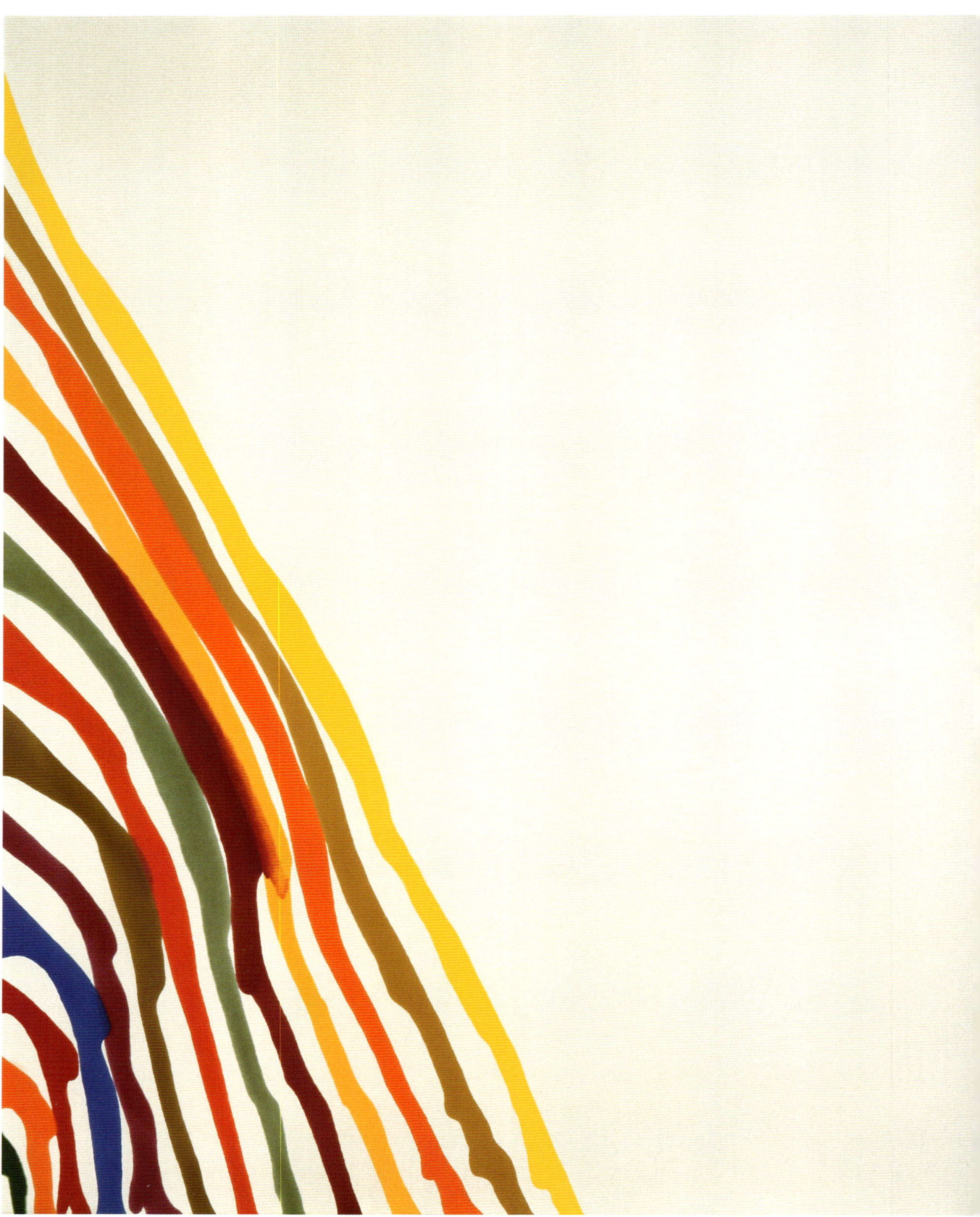

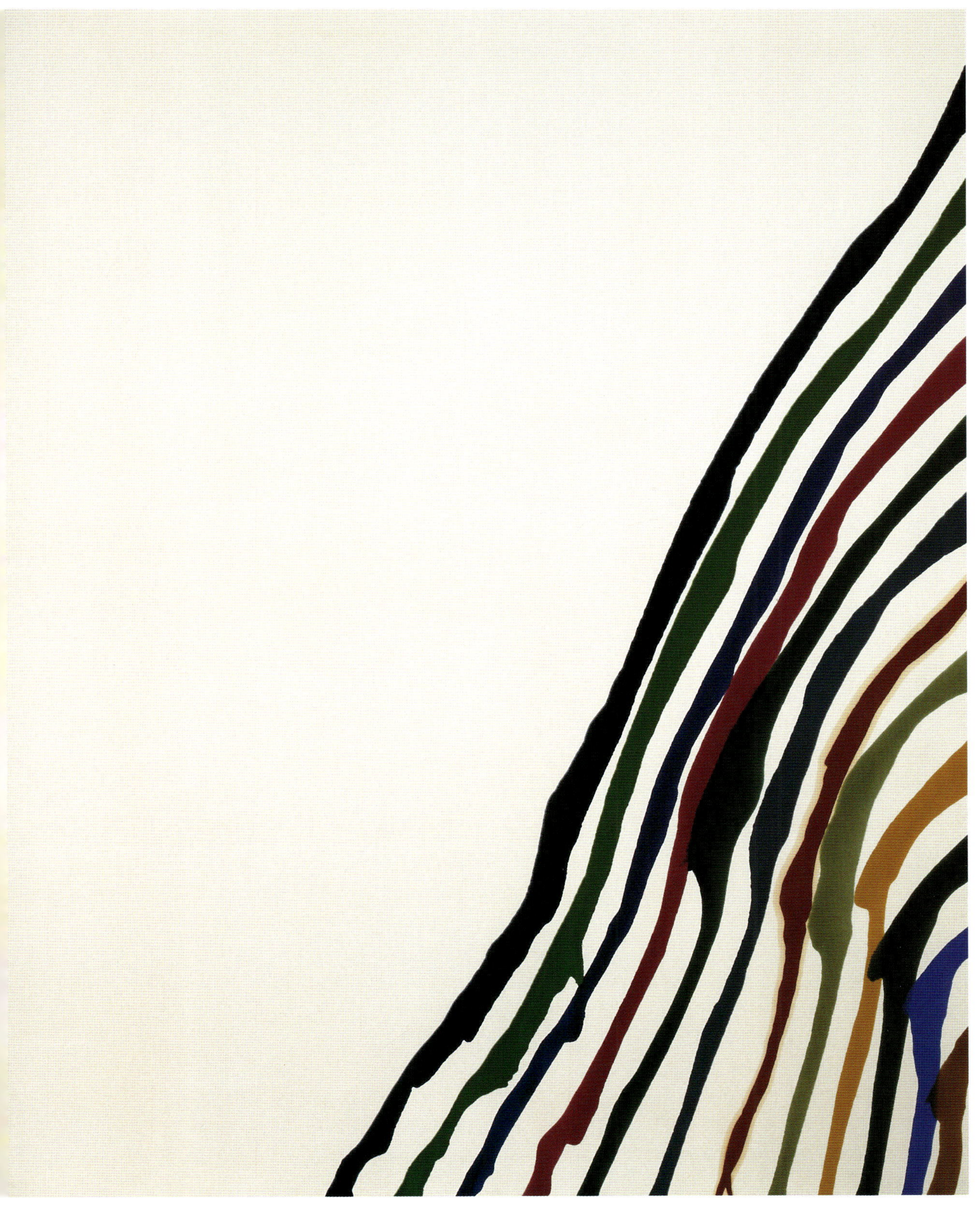

PLATE 18

MORRIS LOUIS

Theta, 1961
Acrylic resin (Magna) on canvas
102 x 168 inches
Museum of Fine Arts, Boston; anonymous gift (67.623)

and conceptions of what a picture could be were both closely related and remarkably diverse.

The primary link among the majority of artists now grouped—however casually—under the label "Color Field" was Clement Greenberg. Just as he had been for the Abstract Expressionists, Greenberg was both a spokesman who championed their efforts and a valued studio visitor whose tough-minded, uncompromising responses to their work they found stimulating and helpful. He steered collectors in their direction and included their work in exhibitions at New York's prestigious French & Co. Gallery, when he briefly served as their advisor. Perhaps most important was his acting as the joint curator of the museum exhibition *Post Painterly Abstraction*, which allowed him to present Color Field's practitioners and define its desiderata for a larger audience.

Frank Stella, *Jill*, 1959
Enamel on canvas, 90⅜ x 78¾ inches. Albright Knox Gallery, Buffalo, New York; gift of Seymour H. Knox, Jr. 1962

Throughout the 1960s, the art historian and critic Michael Fried—much younger but no less high-minded than Greenberg—played a comparable role in articulating the significance of the new type of color-based abstraction. A contemporary of the youngest Color Field painters (he, Stella, and Bannard were all undergraduates at Princeton University at about the same time), Fried's combination of intellectual rigor and passion for every aspect of works of art—manifest in his writings in *Art International* and *ArtForum* and his exhibition catalogue essays on Louis, Noland, Olitski, and Stella—quickly set a standard for illuminating formalist criticism. The exhibition *Three American Painters: Kenneth Noland, Jules Olitski, Frank Stella*, which Fried organized for the Fogg Art Museum at Harvard University, in 1965, significantly expanded the aesthetic distinctions made by Greenberg in his catalogue essay for *Post Painterly Abstraction*. Fried himself was indebted to Greenberg's example; as a student, along with Stella, he discovered Greenberg's writings in periodicals and found him a provocative guide to the New York art world of the period. Like Greenberg, Fried frequented studios and was valued for his perceptive eye by his artist friends.

Further connections were provided by friendships among the artists themselves—who sometimes had met through Greenberg or Fried in the first place. Despite these multiple, if often oblique ties, the Color Field painters never formed a coherent group, yet the interconnections among them are fascinating and often revealing. The close relationship of Greenberg and Frankenthaler—herself something of a lynchpin, as the story of Louis, Noland, and *Mountains and Sea* (1952), among others, suggests—began in 1950, when, newly graduated from Bennington College, in Vermont, the young painter organized an exhibition of works by fellow alumnae for the Seligman Gallery in New York. Through Greenberg, Frankenthaler met and saw the work of an extraordinary cross section of the most adventurous New York artists of the period, both from the Abstract Expressionist generation and her own. (She always acknowledges that this privileged view was crucial to her own evolution.) In the early 1950s, Frankenthaler shared a studio with the German-born painter Friedel Dzubas whose friendship with Greenberg dated from 1948, when the critic rented a building on the painter's Connecticut property for the summer. Superficial resemblances between Frankenthaler's and Dzubas's work of these formative years bear witness to these ties, but Dzubas's large color shapes are more forthright and graphic than Frankenthaler's and his palette of elusive, sometimes acidic colors, wholly original. Dzubas's later paintings, especially those of the 1970s, which most firmly established his reputation, are testimony to his independence of mind. These mysterious canvases, which have been compared to music of the romantic era, are assemblies of color blocks that seem to fray into the surrounding atmosphere, with individual blocks remaining pure and self-contained, like clear ringing notes that form chords but keep their integrity. Like Louis, Dzubas was a near-contemporary of the Abstract Expressionists, yet—again like Louis—he shared the aesthetic aspirations of his younger colleagues. The undertones of brooding drama in Dzubas's paintings are palpable, but there is none of the loading, layering, or implicit histrionics of "the Tenth Street touch."

Olitski's friendship with Greenberg began in 1958, when the critic saw the young painter's first solo exhibition in New York and invited him to take part in a group show, along with Noland, Dzubas, and Louis, among others, at French & Co. The following year, when Olitski had a one-man exhibition at the gallery, he met Noland. That connection became closer in the early 1960s, when Olitski taught at Bennington College and Noland lived in a neighboring town. The mix was enriched by the presence of the British sculptor Anthony Caro, who had temporarily left London to be artist in residence at the college for several years. Caro was especially close to Fried, who had been among the first to write perceptively and enthusiastically about the sculptor's staggeringly original works in steel. The three eager young artists Caro, Noland, and Olitski frequented one another's studios; Greenberg visited regularly. The result was an extraordinary period of innovation, cross-fertilization, mutual criticism, and stimulation. Each artist's work developed in fascinating ways, spurred by the efforts of his colleagues and their heated debates about what Caro calls "the onward of art." It was during one of these intense studio conversations that Olitski, who had been making paintings of concentric "rings" of intense color, so overscaled that they seemed to escape the confines of the canvas, declared that his ideal would be to spray color in the air and somehow have it remain there[14]—which led to his first large painting made with a commercial spray gun and compressor. The resulting spray paintings are among Olitski's best known: seamless, seductive, tonally inflected expanses with superimposed edge-drawing that asserts the difference between the painting's limitless, magical world of color and the banalities of the ordinary environment. These spray paintings are among the most unabashedly beautiful and rigorous abstractions ever made, teetering on the edge of becoming pure optical phenomena, but somehow managing to convince us of the logic of their proportions and inflections. Over the years that followed, Olitski suppressed some of the chromatic opulence of the sprays to concentrate on tonality, not in its traditional role as an adjunct to three-dimensional illusion, but as an independent expressive element. At the same time, he freed his drawing from its task of separating art and not-art, and allowed line to function as independently as tonality.

The idiosyncratic canvases of the Canadian Jack Bush are at the opposite end of the compositional spectrum from Olitski's. Bush first met Greenberg (his exact coeval) in 1956, when

CONTINUED ON PAGE 60

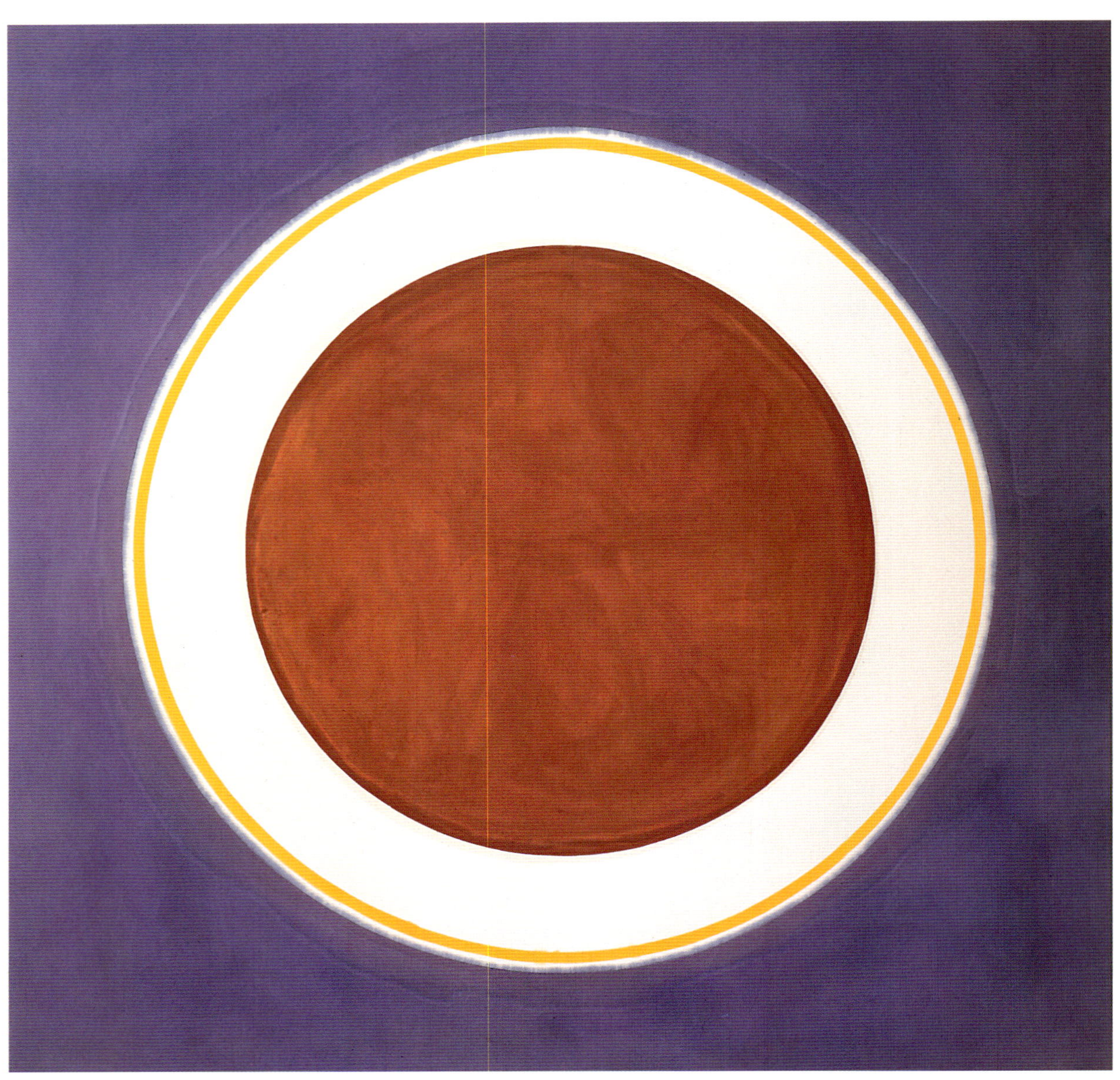

PLATE 19

KENNETH NOLAND

Earthen Bound, 1960
Acrylic on canvas
103½ x 103½ inches
Courtesy the artist

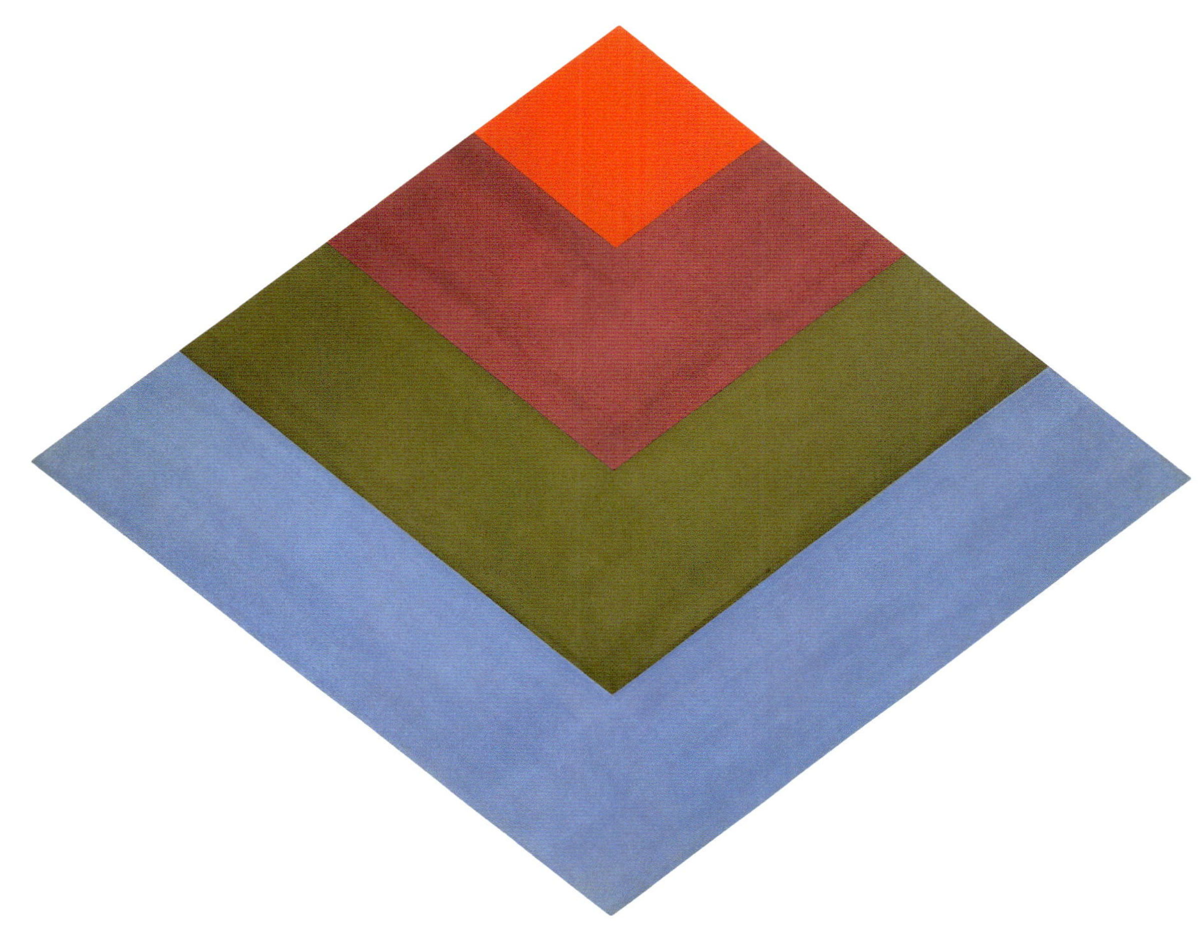

PLATE 20

KENNETH NOLAND

Dark Sweet Cherry, 1966
Acrylic on canvas,
diamond
56 x 70 inches (point to point)
Collection Mr. and Mrs. David Mirvish, Toronto

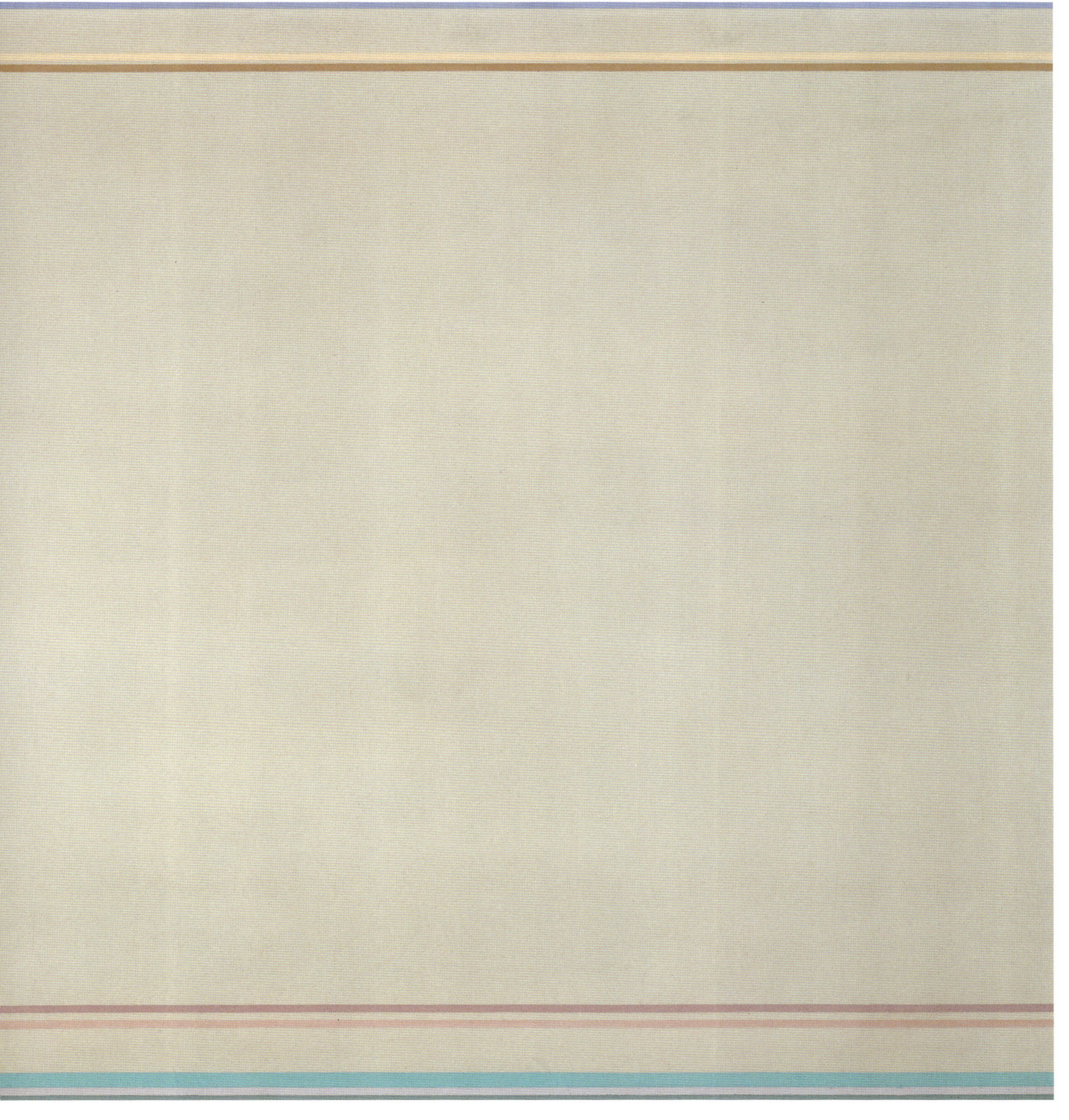

PLATE 21

KENNETH NOLAND

Space Jog, 1970
Acrylic on canvas
74 3/8 x 126 inches
Collection Mr. and Mrs. David Mirvish, Toronto

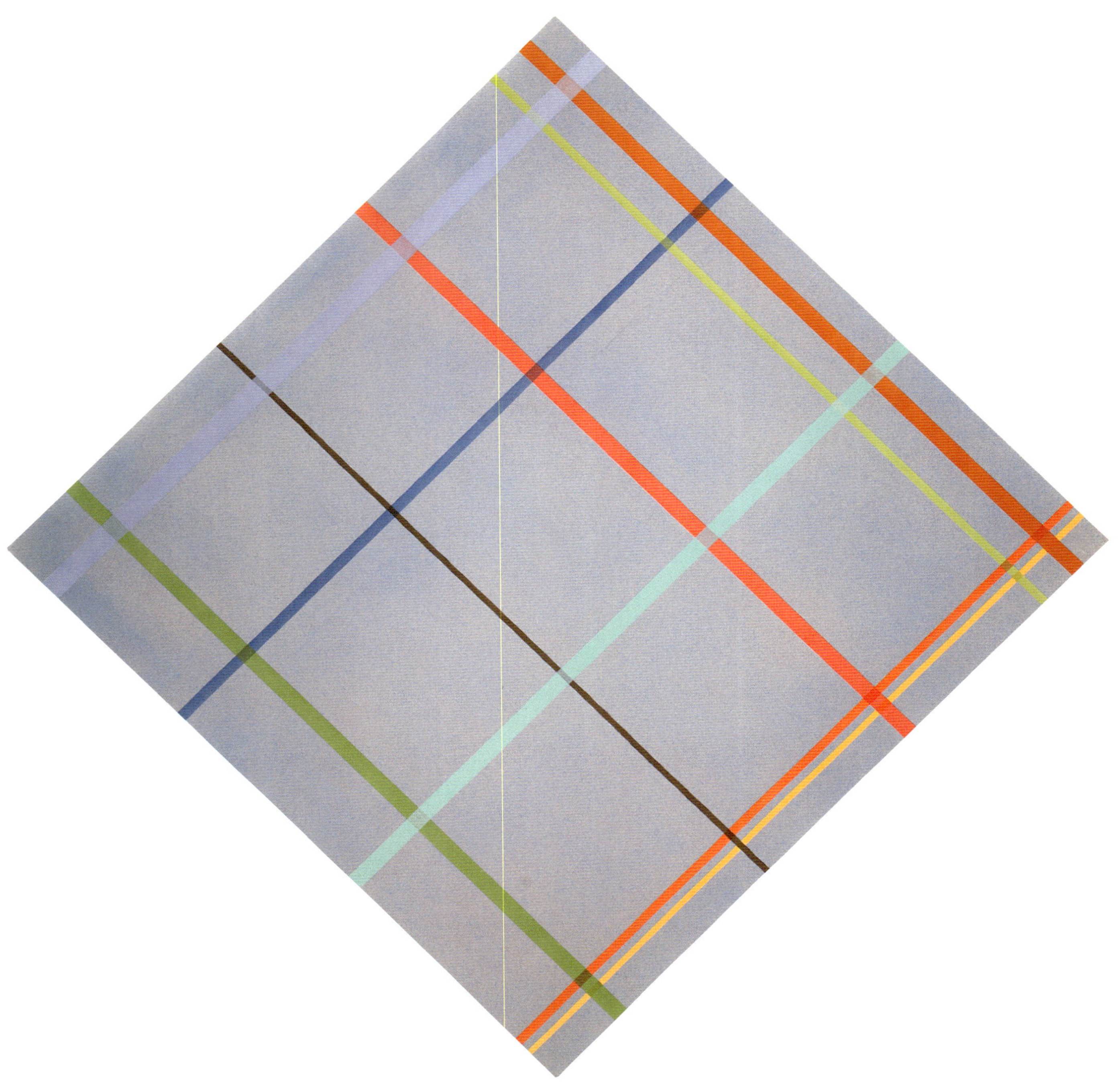

PLATE 22

KENNETH NOLAND

Following Sea, 1974
Acrylic on canvas, diamond
98 ¼ x 98 ¼ inches (point to point)
Collection Mr. and Mrs. David Mirvish, Toronto

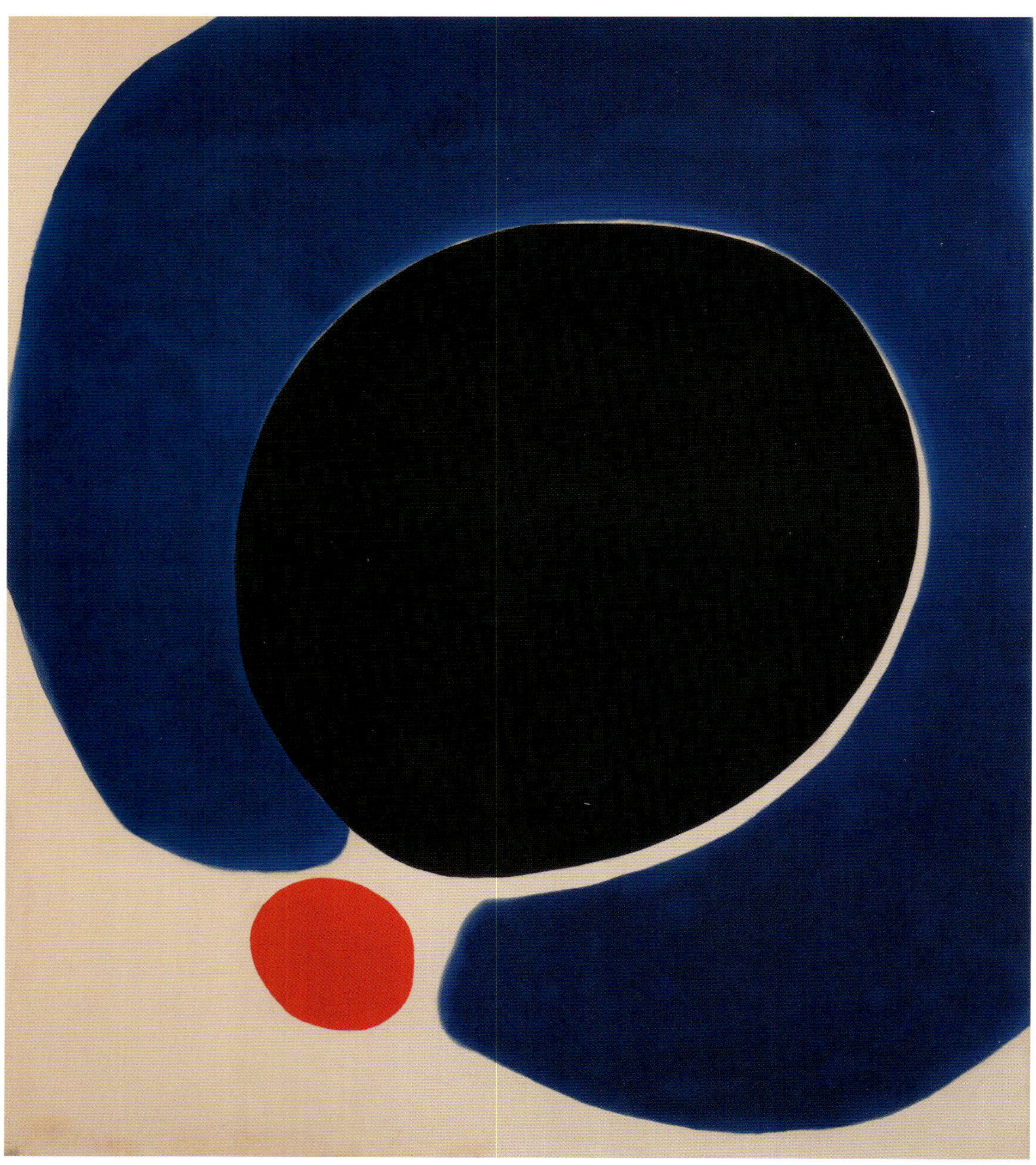

PLATE 23

JULES OLITSKI

Cleopatra Flesh, 1962
Synthetic polymer paint on canvas
104 x 90 inches
The Museum of Modern Art, New York; gift of
G. David Thompson, 1964 (262.1964)

PLATE 24

JULES OLITSKI

Tin Lizzie Green, 1964
Alkyd and oil/wax crayon on canvas
130 x 82 inches
Museum of Fine Arts, Boston; purchased
with the aid of funds from the National Endowment
for the Arts (1977.617)

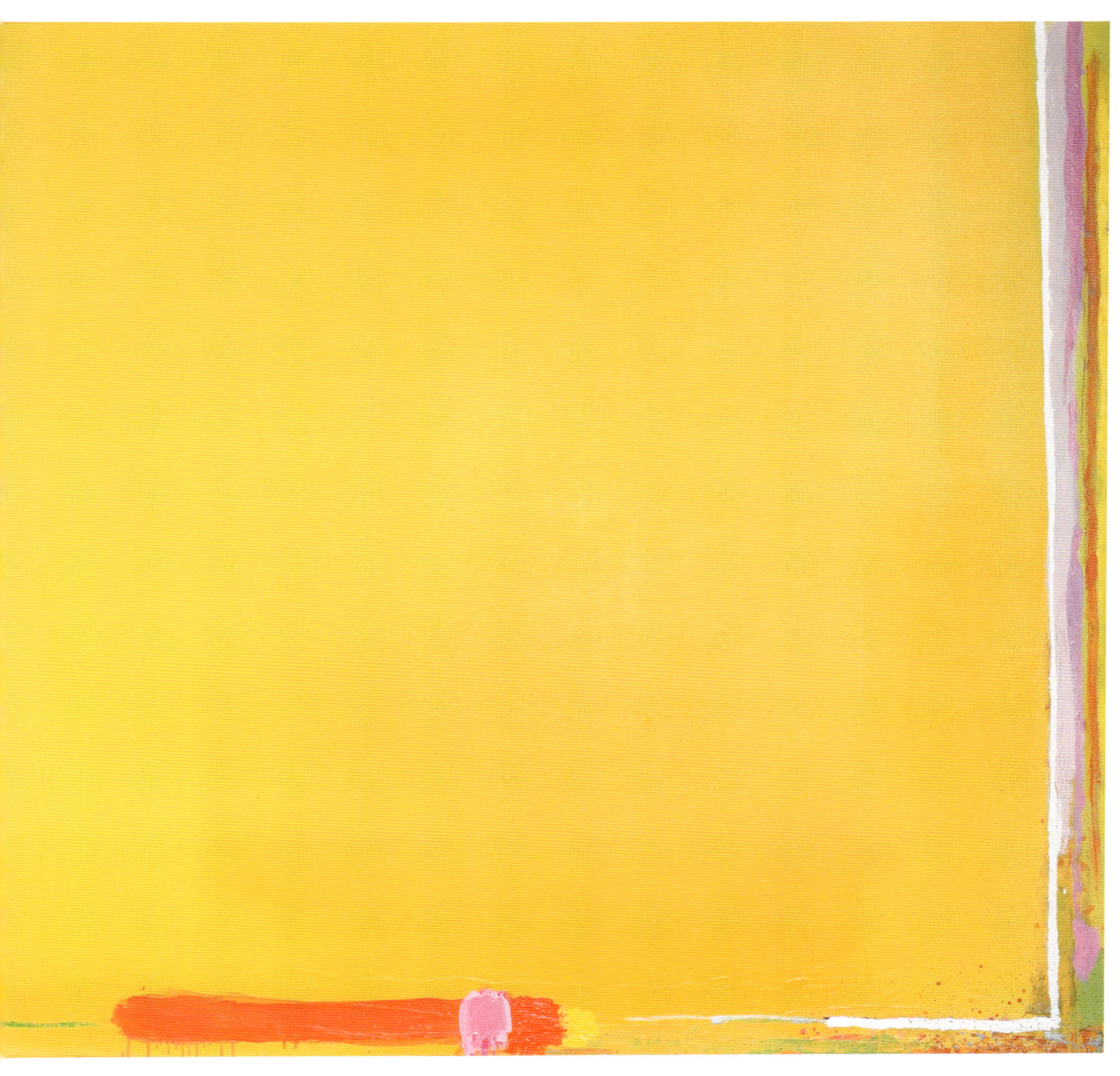

PLATE 25

JULES OLITSKI

Julius and Friends, 1967
Acrylic on canvas
71½ x 149¾ inches
Private collection; courtesy Foley Hoag LLP, Boston

he exhibited in New York with Painters Eleven, Anglophone Canada's first abstract artists. Soon after, Greenberg visited Toronto, invited by the group (with a few abstainers) to spend a half day in each of their studios. Bush always said that his session with Greenberg—the first of many, over the next two decades—was invaluable in helping him clarify his direction. It was also the start of a lifelong friendship that connected Bush with his like-minded peers among the critic's circle. Bush's ability to construct his pictures with virtuoso manipulations of mouthwatering, wholly invented hues plainly allies him with his friends among the Color Field painters, but his works were conceived very differently from those of his American colleagues. Instead of the neutral structures deduced from the proportions of the canvas of Noland or the emptied-out, resonant expanses of Olitski, or the suggestive, elusive pools of Frankenthaler, Bush populated his paintings with quirky stacks of color or free-wheeling calligraphic shapes. They seem improvised, but closer acquaintance reveals them to have been extracted from often improbable sources within Bush's everyday experience—shop window displays of women's clothing, glimpsed from a bus, patterns in giftwrapping paper, his flower garden, etc.—translated into a playful language of energetic abstraction.

The McLuhan-esque "cool," singing color, and declarative structure of the early work of Larry Poons and Walter Darby Bannard—both intimates of the Greenberg-Fried circle—signaled the advent of a vital, younger generation who shared many of the aesthetic aspirations of the older Color Field painters. Poons's early paintings, with their meticulously plotted arrangements of pulsing lozenges of dazzling color, seem at once irrational and ordered, with their elements arrayed according to some kind of ungraspable but persuasive logic. It is impossible to contemplate these uncanny pictures without thinking about Poons's early training as a musician and wondering if the disciplined but always surprising placement of the lozenges might be an arcane visual equivalent of a tone row.

Whether or not the analogy with music holds, Poons's focus on gridding out the canvas and devising systems for positioning the lozenges allowed his color instincts to operate freely and fully—an early iteration of what he calls "getting out of your own way," shorthand for finding devices or methods that encourage working from pure intuition. The explosive paintings that followed, in the early 1970s, were more radical examples of this effort to liberate impulse and set talent free, with gravity recruited to assert order by irresistibly affecting the flow of the extravagant curtains of paint. Calculation and the disciplined order imposed by drawing were replaced by the inevitable action of physical laws, with the artist's intention somehow subliminally influencing the forces of nature. No matter what their final orientation, Poons's use of thrown paint in these pictures makes high drama out of a flung liquid's simultaneous ability to briefly defy the tug of gravity and to flow in response to it. Unexpected, intuitive layerings and collisions of color make the "thrown" paintings notably elusive and alluring. Cascades of indescribable hues seem to shift and recompose themselves as we watch. Gesture is completely detached from the hand, with the visible memory of the throw and the subsequent motion of the liquid paint, at various speeds, turned simultaneously into a feast for the eye and an abstraction of physical laws.

As a student at Princeton in the late 1950s, Bannard shared Fried's and Stella's discovery and exploration of radical abstraction during those formative years. Bannard's paintings of the 1960s, like Olitski's, test the limits of economy, reducing compositional elements to a minimum and restricting the palette of each canvas to a narrow spectrum of high-key, intense hues. The most extreme of this early series are nearly unmodulated rectangles of a single hue, with narrow frames of contrasting colors, bare-bones compositions that anticipate Minimalism. In the works that followed, in the late 1960s and early 1970s, Bannard probed just how subtle chromatic nuances could be before they became an unbroken expanse. In these pictures, even composition could be reduced to a kind of near-negative, an echo of something no longer there. In a series of frontal compositions made by sweeping paint over applied rectangles and then removing the applications, all that remained was a tattered grid of luminous hues, like the memory of earlier, perhaps ephemeral painting incidents.

Among the young New York artists associated with Color Field ideas, Stella stands somewhat apart, despite his having been selected by Greenberg for *Post Painterly Abstraction* and despite the growing importance of near-Fauvist color in his work after about 1964. Independent-minded and fiercely intelligent, Stella has always been interested in working out permutations, proceeding from a more conceptualized point of departure than most painters associated with Color Field. The celebrated black or metallic Pinstripes that first established his reputation were not only doggedly uningratiating but decidedly subdued. Stella appeared to systematically reject such overt seductions as relationships of complex shapes or colors, substituting instead rows of monochrome stripes. When he very occasionally employed full-throttle hues, in the early 1960s, they were usually primaries, chosen, it seemed, as emblems of what Fried might have called "colorness," chromatic equivalents of black and white, rather than for their intrinsic qualities. The Pinstripes turned all-overness into literal surface, presented in terms of aggressive shape and insistent repetitions. In Stella's hands, Pollock's airborne, whiplash pours and drips became slow, broad, clean-edged strokes, his wide-flung spatters and loops of aluminum paint, a continuous expanse. The external, "literal" shape—Fried's term[15]—of this continuous expanse, simultaneously generated and measured by the repeated, regular, nested stripes, took precedence over color.

Yet in the mid-1960s, Stella produced a series termed Irregular Polygons that depended upon complex, interlocking blocks of astringent hues. Their eccentricities could be read as simple geometric shapes imposed on one another and framed with bands of color, but the result seemed nonetheless unpredictable. Fried discussed the Irregular Polygons' compelling fusion of "depicted"—internal—and "literal"—external—configurations[16] and suggested a connection with what Caro was proposing at the time, in his polychrome steel constructions, absent sculpture's need to be self-supporting. The observation is prescient, given Stella's later preoccupation with metaphorical and factual three-dimensional space in his work, but the way the Irregular Polygons flirt with perspectival illusion in their forthright shapes, together with the way color pries their literal flatness apart, also speaks to Stella's longstanding admiration for Hofmann.

The series that followed, the Protractors, moved even further toward a Hofmannesque activation of space—the famous credo of "push-pull" that at once affirms flatness and creates spatial dynamism. The Protractors are based on the familiar propositions of elementary geometry; what, for example, happens when a half-circle is inscribed in a square whose side forms the diameter. The lucid configurations that these exercises produce are elaborated upon with complicated overlappings and fractured with raucous, sometimes fluorescent color. At first acquaintance, the Protractors seem to risk slipping into the decorative—especially in contrast to the severe Pinstripes—but they prove more reticent than their apparently rational, symmetrical layouts and slightly cartoonish palette initially suggest. Despite their generous scale, clarity, and decorative appeal, there is something held back about the series, as if the Protractors refuse to yield up their logic

CONTINUED ON PAGE 66

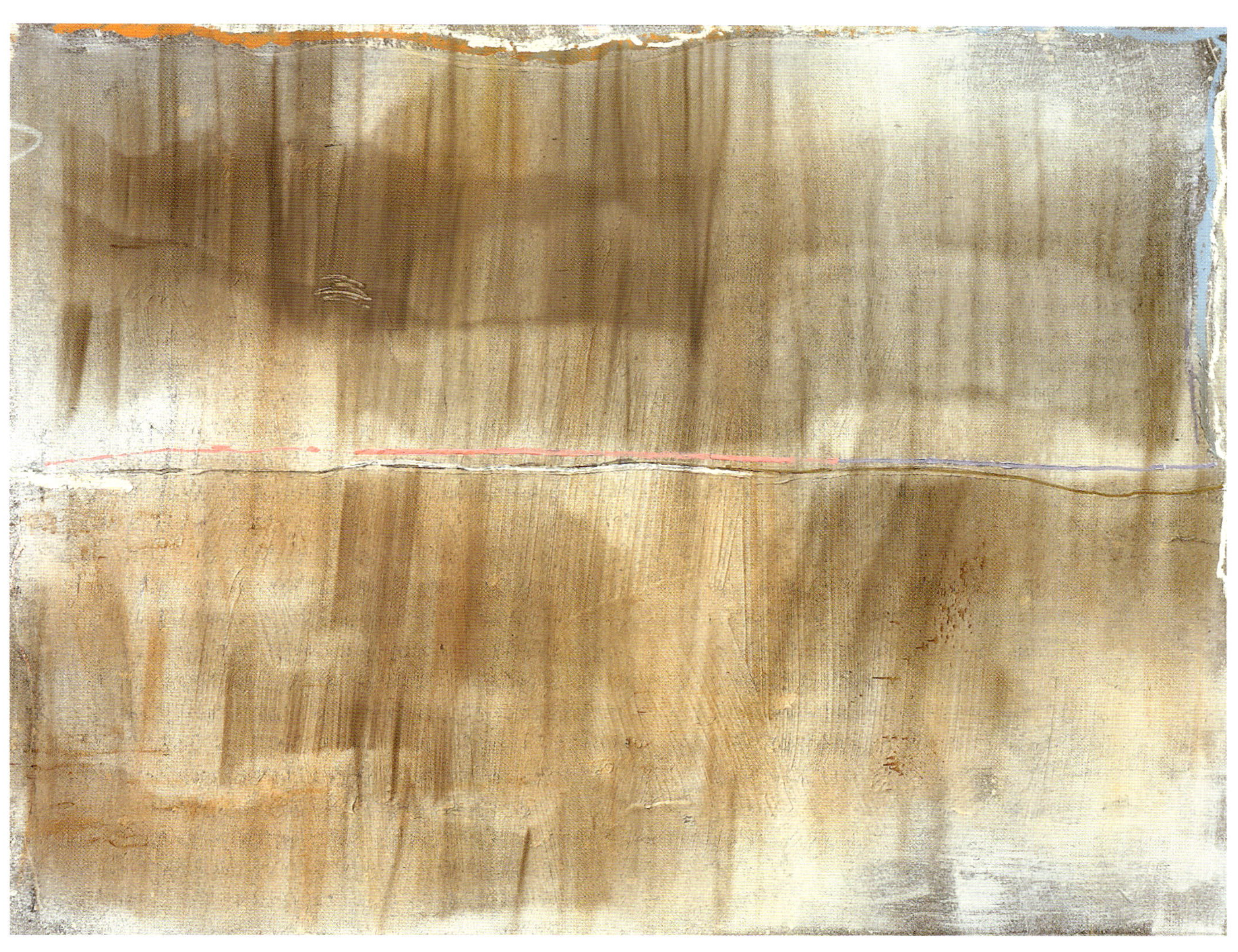

PLATE 26

JULES OLITSKI

Greek Princess–8, 1976
Acrylic on canvas
102⅛ x 132¼ inches
Hirshhorn Museum and Sculpture
Garden, Smithsonian Institution, Washington, D.C.;
museum purchase, 1976

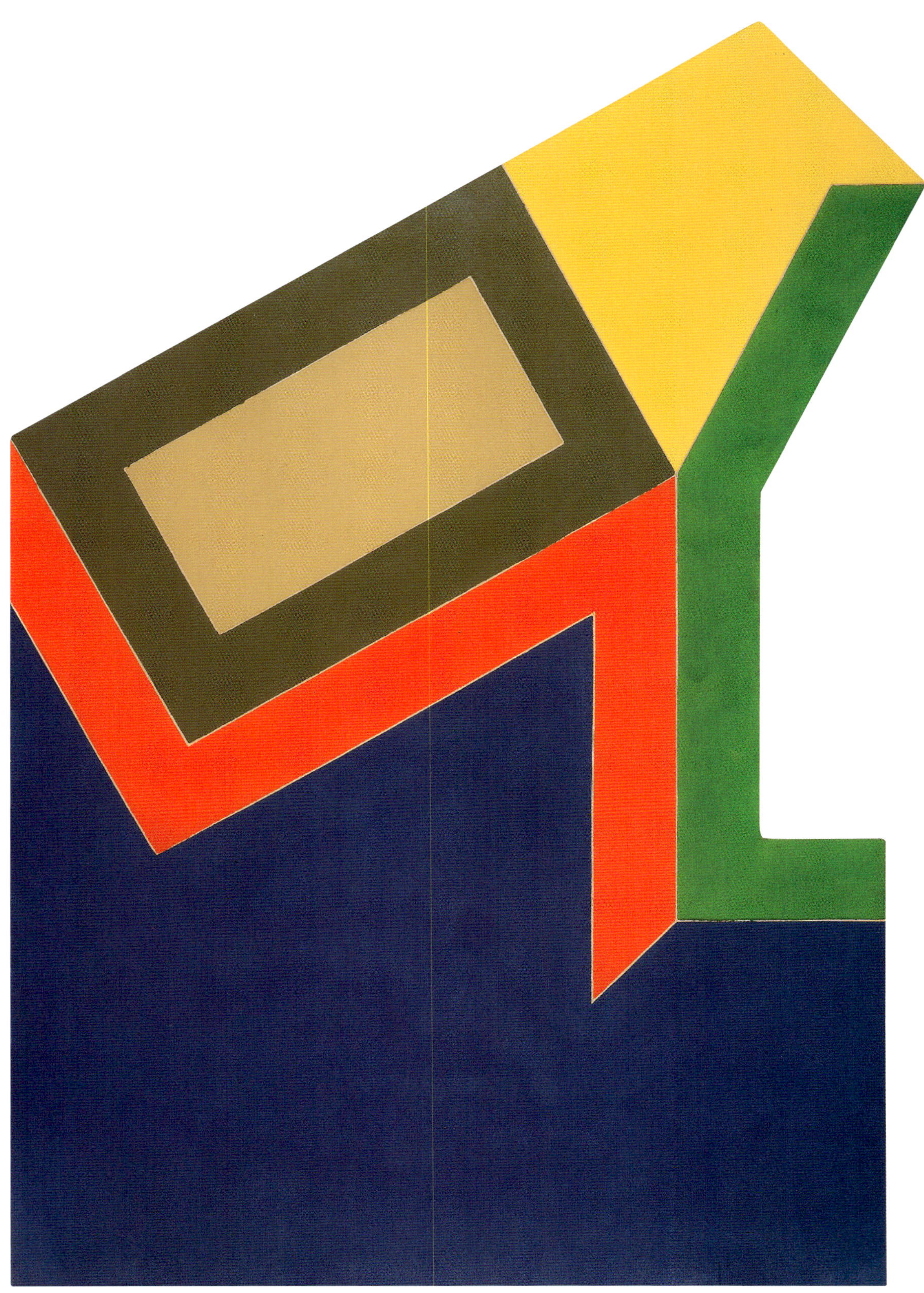

PLATE 27

FRANK STELLA

Moultonville II, 1966

Fluorescent alkyd and epoxy paint on canvas

124 x 86 inches

Collection Mr. and Mrs. David Mirvish, Toronto

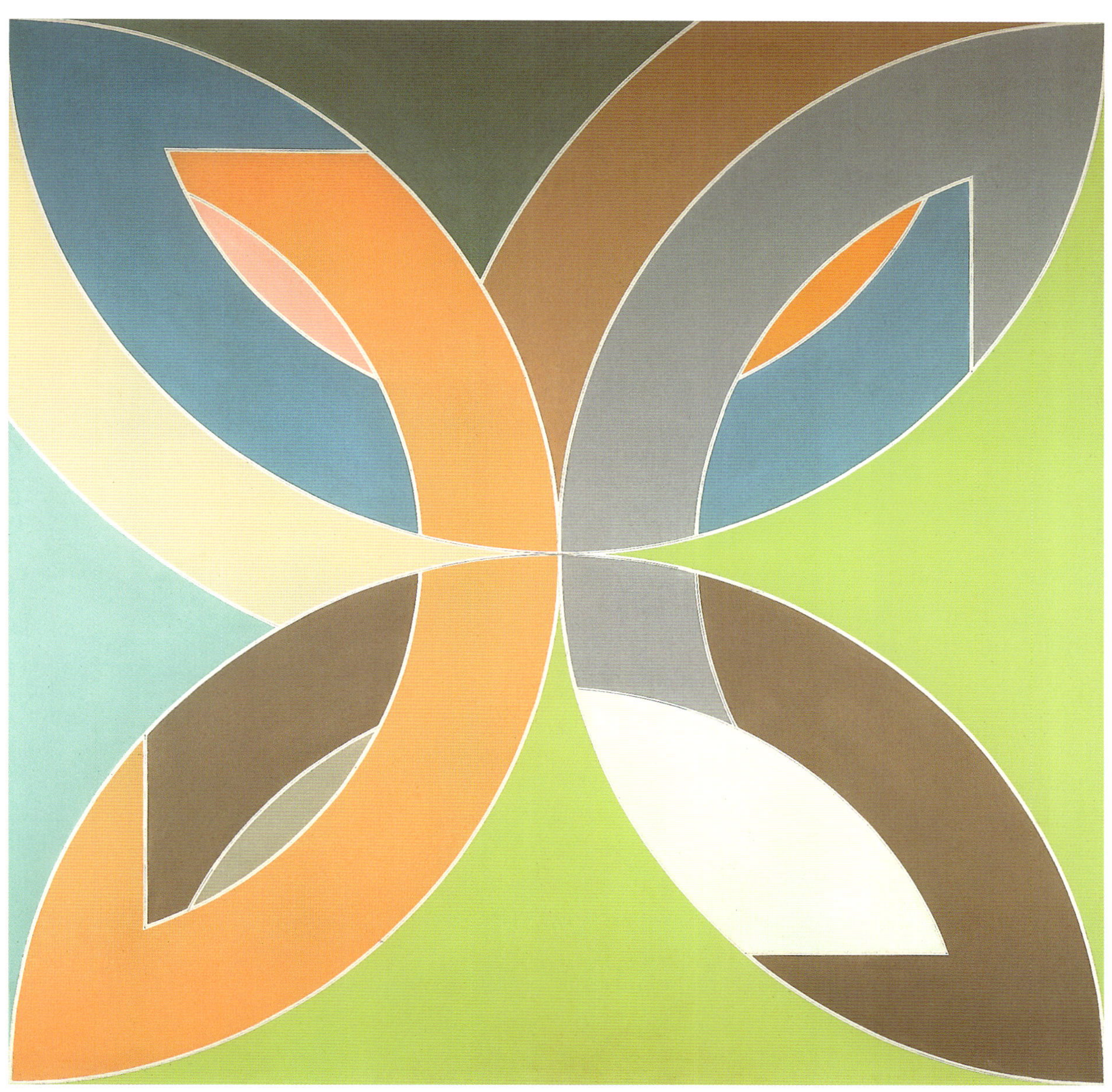

PLATE 28

FRANK STELLA

Flin Flon IV, 1969
Polymer and fluorescent polymer paint on canvas
96½ x 96½ inches
National Gallery of Art, Washington, D.C.; Robert and Jane Meyerhoff Collection (1994.82.1)

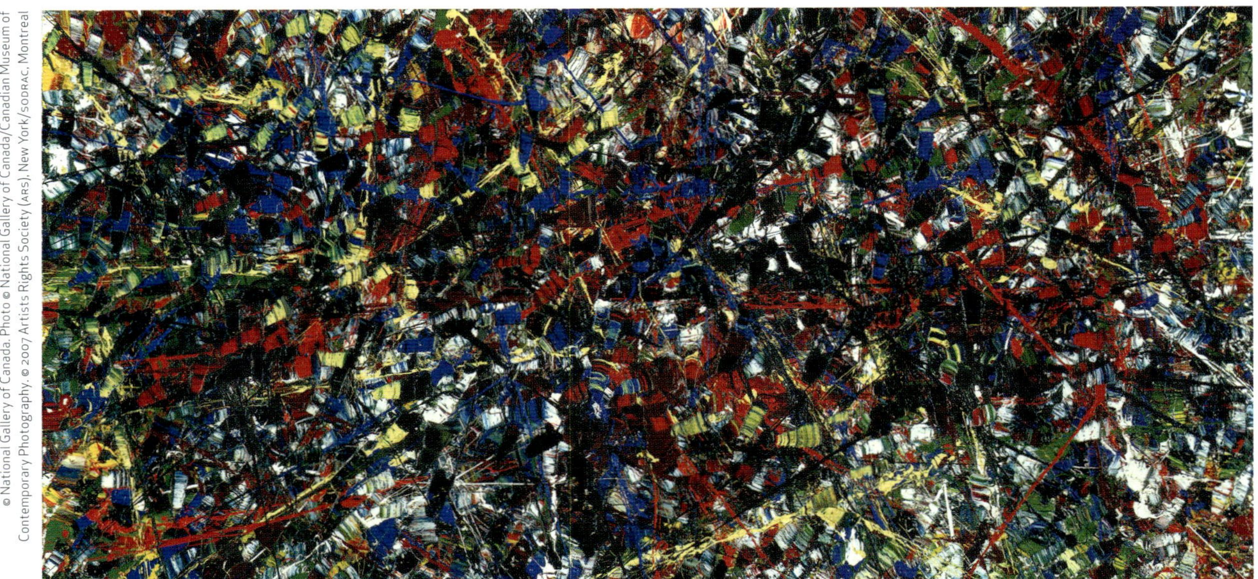

Jean-Paul Riopelle, *Knight Watch*, 1953
Oil on canvas, 38 x 76 ¾ inches. National Gallery of Canada; purchased 1954

entirely. Stella's disclaimer, "what you see is what you see," notwithstanding, both the Irregular Polygons and the Protractors are clearly rooted in the long tradition of Western art, including that of the anti-Malerische Abstract Expressionists. In their determined abstractness and their Greenbergian "openness and clarity," they also have deep affinities with the work of the Color Field painters, yet their near-garish palette, combined with their deadpan, confrontational formats, and their truculence, suggests a dialogue with the vernacular rather different from the high modernist detachment of the rest of the Color Field painters.

Sam Francis stands at a similar remove from the Greenberg circle, not only because of his West Coast affiliations, but also because of his long residence in France, between 1950 and 1957, and his extended travels in Japan; when Francis's work was selected for *Post Painterly Abstraction*, he had been back in California for only two years. Although Rothko, Still, and Pollock were clearly important to Francis, his work reveals the effects of other enthusiasms, perhaps most notably his interest in Japanese art and his friendship, during his Paris years, with the French-Canadian painter Jean-Paul Riopelle. Before moving to France, in the 1940s, Riopelle belonged to Les Automatistes, the Canadian equivalent of the Abstract Expressionists. These young Montreal-based artists were Canada's first abstract painters, part of a rebellious group of progressive thinkers from all professions for whom a devout belief in the creative powers of the unconscious replaced the devout Catholicism of the rest of the province of Quebec. Francis's distinctive way of building a picture with an accretion of rhythmic touches, at once deliberate and loose, seems equally indebted to the legacy of Abstract Expressionism, the slashing "automatic" gestures of Riopelle and his colleagues, and the most spontaneous, inspired Japanese brushwork, with an admixture of reverent homage to the planar strokes of Paul Cézanne's late watercolors.

This dependence on a mark that, like Cézanne's, is at once intimate and anonymous, distinguishes Francis's work. His touch, embodied by the pressure of the brush against the canvas, never announces itself as handwriting. Runs and drips are exploited as small-scale drawing, but the accumulated touches refuse interpretation as rapid or emotion-driven; instead, they insist on being read as the relics of slow, cool-headed, rather formal gestures. In several of Francis's series of the early 1960s, with their Japanese-inspired asymmetrical compositions, clusters of touches seem to try to escape the confines of canvas, suggesting the existence of a larger pictorial space, extending beyond the borders of the image before us. Time slows down as we follow Francis's overlapping touches of disembodied, weightless color across his large expanses of unpainted canvas; it is as if we were travelers in some fictive alternative system of space.

The inclusion of the Washington-based painter Gene Davis's radiant, singing stripe paintings in *Post Painterly Abstraction* allowed for the statement of yet another permutation of the Color Field aesthetic. Davis's bands of color are organized with military precision. In contrast to his colleague Kenneth Noland's groupings of horizontal bars whose spacing and dimensions vary, Davis's crisp stripes are placed vertically and evenly across the canvas, their constant width like the steady drumbeat that set the pace for the marching armies of antiquity. But Davis disrupts this linear order with blasts of intense color, creating irregular rhythms and counterrhythms by means of chromatic relationships. High-contrast bands, pressed side by side, add syncopation. Runs of closely related, more harmonious hues function as chords or broaden into large color zones. Eccentrically placed hues serve as accents. The strict repetitions of Davis's "drawing" are subsumed by rolling waves of color that change, depending on our distance from the canvas. From a close viewpoint, the colors of individual stripes become significant, while from a distance, the larger relationships among families of colors seem more critical to the composition. This is not to suggest that Davis's work depends on optical trickery or effects. Rather, his paintings add a kind of rowdy brass note to the Color Field aesthetic. Davis himself frequently said that he felt an affinity with the Pop Artists, since he thought of stripes as notably ordinary, ubiquitous elements of the everyday world. A more accurate comparison might be with Bush, with his invented configurations drawn from things randomly glimpsed in his daily life, translated into chromatic harmonies, assonances, and dissonances.

Davis's fellow Washingtonian Sam Gilliam is best known for his "drape" paintings, in which lengths of painted canvas are suspended, freed from the stretcher, so that they assume graceful Baroque configurations, determined by gravity's effect on the heavy fabric. Earlier, however, Gilliam worked on more conventionally presented canvases, yet his practice was distinguished by a reliance on the unpredictable—an echo of Poons's desire to get out of his own way—that prefigures his later explorations. After applying thinned-out paint to unstretched canvas, Gilliam folded the fabric and allowed color to soak through the layers, controlling the flow by the timing of the unfolding but otherwise minimizing the evidence of his hand. The loose, lyrical images that resulted read as floods of weightless, disembodied color, at once willed, directed, and found.

A diametrically opposed conception is announced by the work of the California-based painter Ronald Davis. His experiments with resins turned color literally into self-sufficient shape and form. Davis's paintings are things, constructed of solid, translucent hues; in them color becomes self-sustaining mass, its shape willed by the artist. These shapes are unequivocally flat, despite their evident density, but Davis wreaks havoc with our reading of these arresting objects by playing with perspectival illusions. Massive as they are, his color shapes refuse to settle down

CONTINUED ON PAGE 72

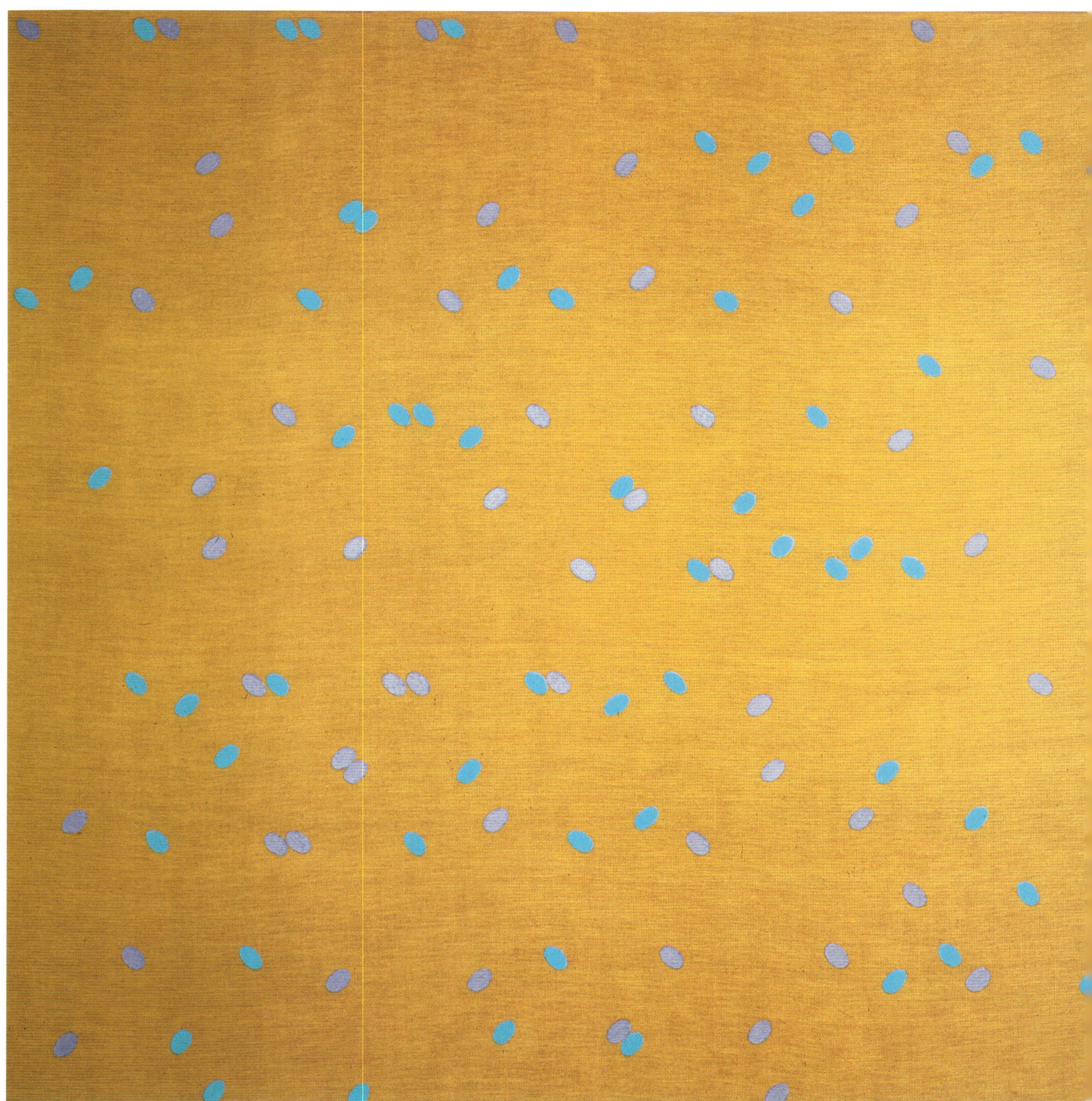

PLATE 29

LARRY POONS

Han-San Cadence, 1963
Acrylic and fabric dye on canvas
72 x 144 inches
Des Moines Art Center; purchased with funds from the Coffin Fine Arts Trust; Nathan Emory Coffin Collection of the Des Moines Art Center (1970.19)

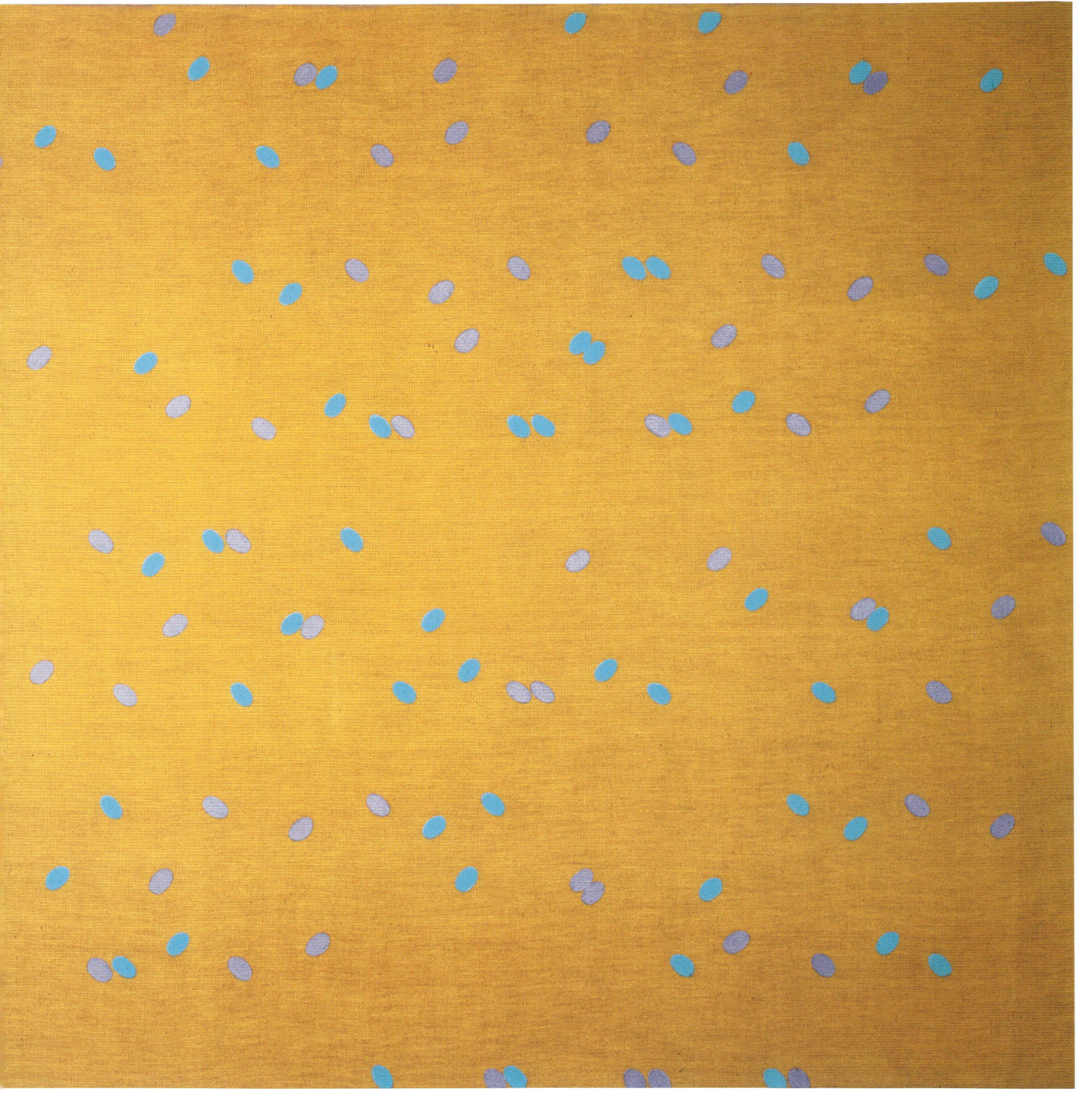

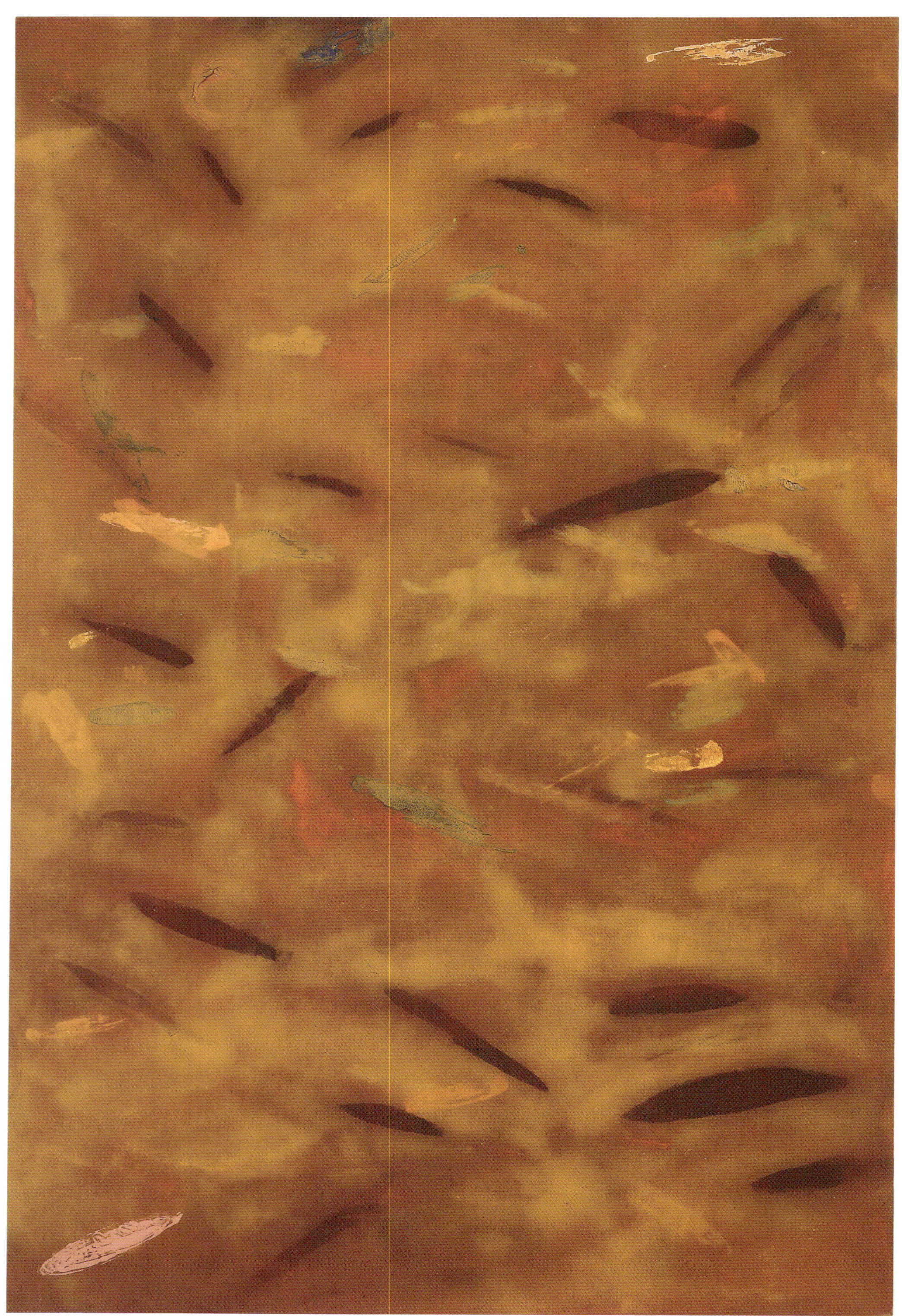

PLATE 30

LARRY POONS

Untitled, 1969
Acrylic on canvas
153 x 101 inches
The Museum of Contemporary Art, Los Angeles;
gift of Ronald Davis (83.35)

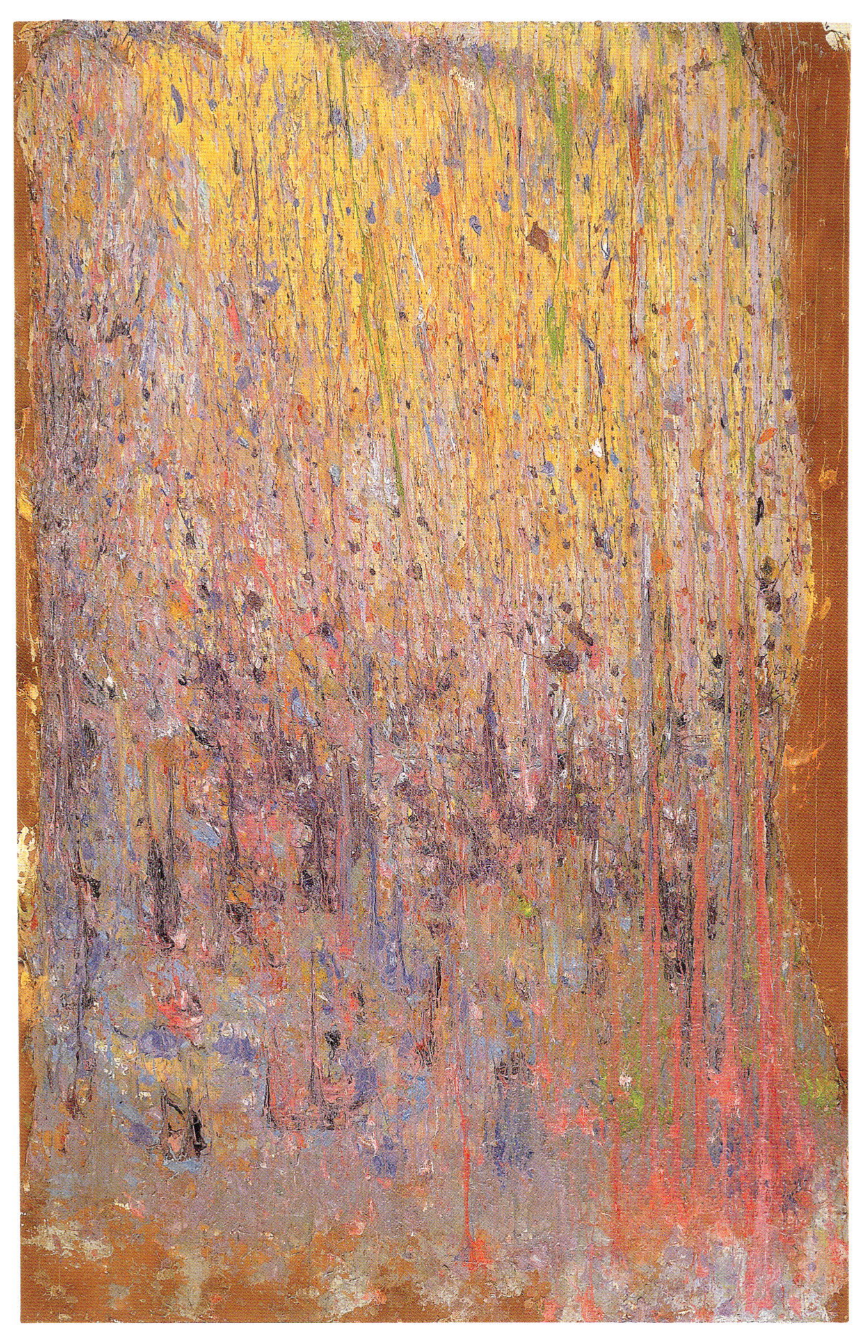

PLATE 31

LARRY POONS

Yellow and Brown Womb, 1972
Acrylic on canvas
118 x 73 ½ inches
Collection Mr. and Mrs. David Mirvish, Toronto

but demand that we remember how geometry is transformed by movement through space. In a sense, these engaging object-paintings are aggressively physical realizations of Olitski's desire to spray color in the air and have it stay there. Davis seems to have carved a chunk out of an infinite universe of inchoate colored matter and presented it for our delectation.

From Frankenthaler's stains to Olitski's sprays to Poons's throws to Ronald Davis's enthusiastic embrace of new mediums, the history of Color Field painting, like the history of modernism itself, can be described in terms of unexpected facture, beginning with Pollock's working with unstretched cotton duck, spread on the floor. Ideologically, Pollock's removing the support from the stretcher freed the painter to work from all directions and allowed boundaries and the orientation of the picture to be decided only at the end; practically, it permitted pouring and staining. Pouring and staining, of course, imply that gravity is also part of the painter's arsenal. Louis's pictures depend, in their execution, on paint's response to this elemental force but defy its power with inverted configurations that can place the spreading bottom of a pour at the top of a rivulet of color. Olitski defied gravity when he sprayed color on his canvases—the next best thing to spraying it in the air and having it remain there. Poons's "thrown" pictures of the 1970s, by contrast, not only acknowledged the effect of gravity on paint but also made it the primary agent of drawing, as well as one of the determining factors in the relationship of superimposed colors. Gilliam's staining and folding harnessed gravity in a different way, slowing down its effects on liquid paint to create multiple versions of the same color passage on the same canvas, once it was unfolded. Ronald Davis's resin paintings made gravity irrelevant.

Much has been written about the visual weightlessness of Color Field painting, about the way thinned-out paint, soaked into unprimed canvas, becomes contiguous with the fabric itself, creating zones of color that appear to have little or no physical presence—that are, in short, for the eye only. The unpainted spaces between these zones, like intervals of silence between notes, can seem as important and evocative as the painted elements, further disembodying the abstract images. When paintings of this type were first exhibited, their clarity and brilliance, along with their insubstantial, almost anonymous surfaces made them appear so different from the gestural abstractions of the preceding generation that whatever evidence of the hand remained visible seemed unimportant. The novelty of paint that had been applied by pouring or with spray guns, squeegees, and spreaders, in place of traditional tools, may also have encouraged the first viewers of these paintings to ignore traces of handwriting. Today, when such methods are commonplace, the residual gestures of some Color Field pictures are starting to reveal themselves, perhaps in contrast to the proliferation of computer-generated and photo-based images whose surfaces are truly mechanical and anonymous. When, for example, Noland's earliest thinly painted, spare Circle paintings, with their concentric rings of color, were initially shown, any deviations from symmetry, impure edges, or occasional splatters seemed less important than the pictures' amazing fragility of surface, radiance, and chromatic fullness, probably because the cumulative effect was of their striking difference from the prevailing norms of second-generation Abstract Expressionism. Noland himself chose to emphasize that difference, making the edges of color bars in his subsequent paintings meticulously crisp and clean, yet with the passage of time, the animating irregularities of some of his earliest Circles have become newly visible and newly eloquent.

Other perceptions of color-based abstraction are subject to change, as well. From today's

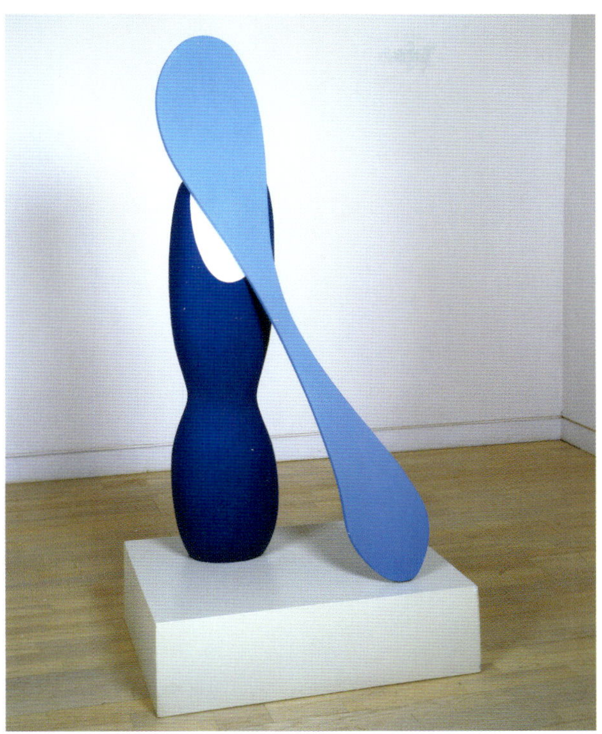

Isaac Witkin, *Alter Ego*, 1963
Painted wood and plastic, 65½ x 27¾ x 18½ inches
Private collection, courtesy Locks Gallery, Philadelphia

perspective, some of the unmistakable earmarks of Color Field painting turn out not to be solely specific to post-painterly abstraction but generally characteristic of painting of the late 1960s. It is possible, for example, to find parallels between Color Field's quest for radical simplicity and transparency of intention with Minimalism's striving for economy or to see that the Color Field painters and their contemporaries, the Pop artists, shared a taste for clarity and anonymous facture. Gene Davis's contention that he thought of himself as connected with Pop artists is not altogether facetious. Yet these large similarities coexist with profound differences. No matter how simplified, Color Field painting was never reductive in the way that Minimalism is. The Color Field painters remained faithful to the idea of working as closely as possible out of pure intuition, on the assumption that the resulting painting would be revelatory of its maker; they rejected Minimalism's fascination with preconception and systems. Similarly, Color Field painting and Pop Art are separated by fundamentally different attitudes, not only toward imagery but also toward material means. The "cool" immaculate surfaces and discrete color areas of Color Field painting are intended as expressive elements in themselves, not as in Pop Art, as equivalents for the machine-made, mass-produced artifacts of popular culture, advertising, and the mass media.

There are, however, deep connections between the evolution of Color Field painting and the evolution of sculpture in the 1960s, most notably in the work of Anthony Caro and his immediate circle. Caro drew upon the legacy of Pablo Picasso and Julío González's open construction in metal, by way of David Smith, and moved this inheritance into the realm of complete abstraction, with polychrome steel structures that apparently defied gravity to hover above the ground. The impetus for Caro's radical reinvention of what sculpture could be came, in part, from his encounters with the paintings of Frankenthaler, Noland, Gottlieb, and others, on his first trip to the United States from his native Great Britain, in 1959. Like his painter colleagues, who later became his close friends, Caro made eloquent dramas out of interval, extension, and edges, realized in wholly sculptural, spatially articulate terms; he adopted industrial materials and rendered them optical and seemingly weightless by virtue of their placement and color. At the time Caro was taking his own work in unprecedented directions and expanding conceptions of the nature of sculpture, he was teaching at London's Saint Martin's School of Art. He encouraged his students, who were not much younger than he, to join him in his explorations, urging them to experiment with new materials: glass, wood, fiberglass, colored Plexiglas. The results suggested new possibilities for

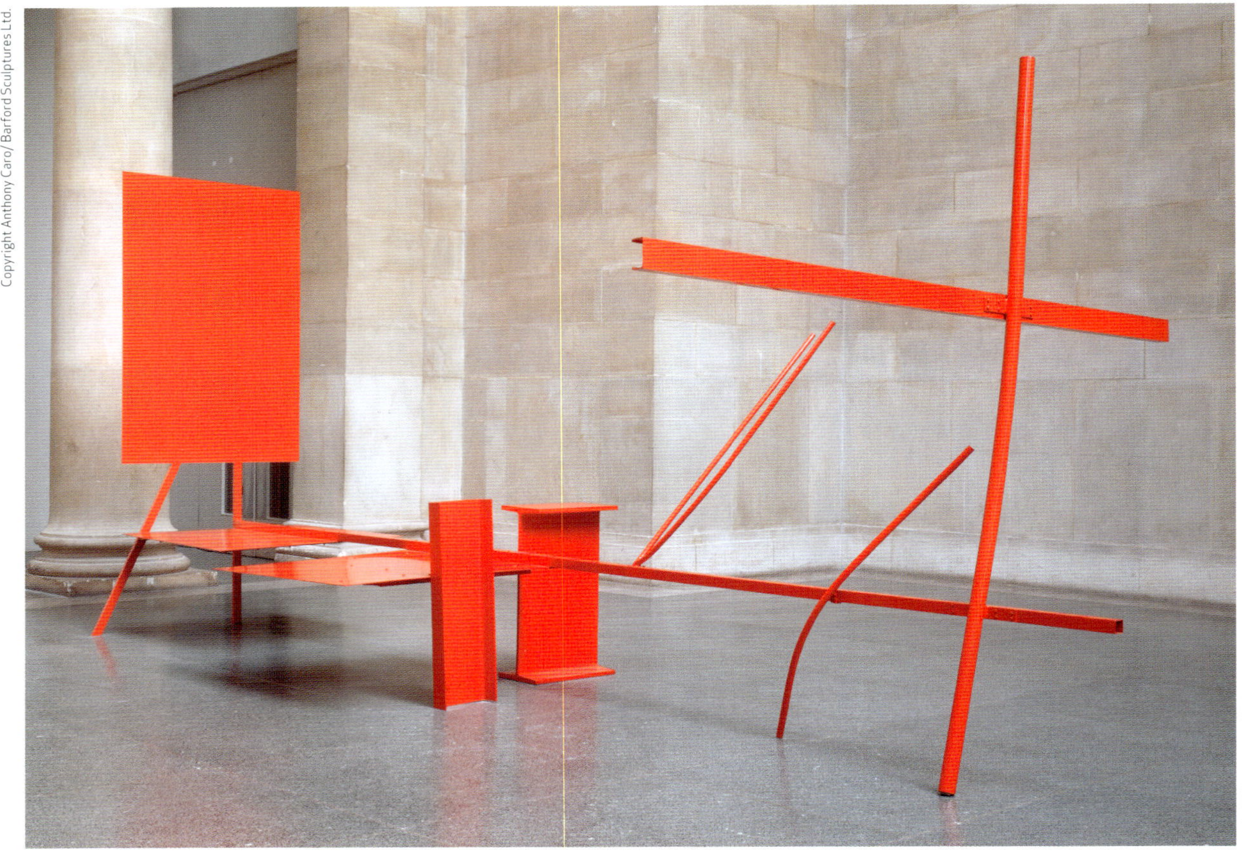

Anthony Caro, *Early One Morning*, 1962
Painted steel and aluminum, 9½ x 20 x 11 feet. Tate Gallery, London; presented by the Contemporary Art Society, 1965 (T00805)

the fusion of color and form, and received, like Caro's own work, wide international attention. The dialogue between what was termed "the new sculpture"—a largely British phenomenon, in the early 1960s—and American painting was expanded when Caro began to spend more time in the United States, beginning with his stint at Bennington College, in 1963, which brought him into close contact with Noland and Olitski. The way the conversation among all of these artists was made visible by their work of the 1960s and 1970s is complex, provocative, and warrants more focused attention.

Over the past decade and a half, and until recently, when astute eyes have begun to reevaluate what remains a living tradition, the reputation of the Color Field painters has sometimes seemed problematic. Greenberg's enthusiasm for their work has been detrimental, in many respects. Even when he was at the height of his powers and influence, the outspoken critic was often seen as authoritarian, the tacit "in my opinion" that underlay all of his value judgments, ignored. By the 1980s, until his death in 1994, his subtlest observations were misconstrued as prescriptions, most often, it must be acknowledged, by those who had not read his work. Greenberg's view, for example, that modernism squeezed deep space out of painting, as each medium gradually purged itself of everything not intrinsic to itself, was interpreted by many not as a conclusion based on a wide experience of looking at art, but as a simplistic directive—as in the often repeated assertion that Greenberg said paintings ought to be flat. He was accused of telling artists what to do, when, in fact, they urged him to come to their studios because they valued his responses—whether or not they acted upon them, which they often didn't. Even today, a decade after his death, the personal animosities aroused by this difficult, thorny man can seem to get in the way of objective judgment of his achievement, and by extension, to obscure the excellences of the art with which he was most closely associated.

In the 1980s and 1990s, Color Field abstraction, with its deliberate avoidance of specific narrative and nonvisual issues, was often accused of being reactionary, patriarchal, and phallocentric—among other things. Modish critics and art historians, reared on a diet of art that insists on elaborate verbal explication, and deeply mistrustful of anything that doesn't come fully bolstered with words, have decried Color Field painting as merely decorative, a charge, it is worth noting, that has also been leveled at Matisse and his profound investigations of the tension between his acute perceptions of space and mass, and the fact of the flat surface of the canvas or sheet of paper. More politically or sociologically-minded critics have faulted the work produced by Color Field artists as "corporate" or "bland," bolstering their conclusion, through a stunning leap of logic, by assuming that if the paintings of Noland or Louis were acquired by public and corporate collections it was not because of the work's aesthetic potency, but rather because it did not disturb, threaten to fall apart, or shout. We can hold Marcel Duchamp responsible for this point of view; made uneasy by what he scornfully called "aesthetic delectation," he claimed that, as a corrective, he wished "to carry the mind of the spectator toward other regions more verbal."[17] Unfortunately, the minds of many spectators, who include makers of art, as well as art historians, critics, and curators, have been carried so far into regions so purely literary that they seem to have forgotten that the visual is as much a cerebral function as the verbal. Perhaps, today's renewed interest in painting, posited on the conviction that the eye, the intellect, and the emotions are inextricably connected, is an indication that art is retreating from "regions more verbal" back to the complex, subtle, endlessly fascinating, wordless realm of the visual. "Aesthetic delectation" is neither a bad thing nor a simple one. The eye, after all, is directly connected to the brain.

NOTES

All quotations or paraphrases attributed to various artists and not otherwise documented come from conversations with the author, ca. 1975 to the present various dates.

1 Clement Greenberg, "After Abstract Expressionism" (*Art International*, October 25, 1962), in *Clement Greenberg: The Collected Essays and Criticism*, vol. 4, *Modernism with a Vengeance, 1957–1969*, ed. John O'Brian (Chicago: University of Chicago Press, 1993), 123.

2 Clement Greenberg, *Post Painterly Abstraction*, exhib. cat. (Los Angeles County Museum of Art, 1964), in O'Brian, *Clement Greenberg*, vol. 4, 192.

3 Ibid., 195.

4 Greenberg selected all the participating artists with the exception of those from California. The Californians, who included Sam Francis and Ronald Davis, were selected by James Elliott, curator at Los Angeles County Museum of Art, the organizing institution. The exhibition included a number of artists who today are considered to have been interested in conceptions of painting quite different from those generally associated with the majority of those exhibited; they include, among others, Ellsworth Kelly, Arthur McKay, and Ludwig Sander.

5 Ibid., 192.

6 Obviously, these associations vary with each viewer and may or may not correspond, even tangentially, to those of the painter himself. Rothko, for example, always insisted that there was a mystical, rhetorical, "tragic" subtext to his work.

7 Since, according to Greenberg's model, the non-essentials of painting, included illusionism and narrative, the "ultimate" reduction would, logically, be a flat surface covered with a single hue; Greenberg, frequently asked if this would be a painting, would reply "Yes, but not necessarily a good one."

8 Quoted in Lucy R. Lippard, ed., "Questions to Stella and Judd," *ArtNews*, September 1966, 59.

9 Greenberg, "After Abstract Expressionism," in O'Brian, *Clement Greenberg*, vol. 4, 131.

10 Henry Geldzahler, "An Interview with Helen Frankenthaler," *Artforum*, October 1965, 37.

11 Quoted in Karen Wilkin, *Kenneth Noland* (New York: Rizzoli International Publications, 1990), 8.

12 Quoted in Karen Wilkin, *Frankenthaler: Works on Paper, 1949–1984*, exhib. cat. (New York and Washington, D.C.: George Braziller and International Exhibitions Foundation, 1984), 66.

13 Louis, who died in 1962, was included posthumously in *Post Painterly Abstraction.*

14 Kenworth Moffett, *Jules Olitski*, exhib. cat. (Boston: Museum of Fine Arts, 1973), 34.

15 Michael Fried, "Frank Stella's Irregular Polygons" (1966), in *Art and Objecthood: Essays and Reviews* (Chicago: University of Chicago Press, 1998), 81.

16 Ibid.

17 Quoted in Dore Ashton, ed., *Twentieth Century Artists on Art* (New York: Pantheon Books, 1985), 21.

Fields of Dreams

Carl Belz

I. THE 1950S WERE PROSPEROUS BUT DREARY. AMERICA EMERGED after World War II as a global power, confident in its promise of the good life in suburbia. What we got instead was Levittown, the cold war, Eisenhower, the McCarthy hearings, Korea, *The Man in the Gray Flannel Suit*, Ed Sullivan, the silent generation, and the Ivy League look—trim and buttoned-down for success. Young people were eager to grow up and become adults. True, they got a countercultural buzz from *On the Road*, and true, too, they had their own music— rock 'n' roll—which caused a ruckus when it emerged early in the decade and briefly pitted them against their parents. They even found a spokesman in Elvis, but the trajectory of the King's enormous commercial success throughout the 1950s reflected their underlying ambition, which was to emulate their elders and share their material comforts. Elvis was a raw country talent, brash and sexy, when he first recorded on the Sun label, but RCA quickly smoothed out all the rough edges, made him acceptable to an increasingly moderate audience, and diluted his originality in the process. It all felt like a letdown.

In comparison, the 1960s spawned an outspoken generation that was as hedonistic as it was activist, as determined in pursuing pleasure as in remaking the world—a generation whose excesses were coupled in the call to make love, not war, and the warning not to trust anyone over thirty. The 1960s were self-indulgent, yet, equally, were they idealistic, a seemingly win-win moment. But it didn't turn out that way; instead it turned ugly. We got the unthinkable assassinations of John F. Kennedy, Martin Luther King, Jr., and Robert F. Kennedy, the destruction of the Watts riots, and the tragedy of Vietnam. We reveled in a summer of love but closed out the decade with student protests erupting on college campuses all across the country and giving us the horror of Kent State in 1970. It was the start of a new decade, but the 1960s weren't finished. Jimi Hendrix, Janis Joplin, and Jim Morrison were all dead within a year, their meteoric careers senselessly extinguished. The utopian dreams that started with Camelot had fizzled.

Against this backdrop, we were presented with some of the great painting of our time, the painting of the New York school, which inexorably took its place alongside the great painting of the school of Paris, where modernism had originated a full century earlier. Hard to believe of a culture that had been largely provincial be-

CONTINUED ON PAGE 80

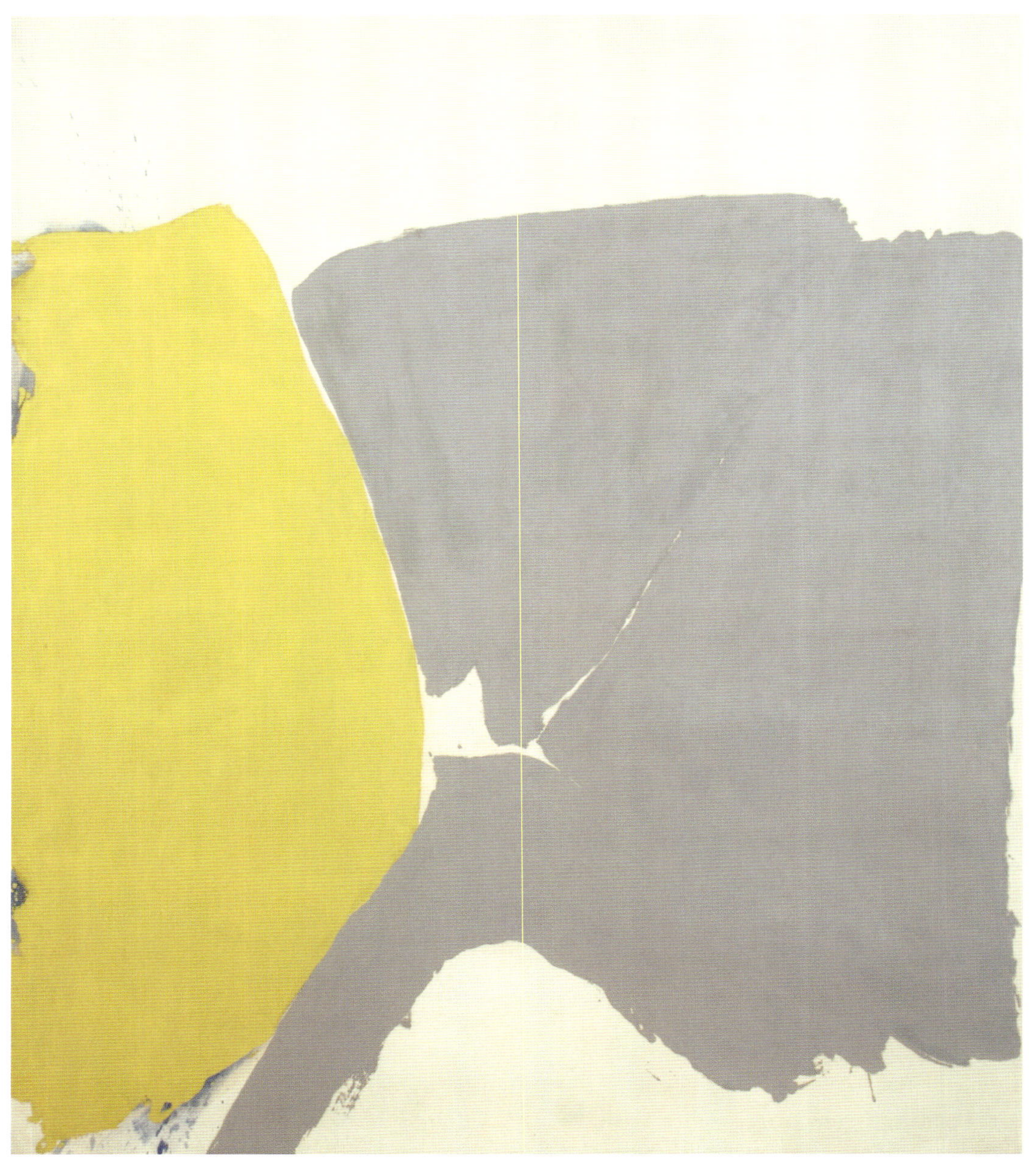

PLATE 32

FRIEDEL DZUBAS

Lotus, 1962
Oil on canvas
80½ x 68½ inches
Estate of Friedel Dzubas; courtesy Jacobson
Howard Gallery, New York

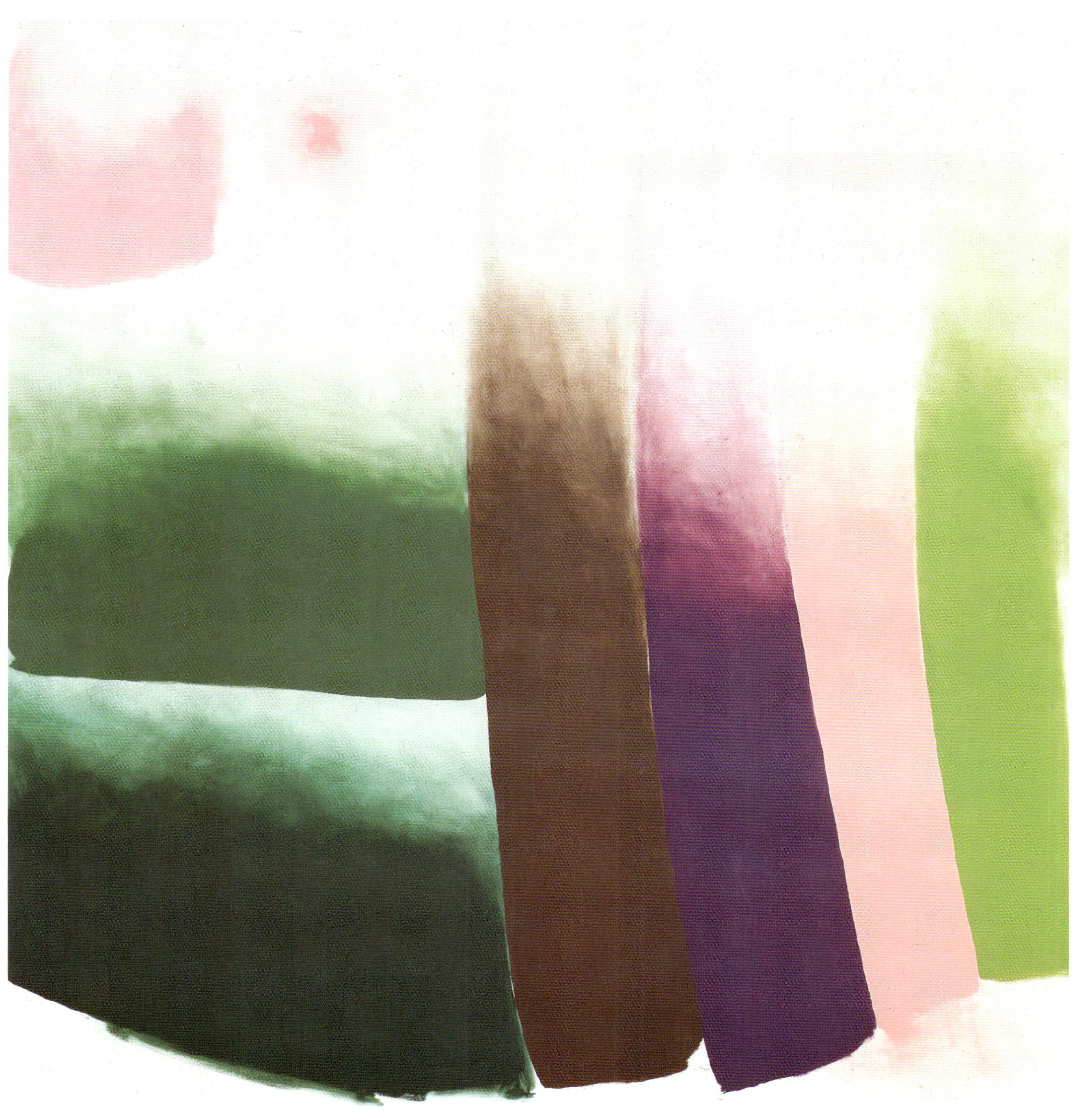

PLATE 33

FRIEDEL DZUBAS

Trough, 1972
Synthetic polymer on canvas
96¼ x 98⅜ inches
Hirshhorn Museum and Sculpture Garden, Smithsonian Institution, Washington, D.C.; museum purchase with funds donated by the Smithsonian Resident Associates Program, 1975

fore the war and then became so conservative on the one hand and so radical on the other. Not so hard to believe, at the same time, is the fact that the painting in question was unabashedly abstract. Consisting of lines and shapes and fields of color, it imaged none of the subjects available on the cultural landscape of the time, seeming instead to be utterly detached from them, as if it were merely art for art's sake that had nothing to do with lived experience. Yet, those same paintings—and the artists who made them—were in their own way as radical and conservative as the culture in which they flowered, displaying a vitality unmatched by any other paintings made in the years between 1950 and 1975, a vitality that is about nothing if not lived experience, either then or now.

II. My reflections on color-based painting between 1950 and 1975 begin with the later 1950s when, as an impressionable college undergraduate, I was first introduced to the new American art that had emerged in New York in the aftermath of World War II—to Mark Rothko and Hans Hofmann, for instance, and, with them, Abstract Expressionism. The discourse at the time, openly and irresistibly romantic, was laden with existential rhetoric and images of the artist operating on the edge of the abyss, risking all in the all-or-nothing stakes posed by each blank canvas, a scenario for which Rothko and his work were made to order. Rothko's personal struggle against anxiety and isolation, like the hovering rectangles he painted, embodied an urge to lift himself and his artistic voice to a spiritual level that transcended the humdrum concerns of the everyday world and in doing so demonstrated what artistic expression was all about for members of his generation, the first generation of the New York school.

Hofmann was more earthbound. A full generation older than the abstract expressionists among whom he circulated—and by whom he was highly respected—his firsthand experience of Matisse and Picasso inured him to the cultural alienation that haunted many of his younger colleagues and too often propelled them toward lives of self-destruction. In contrast, Hofmann was comfortable with the meaning of his enterprise; he had nothing to prove and was content to move his painting along at its own pace. He was said to be an influential teacher who encouraged his students to address every square inch of every canvas via his theory of push and pull—if an area recedes over here, pull it back over there; if it projects at the top, push it back at the bottom, and so on, but in any case keep the surface everywhere taut, every part in dynamic tension with every other part in order to make the picture whole. In the darkened lecture hall where I initially heard about Hofmann and saw reproductions of his work, the push-pull theory was altogether clear; I could actually point to its workings. But there was no romance associated with that, the theory seeming instead to border on the academic, like a formula for making pictures.

Such was my experience of painting in the 1950s as the enthusiasms of its critics filtered from the art magazines into the classroom. Terms such as Color Field painting and post-painterly abstraction were not then used to describe the art, but they would soon be forthcoming from the pen of Clement Greenberg, and they would increasingly gain currency as the next decade unfolded. Also forthcoming would be my increased firsthand encounters with the pictures I had initially learned about in school. A particularly memorable example was a Hans Hofmann exhibition at the Museum of Modern Art in 1963. Towering before me was a painter whose work blew away one after another of the critical theories I'd been absorbing and gave the lie to my naïve assumption that they were in any way formulaic. There were pictures clearly based on landscape that also featured rectangular slabs of color, thus challenging the abstract versus-representational divide that supposedly signaled self-conscious modernist autonomy. There were pictures that combined troweled pigment with thin washes of color, thus questioning the then-current impulse toward singularly unified surfaces. There were pictures in which impulsively dripped lines suggested human figures or animals, thus recalling a surrealist practice that had presumably been buried in the 1940s. And one after another there were pictures in which color eclipsed all of the above—including Hofmann's own push-pull dictum—pictures whose sheer exuberance celebrated painting in and of itself and left no doubt about its primary resource. The exhibition was at once stunning and unsettling—stunning in the way pictures I thought I knew assumed an entirely new significance, unsettling in the way those same pictures disrupted my overall thinking about painting in the 1950s and early 1960s. On top of that, there was the fact that the pictures were painted by an artist who hit his stride in his seventies and whose powers were undiminished while he was in his eighties, which was nothing less than inspirational.

Hofmann could fling paint as well as anyone around in the 1950s—paint-flinging being a conventional sign of an artist's signature identity then—but in the end his pictures were more detached than Rothko's, which was surprising insofar as Rothko didn't fling paint at all. By detached, I mean not that they weren't expressive, even ebullient—as so many of Hofmann's works were, giving the impression that, whatever their challenges, the artist experienced deep pleasure in making them—rather, that they were expressive in a different way. While Rothko's softly brushed pictures were highly evocative, transporting you into his radiant fictive world—the Rothko world, pure and simple, that was so unmistakably his—Hofmann's kept one riveted to what was right before your eyes. Although the artist's personal touch was evident in each one, Hofmann's pictures were not first of all personal; they seemed as separate from him as they were from any beholder, as though, once they were brought into being, their meaning existed independently of maker or viewer and was utterly self-contained, even when they included allusive imagery. Hofmann, especially in his dignified "slabs" of color, occasionally got me thinking about the music I was listening to at the time, the cool trumpet of Miles Davis, for instance, and the concerts of his I'd been to in which he would wander the stage, aloof, spinning his improvisatory magic, oblivious of his audience and his band alike, alone, fully absorbed in the sound itself. Whether it was painting or music, I found that kind of experience exhilarating; its "impersonalness" even offered a fresh glimpse of freedom—instead of romanticizing about the artist's intent, I could focus first of all on what the artist had actually done.

So painting in the 1950s began to simmer down in my understanding, which meant retooling some of the concepts I had been presented with earlier. Like the "one-shot" painting, for instance. In the heyday of gestural abstraction, the one-shot painting was the one that, however many hours or days had actually been consumed in bringing it to completion, looked as though it had been created during a single burst of inspiration. Willem de Kooning's late 1950s pictures were archetypes of this look and, in appearing to have come about as an existential, instantaneous assault on the canvas—which is how Harold Rosenberg had evoked it in his 1952 *Art News* article "The American Action Painters"—the look became inseparable from the picture's meaning. For the young Kenneth Noland, by comparison, the one-shot painting wasn't identified with how

CONTINUED ON PAGE 90

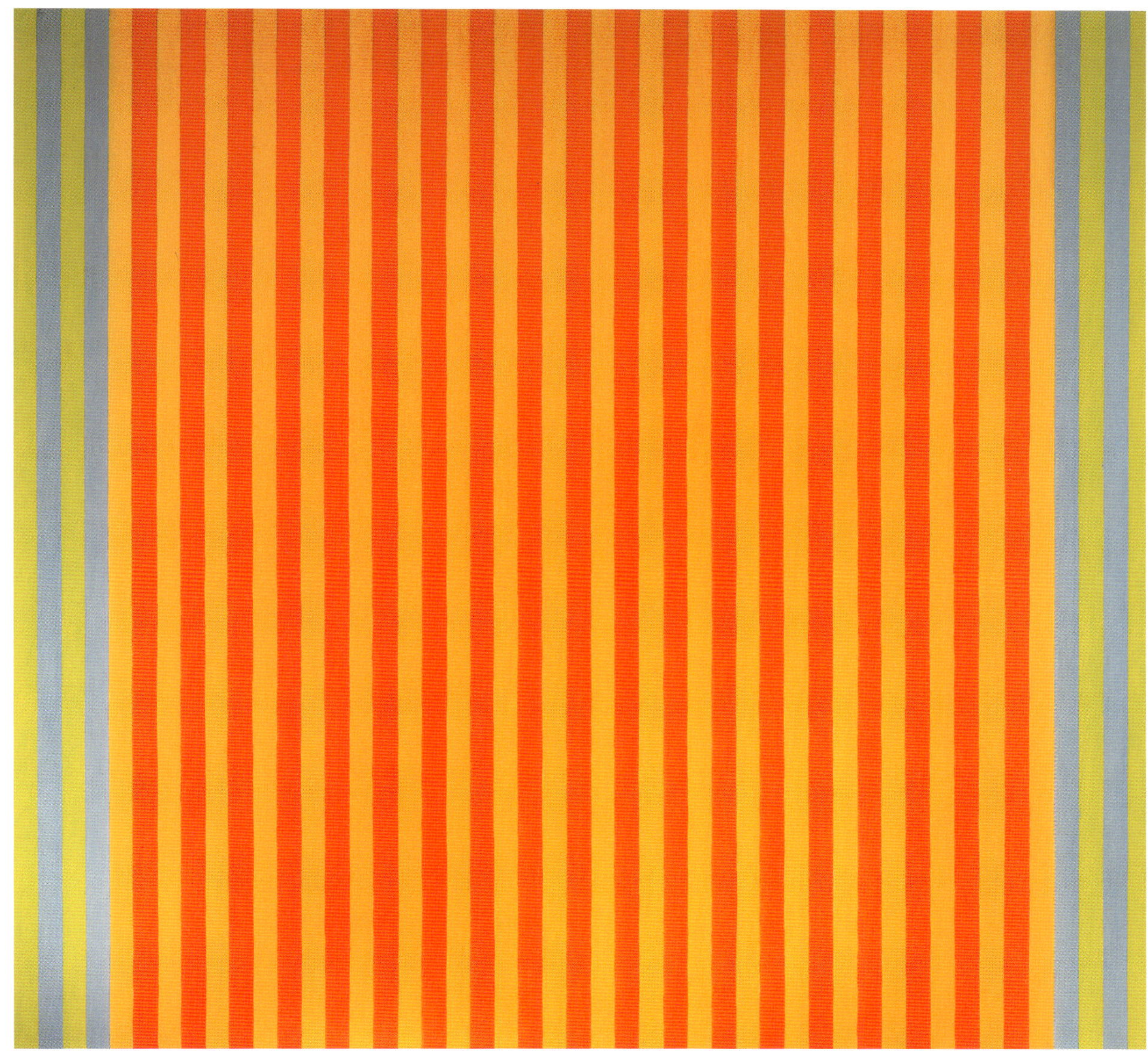

PLATE 34

GENE DAVIS

Sun Ball, 1960
Magna on canvas
88 x 93⅝ inches
Courtesy Charles Cowles Gallery, New York

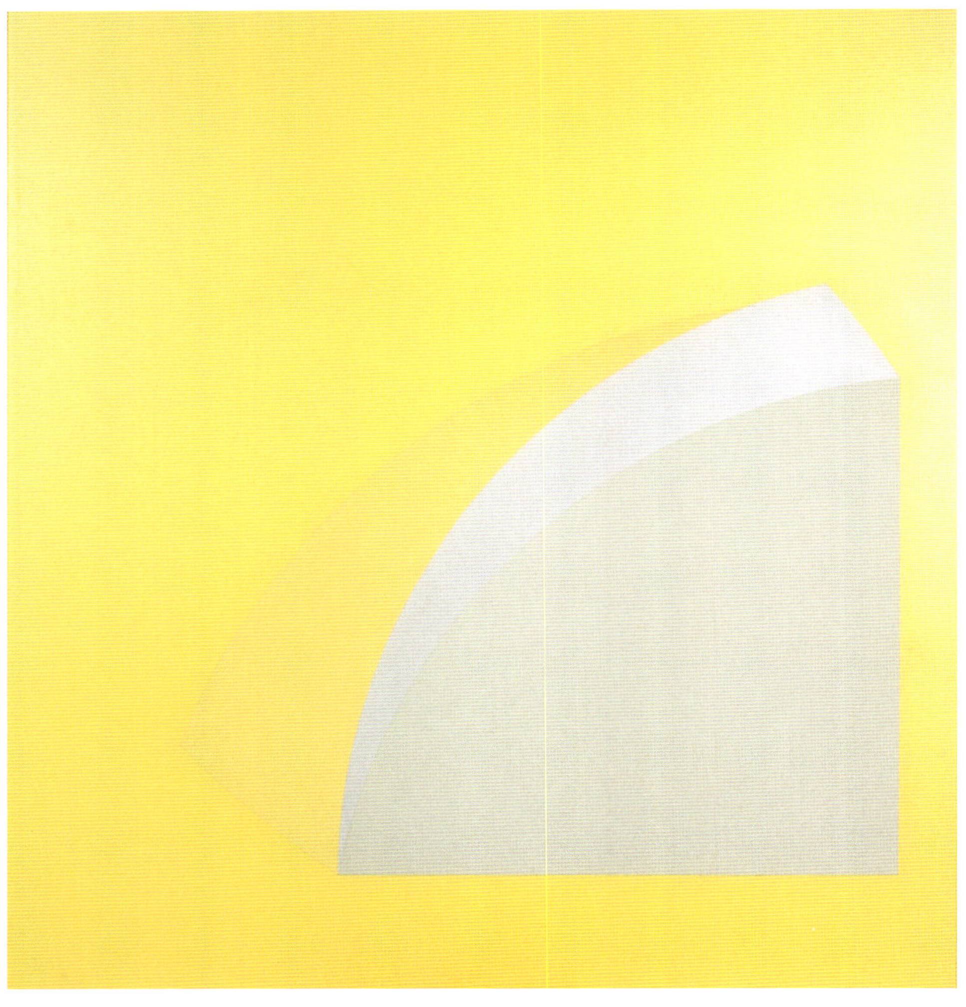

PLATE 35

WALTER DARBY BANNARD

Yellow Rose #4, 1965
Acrylic on canvas
68 x 62 inches
Private collection; courtesy
Jacobson Howard Gallery, New York

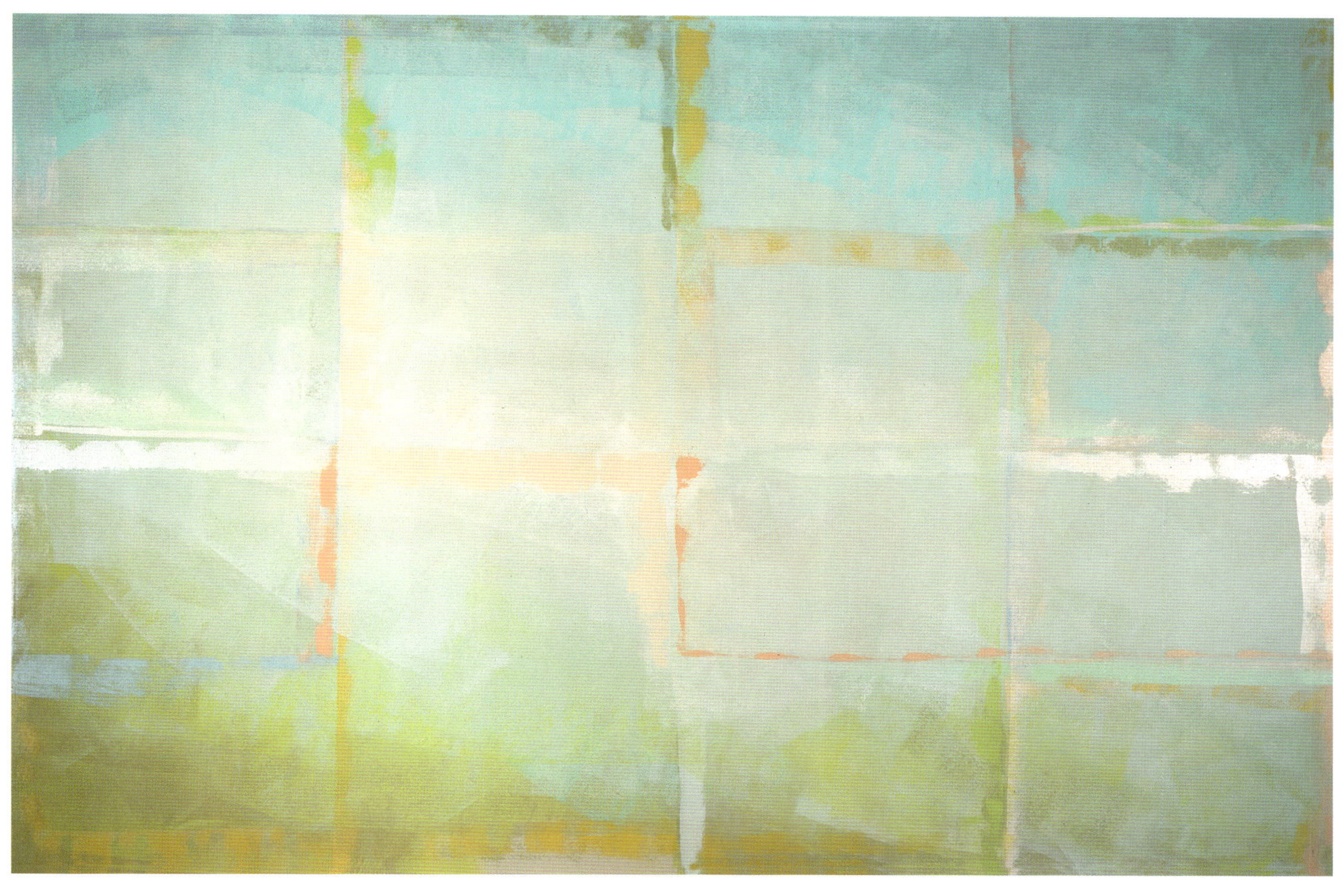

PLATE 36

WALTER DARBY BANNARD

China Spring #3, 1969
Alkyd resin on canvas
66 1/8 x 99 1/4 inches
The Baltimore Museum of Art;
National Endowment for the Arts and Matching
Trustee Funds (BMA 1972.11)

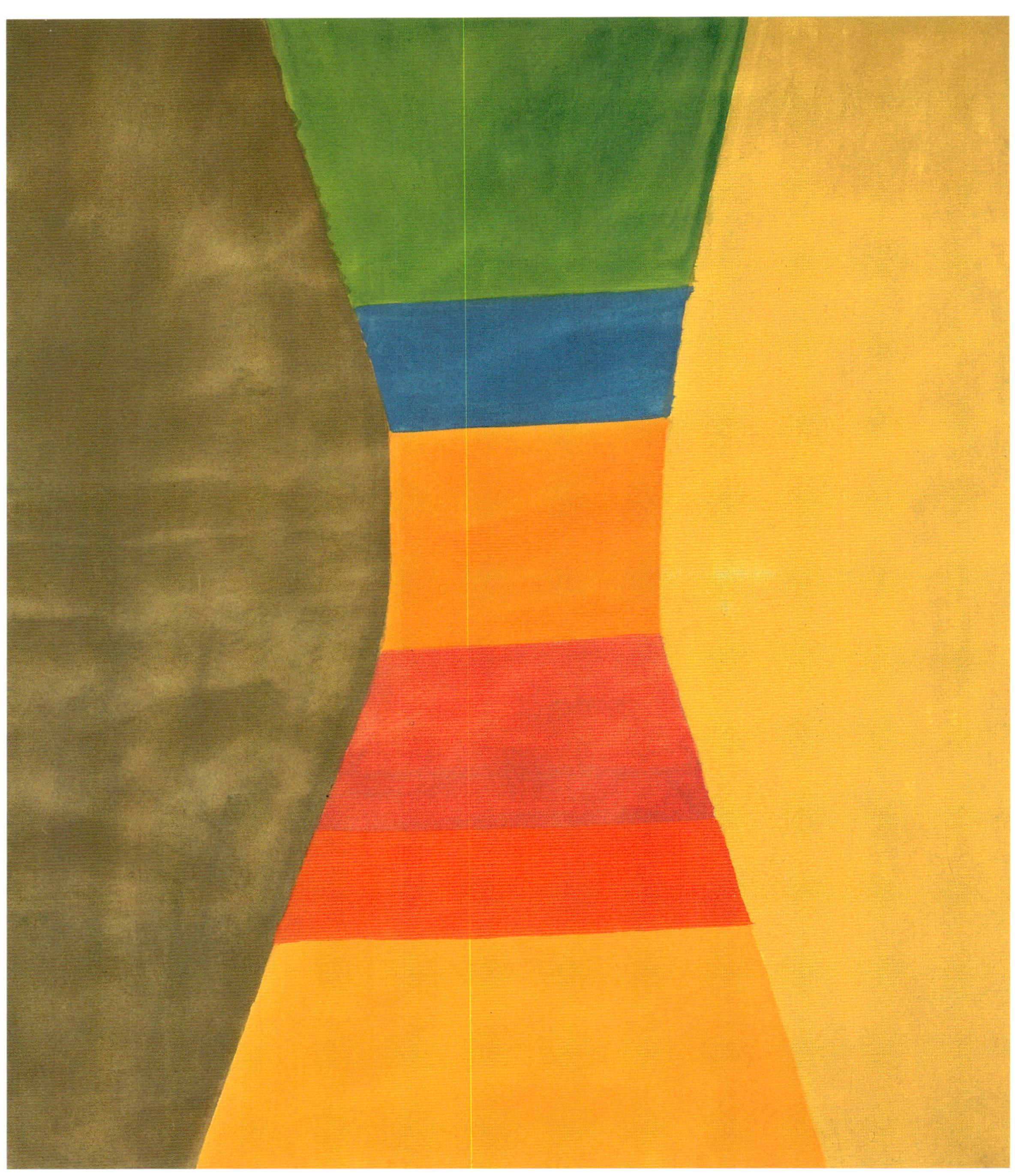

PLATE 37

JACK BUSH

Orange Centre, 1964
Oil on canvas
81 x 68½ inches
Art Gallery of Alberta Collection,
Edmonton (79.22)

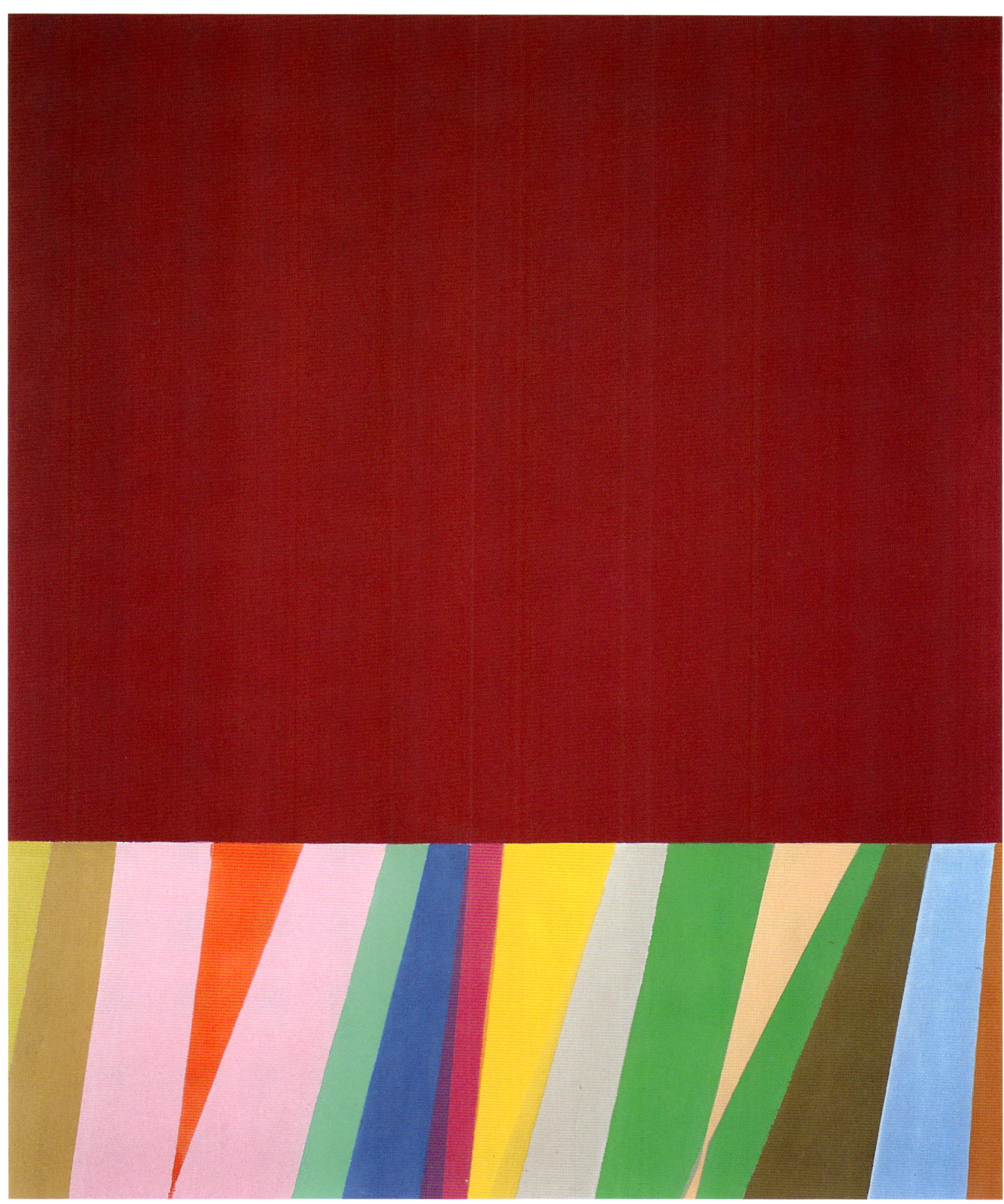

PLATE 38

JACK BUSH

Burgundy, 1968
Acrylic on canvas
84 x 68 inches
Collection Cam Allard, Edmonton

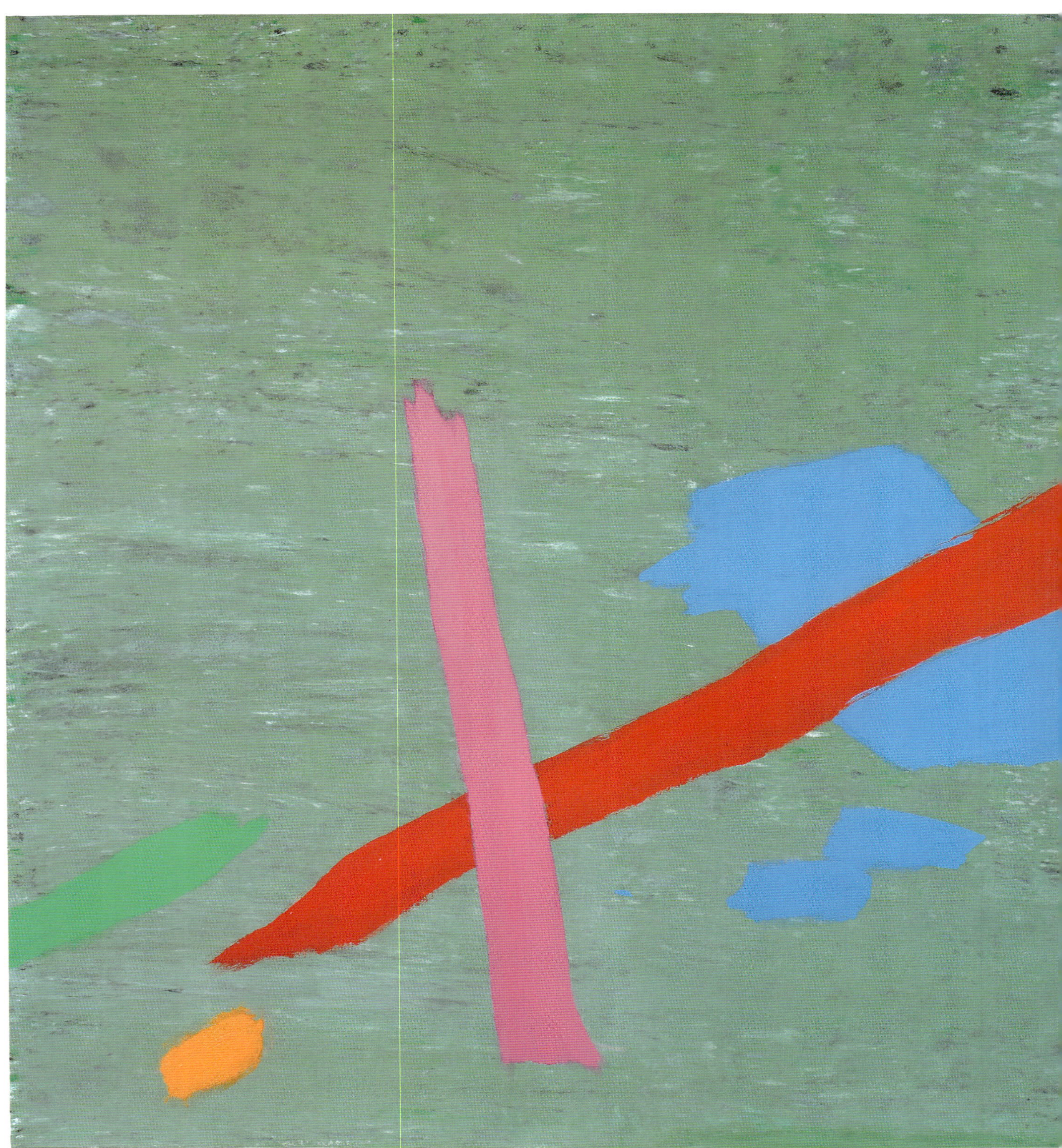

PLATE 39

JACK BUSH

Red Pink Cross, 1973
Acrylic on canvas
66 1/4 x 89 inches
Private collection;
courtesy Foley Hoag LLP, Boston

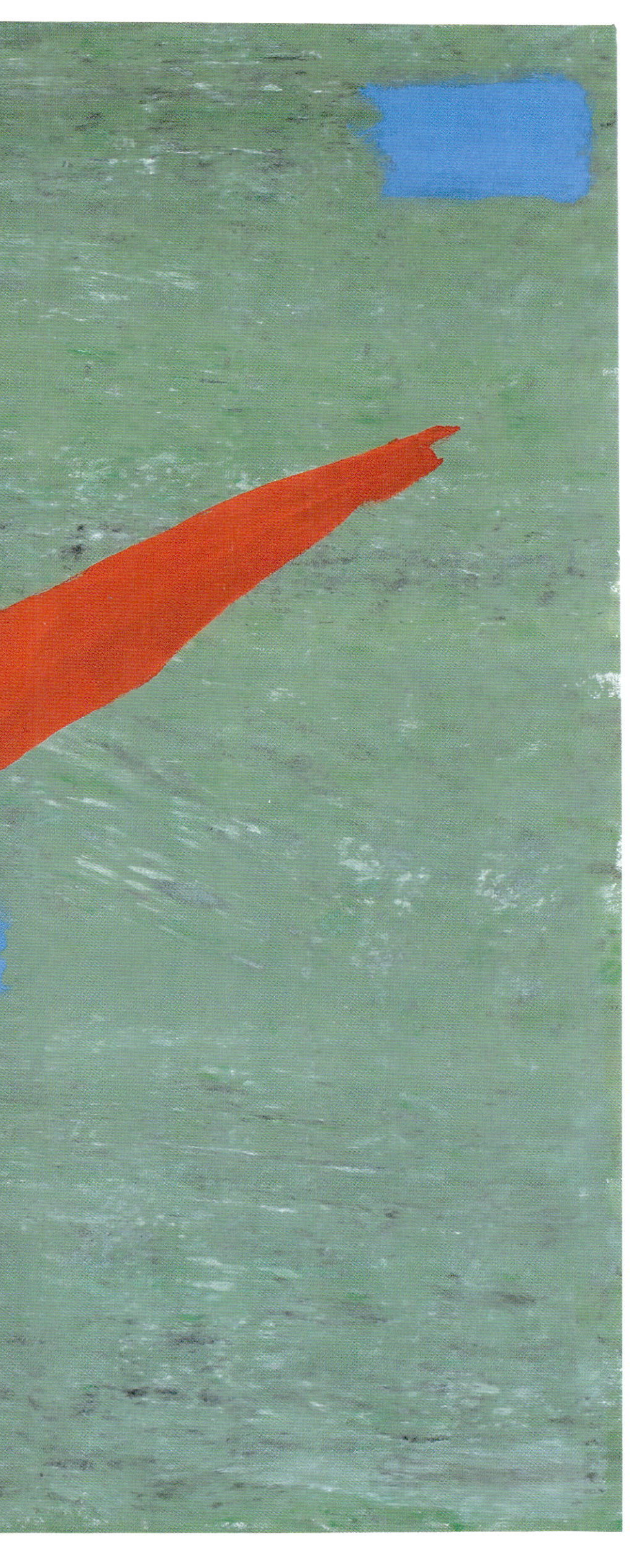

effectively it had been composed but how effectively it could be seen. His series of concentric bands of circles were centered on square canvases, which meant that, while the bands varied in width and color, their composition had been neutralized, made to function like the control in a scientific experiment. Compositionally speaking, the pictures could be seen in an instant, one shot, dead center. Which in turn meant that the impulse behind them, color expression—the singularly isolated variable on which their success or failure was staked in its entirety—could be unequivocally experienced in and of itself.

III.

The artist who grew increasingly central to color-based painting as my thinking about it evolved, beginning in the 1960s, was Helen Frankenthaler. I had missed her first retrospective at the Jewish Museum in 1960—her name had yet to become fully etched on my Color Field, Post-Painterly radar screen—but saw the second at the Whitney Museum of American Art in 1969. This was within a year after seeing a Morris Louis retrospective at the Los Angeles County Museum of Art, which meant I was primed to experience fully the Frankenthaler side of the Frankenthaler-Louis connection associated with her *Mountains and Sea* (1952)—the picture that Louis, during a visit to Frankenthaler's studio in the company of Greenberg and Noland back in 1953, had famously seen, and been radicalized by, citing Frankenthaler as "a bridge between Pollock and what was possible."[1] By 1969 the picture had become the legendary cornerstone for "soak/stain painting," the kind of Color Field painting with which both Frankenthaler and Louis had become identified.

Shared concerns notwithstanding—in their staining, for instance, their size and scale, and their exalted color—the Louis and Frankenthaler retrospectives presented two very different artists and two equally different experiences. Louis's mature career had been tragically brief, spanning only eight years from 1954, when his epiphany in the presence of *Mountains and Sea* first became manifest, to his death in 1962. At his retrospective, we saw earlier pictures that were cubist-based or derived from Pollock's drip technique, and then encountered the Veils from 1954 and 1958–59, the Florals and Unfurleds that followed, and the Stripes that were ongoing at the time of the artist's death. The pictures in each series were astonishingly beautiful—one-shot wonders that seemed to have come into being on their own, like natural phenomena that were detached from human intervention and, as such, embodied Gustave Flaubert's dictum that the artist's relationship to his work should be like God's relationship to his universe: everywhere present but nowhere visible. In addition, each series appeared fully realized, as if each format, once arrived at, had enabled the artist effortlessly to create picture after picture, each sustaining the high quality of the others, yet each complete in itself. It was as though, following his breakthrough, Louis never had a bad day.

The Frankenthaler retrospective spanned the artist's first two decades, revealing her at mid-career and in full command of her powers. Frankenthaler had inspired Louis and Noland alike, but, unlike them, she didn't work in series. While there were clusters of pictures that were clearly in dialogue with one another, each just as clearly presented a world unto itself, a world articulated not only by color but by drawing as well, even pictures constructed with only a handful of discrete shapes or areas. Her pictures were, in other words, more individualistic. Credited with having "invented" soak/stain painting for a new generation, she nonetheless didn't rely exclusively on it in her own practice—not in the 1950s, not even in the 1960s when its usage had become widespread in modernist abstraction—but was instead regularly willing to couple its disembodied images with marks or shapes or areas that acknowledged the substance of her medium, the physicality of the paint she actually worked with. Not surprisingly, this meant that as an artist, she was as individualistic as the individual pictures she painted, which is to say she eluded the categories that were employed at the time to describe advanced American painting. Was she a second-generation Abstract Expressionist or a first-generation Color Field painter? What was more important in her work, drawing or color? And above all, did she "belong" to the 1950s or the 1960s? Whichever, her work complicated the bigger picture and in doing so exposed some basic assumptions in the discourse surrounding it.

This is evident in the criticism that tracked Frankenthaler's career during the two decades in question. Here, for instance, is Donald Judd—soon to emerge as a leading practitioner of minimalism and a spokesman for the kind of one-shot picture mentioned above in connection with Kenneth Noland—comparing Frankenthaler to Pollock on the occasion of her Jewish Museum retrospective: "Pollock's paintings are hardly quiescent; both marks and bare canvas are equally positive, almost in competition for frontality; the result is cool, tough, and rigorous. It has implications of objectivity and, as alien as that is, Frankenthaler may eventually need a form of it to continue."[2] Judd went further along these lines in reviewing a solo exhibition at the Andre Emmerich Gallery in 1963: "There is nothing wrong with these paintings. Frankenthaler's softness is fine but it would be more profound if it were also hard. Bonnard's and Watteau's paintings, for example are soft, essentially as soft as Frankenthaler's, if the quality and nothing else is considered; but their work is also tough and the softness is one aspect."[3] And here, in response to the Whitney Museum retrospective, is Harold Rosenberg, spokesman for Abstract Expressionism-as-action painting and the one-shot picture cited in connection with Willem de Kooning:

The early paintings, with their borrowings from Pollock, Gorky, Kandinsky, and other occasional stainers, are sensitive, but more timid than sensitive...with Frankenthaler, the action is at a minimum; it is the paint that is active. The artist is the medium of her medium; her part is limited to selecting aesthetically acceptable effects from the partly accidental behavior of her color. Apparently, Miss Frankenthaler has never grasped the moral and metaphysical basis of Action painting, and since she is content to let the pigment do most of the acting, her compositions fail to develop resistances against which a creative act can take place.[4]

So, Frankenthaler didn't grasp the metaphysics of action painting, and her softness lacked objectivity. Not physical enough on the one hand, she was not rational enough on the other, which meant, in Bob Dylan's memorably sung words, she was "just like a woman." Back in those days, however, they weren't Dylan's words alone; they were the words of men generally, stereotypes for how men living in a man's world looked upon women at a time when qualifiers such as "She's a pretty good painter, for a woman" were commonplace. In her 1970 monograph on Frankenthaler, Barbara Rose described the artist as "running against the pack"[5] and as experimenting with "techniques and forms that consistently contradicted the prevailing tastes"[6] of the 1950s. She could have said the same about Frankenthaler in the 1960s, though by then the contradictions were less dramatic. But what Rose nonetheless meant, as I came to see, was that Frankethaler's voice struck a different chord than the predominantly male critical voices of either decade; it was a voice whose unique reso-

CONTINUED ON PAGE 96

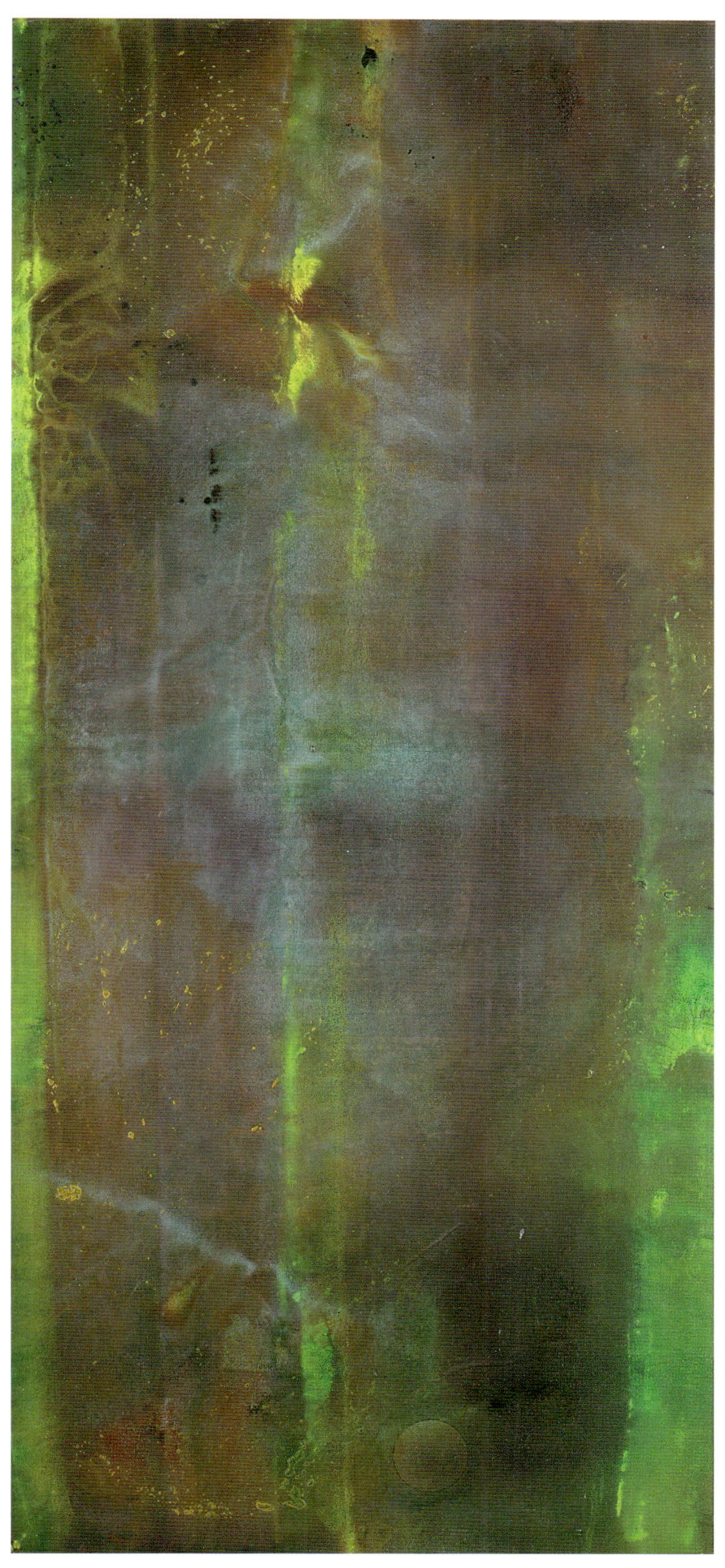

PLATE 40

SAM GILLIAM

Green Web, 1967
Acrylic on canvas
90½ x 39¾ inches
Smithsonian American Art Museum; gift of the Woodward Foundation (1977.48.3)

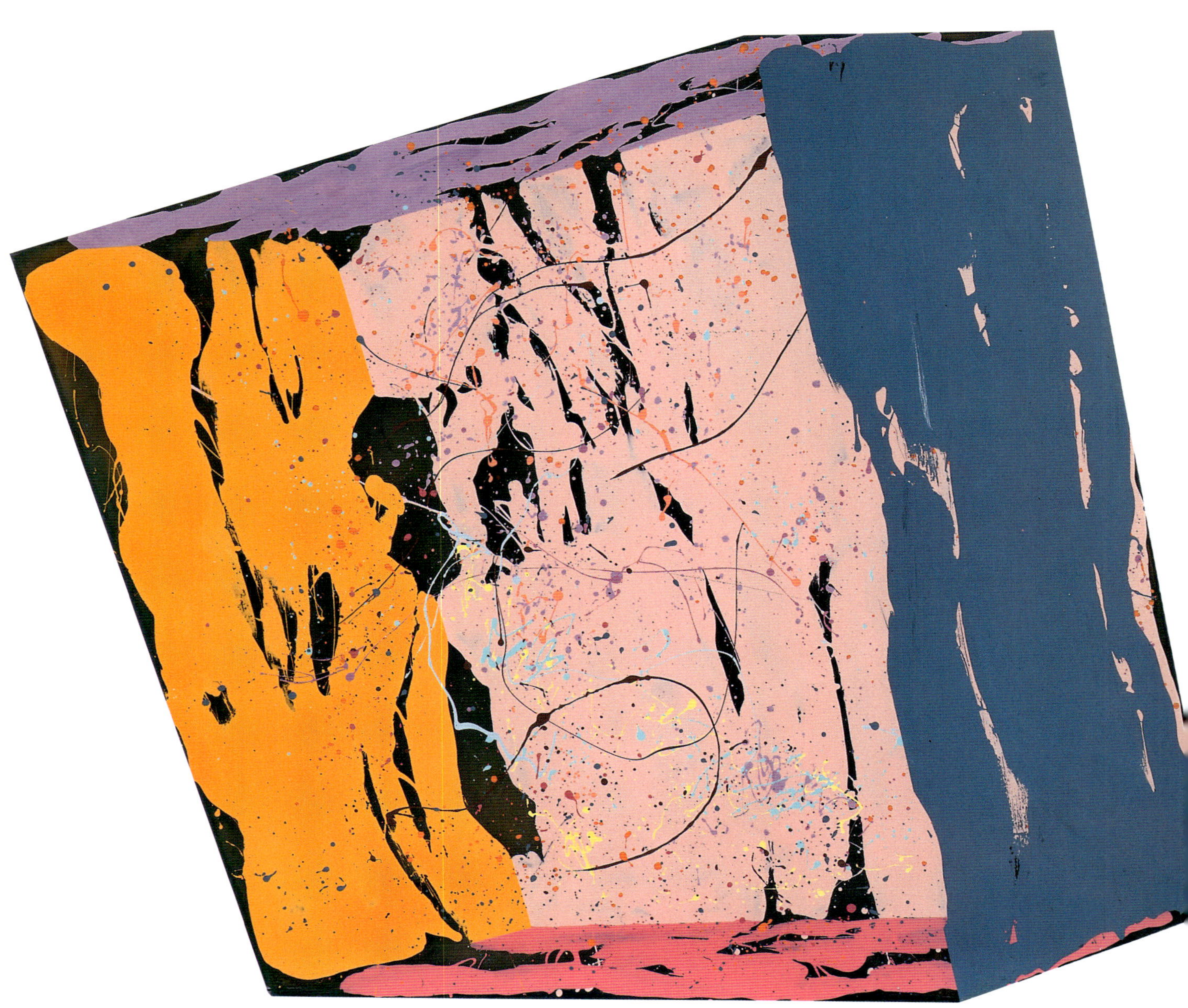

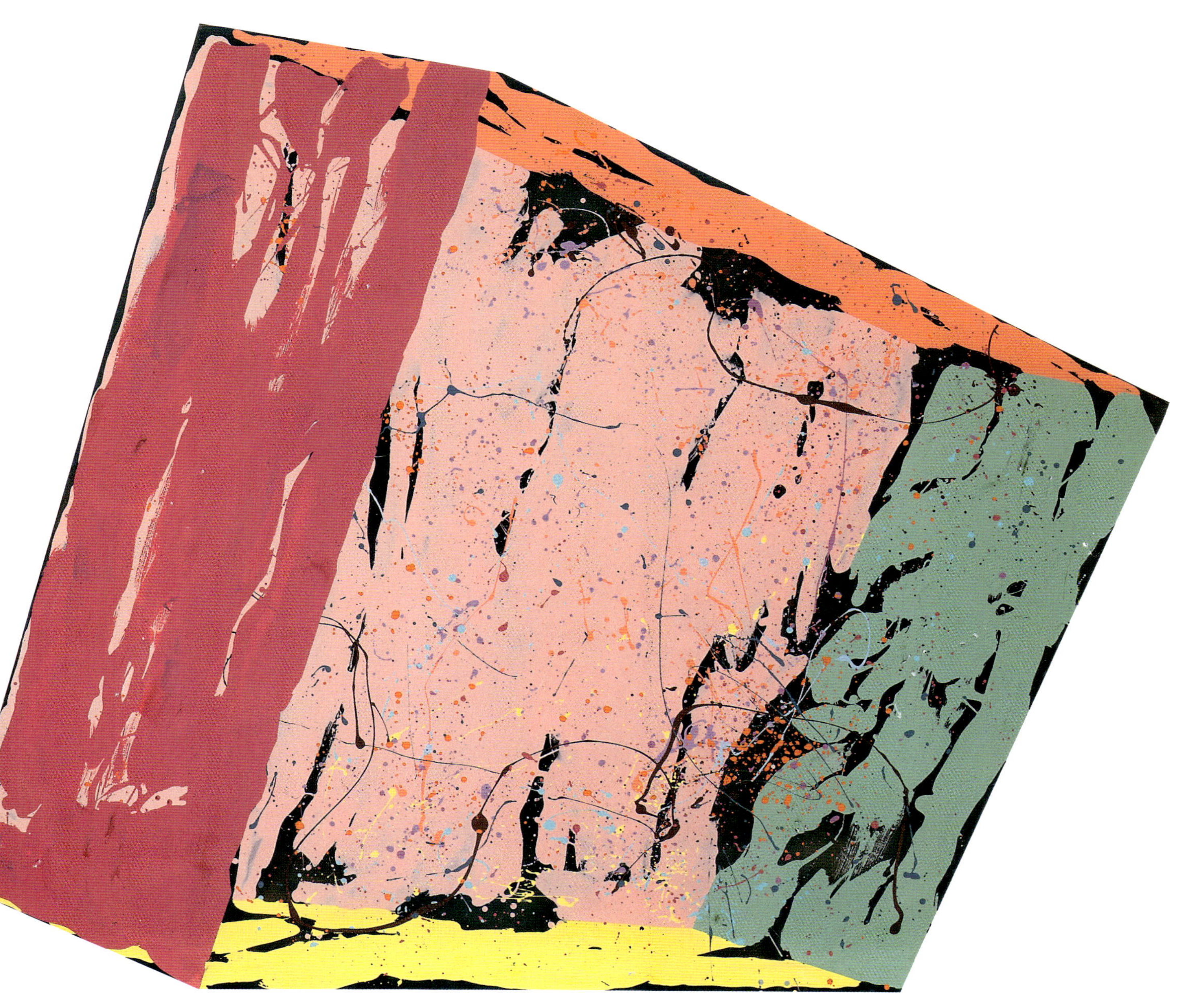

PLATE 41

RONALD DAVIS

Double Pink Slab, 1969
Polyester resin
58 x 129 inches
Collection Mr. and Mrs. David Mirvish, Toronto

nance was not fully accessible to theirs. As to the question of where she "belongs," the 1950s or the 1960s, I look today at pictures such as *Seven Types of Ambiguity* (plate 8) and *Flood* (plate 10), from 1957 and 1967, respectively—both pictures as confident as they are moving, both as convincing in the present as they were when I saw them and the answer seems clear: she belongs equally to each decade, for she seems in each picture to have been fully of her time, inventively drawing with color in the first, generously allowing it to spread in the second. More important, what's clear is that such pictures not only *reflect* those decades but they also have become central to how we *define* them. In response to Frankenthaler's comment about the 1950s, for instance, that "It was a relatively trusting and beautiful period,"[7] we can say now that her pictures from that decade *reveal* a beauty we hadn't seen there before. About the 1960s, we can in turn say that her pictures embodied our aspirations in ways we hadn't imagined.

IV.

The Hofmann experience—that is, the questions raised by his theory on the one hand and the actual experience of his paintings on the other—lingered both before and after seeing the paintings of Frank Stella, who I knew was passionate about Hofmann and would in his own later writings even single him out as *the* great painter of the twentieth century. The first Stella show I saw took place in the glass-walled atrium of McCormick Hall at Princeton University, where the artist was a student, during the spring of his senior year in 1958. The pictures contained a lot of stripes, some vertical, some horizontal, some in combination, but I didn't have a clue about what they were supposed to mean. I next saw *Sixteen Americans*, the exhibition that marked Stella's controversial debut at the Museum of Modern Art in the winter of 1959–60 and included four of the Black Stripe Paintings he was working on at the time. Those paintings shed some light on the ones that had earlier baffled me; it became clear, for instance, that he had already been circling around the kind of one-shot pictorial experience already mentioned in connection with Noland, which Stella himself famously distilled as, "What you see is what you see."[8]

Following the Black Paintings, there were the Aluminum, Copper, Purple, and V series, each presenting stripes in more radically shaped canvases than the series that came before it, which occasionally recalled my experience of the exhibitions at Princeton and MoMA, namely, that each new series clarified the series preceding it. The series all came together in *Three American Painters*, a 1965 exhibition at Harvard's Fogg Art Museum, curated by Michael Fried, that included Stella, Noland, and Jules Olitski. In his ambitious catalogue essay—which remains a position paper on the state of modernist painting at that moment—Fried describes Stella's work in terms of the "deductive structure" whereby the artist deployed his stripes in patterns that not only acknowledged but also, in fact, had been orchestrated by the ever-changing shapes of the supports on which they were painted. The supports became expressive; they were no longer neutral. In turn, the one-shot picture assumed a new significance: it was not just a picture containing a holistic image that could be *seen* in an instant; it was a picture whose shape became inexorably bound to its image—shape and image became stamped on the wall as a *singular* entity. An underlying logic was at work in Stella's enterprise between 1958 and 1965, a logic that was central to the satisfaction of looking at his pictures and was made for the kind of painting that Donald Judd could fully endorse. Its rigor acknowledged the high ambition of the 1950s and thereby sustained it, but its look was utterly different, different enough to make any such connection to the past seem implausible.

Stella disrupted that satisfying logic with the Irregular Polygons he exhibited in 1966. As the title of the series suggests, the new pictures were still shaped, but the images depicted on their surfaces were no longer deduced from those shapes alone. There were identifiable geometric units among them—triangles and parallelograms and so forth—but most of the images were more abstract, comprising straight-edged but unnamable bands and fields that sometimes coincided with the literal support but just as often seemed to disregard it entirely. They were as "irregular" as the "polygons" that contained them. And then there was their color, fields and vectors of color that conformed to no program—as it was generally made to do when the artist had used multiple hues in earlier series—color that was everywhere effusive, color that marked a new dimension in Stella's thought. As it generated the bands and fields and tightened each picture into a frontal image that was right before your eyes, Stella's use of color in the Irregular Polygons inevitably brought me back to Hofmann once again. Through Stella, Hofmann's painting looked even stronger in 1966 than it had looked at MoMA in 1963—just as it's continued to look stronger ever since.

To me, Stella's Irregular Polygons marked a radical departure from where he'd been before, which was on the road to what Michael Fried called "literalism" in his still-seminal article "Art and Objecthood," an assault on minimalism that was published in *Artforum* in 1967. Although he's now lodged in art-history texts as essential to the minimalist sensibility, Stella abruptly veered off that road at the very moment when he was being widely recognized as its pictorial spokesman. In 1966 he reminded me of Bob Dylan at the Newport Folk Festival just a year earlier when he came out "electric" for the second part of his performance and was roundly booed. Since the start of the 1960s, Dylan had become identified with the revival of folk music in America, with Woody Guthrie and Pete Seeger anchoring its past, and Joan Baez and Paul Simon and Art Garfunkel representing its present. Their music, old and new, was said to offer an antidote to the sound of rock 'n' roll that had dominated popular music since the 1950s, from Chuck Berry and Little Richard all the way up to the Beatles and the Rolling Stones, and Dylan, by 1965, had become its leading voice—he was the spokesman of his generation. But he seemed suddenly to have turned his back on all that, as if determined to go his own way regardless of the outcry from his fans, whose number had grown to legions. Which is not to suggest that Stella met a response quite like Dylan's when he exhibited his Irregular Polygons at the Leo Castelli Gallery a year later, only that both artists possessed visions for their art that were far larger and more embracing than their audiences had realized. As each radicalized his art and deepened it by taking inspiration from his art's past and extending it into the present, each revealed the past in a fresh light. In doing so, each took me along to places that were at once familiar and new.

On the heels of the Irregular Polygons, Stella's new absorption in color became even more dramatically evident in his Protractor series. As the designation suggests, the paintings' structural scaffolding—the drawing underlying each composition—consisted of circles, half-circles, arcs, and segments of arcs that interlaced one another in rainbow-like bands unprecedented in the artist's earlier work. In and of themselves, the bands were lyrical; colored as they were, they became celebratory; in combination, they served up pictures that were irresistibly ravishing. Matisse was unavoidably behind these works, as Stella made clear in talking with Museum of Modern Art curator William Rubin on the eve of his retrospective at MoMA in 1970:

> *My main interest has been to make what is popularly called decorative painting truly viable in unequivocal abstract terms. Decorative, that is, in a good sense, in the sense that it is applied to Matisse. What I mean is that I would like to combine the abandon and indulgence of Matisse's* Dance *with the over-all strength and sheer formal inspiration of a picture like his* Moroccans.[9]

Seeing the MoMA show was an enormously gratifying experience—because of the quality of the pictures themselves, but also because I had been fortunate enough to be around to see and admire all of the pictures at the time they were made. I felt privileged to have had that opportunity.

V. A Jules Olitski retrospective curated by Kenworth Moffett took place at Boston's Museum of Fine Arts in 1973. A joy to behold in and of itself, it also triggerered reflections on what it had been like to experience soak-stain, color-based paintings during their halcyon days in the 1960s. Whether by Frankenthaler, Louis, Noland, or Olitski himself, their look was like nothing else I saw at the time—such was its irresistible appeal. Art criticism in those days stressed the paintings' disembodied flatness—the way the soak-stain technique unified figure and ground—along with what was referred to as their opticality—the way they addressed themselves to eyesight alone. The combination was offered as exemplary of modernist painting's urge to define itself from within and in the process demonstrate its uniqueness as a medium of art. While all this was convincing, what floored me was the feeling of release I experienced while standing before the pictures themselves, a feeling I associated above all with their color, which was everywhere flowing and spreading naturally, everywhere clear and open, everywhere emitting life-giving light, everywhere generous. To borrow from Matisse, who had in turn borrowed from Baudelaire, I felt I'd glimpsed a world of luxury, calm, and sensual delight—a world not so much utopian as Edenic.

The Olitski exhibition began with the artist's heavily encrusted but sparsely colored pictures from the late 1950s and extended into the early 1970s when his pictures displayed a renewed interest in surface tactility, albeit one that was, at the start of the new decade, fully informed by the gift for color he had revealed during the years in between. And fully revealed it surely had been—with color robustly soaring and swirling in the Core series of 1961–62, spreading laterally or gently descending in limpid veils in the pictures that followed—check out *Tin Lizzie Green* (plate 24), for example—becoming vaporized and ethereal in the Spray Paintings of 1965–68, and then gaining physicality once again as the end of the decade approached. As these series unfolded, they displayed a range of thought and feeling seemingly beyond the capacity of a single artist, as though a different artist had produced each set of pictures. Facing them, I felt they swept away the lesson about artists I'd learned in the classroom, the lesson that each artist possessed a singular voice, a singular style, a singular identity that had only to be grown into—or broken through to—whereupon they took their place in art's history, and students like me could then identify them during slide examinations in darkened lecture halls. I felt far removed from the 1950s. Yet, in the same moment, I felt that Olitski's restless, many-sided artistic personality confirmed the other lesson I'd picked up early on—from Hofmann, Frankenthaler, and Stella, to name a few—the one about artists taking risks, drawing inspiration from colleagues whose work was ostensibly worlds apart, and coming up with audacious, unpredictable pictorial moves that didn't conform to any pattern of stylistic consistency. Thus did some of my schoolboy romance linger.

I suggested at the outset of this essay that the great color-based paintings of the 1950s and 1960s and the early 1970s were in their own way as radical and as conservative as the times during which they were made. By this, I didn't mean they illustrated, let alone subscribed to, the conventional values of our society in those years—they weren't about hippie activists any more than they were about President Eisenhower—for their very abstractness precluded any such connection. You could even say that their abstractness made clear their distancing of themselves from the culture-at-large in which they slowly but steadily flourished, which is to say their relationship to it was from the beginning oblique. Consider once again the one-shot painting. We hear regularly today about how we're everywhere bombarded with visual images—on television, in newspapers and magazines, on the Internet, all of them competing for our attention in the moment they're allotted, all of them requiring punch, speed, an instant impact. That visual blitz, in fact, started back in the 1950s, and painting was not exempt from the competition. What better way to compete than with the holistic one-shot painting? The compositional overallness that characterizes so many of these pictures—the way one part carries as much weight in relation to the whole as every other part—likewise references obliquely the non-hierarchical culture we generally associate with modern experience. Imagine doing a jigsaw puzzle based on one or another of them and you'll see what I mean.

The paintings were radical in that they went to the root of painting as it was experienced by the artists who made them, by which is meant painting as it was practiced by the first generation of the New York school and by the old masters of the school of Paris before that. This entailed critically assessing painting's past achievements and taking from them the issues and ideas that were felt to be most vital in bringing painting into the present and sustaining its tradition. In this way the paintings were at once radical and conservative. You might say that what the paintings were about, then, was themselves—like art for art's sake—but I want to say the stakes were higher than that; I want to say they were *about* us. Think about what you value most in your past, think about how you'd like to extend that value into your present—think about these paintings as a model for lived experience.

NOTES

1 Quoted by Gerald Nordland in *The Washington Color Painters* exhib. cat. (Washington, D.C.: The Washington Gallery of Modern Art, 1965), 12.

2 Donald Judd, "Helen Frankenthaler," *Arts Magazine*, March 1960, 55.

3 Donald Judd, "Helen Frankenthaler," *Arts Magazine*, April 1963, 54.

4 Harold Rosenberg, "Art and Words," in *The De-definition of Art* (New York: Horizon Press, 1972), 64.

5 Barbara Rose, *Frankenthaler* (New York: Harry N. Abrams, 1970), 14.

6 Ibid., 11.

7 Quoted in Eleanor Munro, *Originals: American Women Artists* (New York: Simon and Schuster, 1979), 216.

8 Quoted in Bruce Glaser, "Questions to Stella and Judd" (1964 interview), in Gregory Battcock, ed., *Minimal Art: A Critical Anthology* (New York: Dutton, 1968), 158.

9 Quoted in William S. Rubin, *Frank Stella* (New York: The Museum of Modern Art), 149.

Artist Biographies

Hrag Vartanian

Walter Darby Bannard

AMERICAN, B. 1934 | Born in New Haven, Connecticut, Bannard was educated at Phillips Exeter Academy and Princeton University. As an undergraduate, he met fellow students Frank Stella and Michael Fried and later the critic Clement Greenberg. A respected "painter's painter," Bannard is also highly regarded for his writings about art. Working as a contributing editor to *Artforum* and a regular contributor to *Art International*, Bannard was an important formalist critic during the 1960s and 1970s and continues to write occasionally. In his opinion, "Writing about art is only useful when it leads into the experience of art."[1]

A largely self-taught artist, Bannard demonstrates a subtle sophistication in his work. He abandoned the gestural brushwork that characterized his art of the 1950s for a simplified compositional strategy that emphasized geometric forms and freely organized shapes.

In 1964, Bannard's work was included in Greenberg's seminal exhibition *Post Painterly Abstraction* at the Los Angeles County Museum of Art. Bannard began exhibiting in New York in 1963 and moved to the city three years later. Beginning in the 1970s, his painting surfaces became more complex as he fragmented the painting field with modulations of texture and the inclusion of drawing. He explained, "I wanted one color to do something with another color—not in a direct, relating way, but to set each other off. I was after a presenting quality rather than a space-relating quality. I wanted the intense feeling I had for a particular color to come right across, unhindered, undifferentiated, unalloyed."[2]

Walter Darby Bannard, Nantucket, Massachusetts, summer of 1970

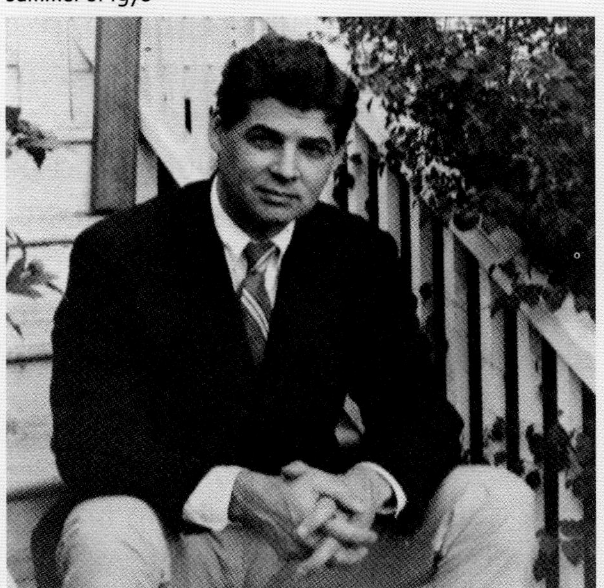

Photo Bruce Johnson

In 1987, Bannard began what he calls his "brush-and-cut" painting. Using a transparent tinted gel medium applied with large street brooms and industrial squeegees onto very large canvases, these works contain three-dimensional illusionism and vigorous brushwork. His painting through the 1980s became more expressionistic and graphic, as he came to prefer a subtler handling of color and surface.

In the early 1990s, Bannard moved to Miami, where his preoccupation with strong color—inspired by the light and colors of south Florida—resurfaced. During a 1999 retrospective of his work, he wrote, "I have always felt that art represents the best of ourselves to ourselves, and that this comes across through intuition and feeling rather than words and meaning."[3]

A former member of the graduate faculty at the School of Visual Arts, New York, Bannard currently serves as professor and head of painting at the University of Miami, Coral Gables.

1 Artist's statement for the retrospective exhibition *Bannard Paintings* (Tampa, FL: University of Tampa's Scarfone Art Gallery, 1997).
2 *Walter Darby Bannard*, exhib. cat. (Baltimore: Baltimore Museum of Art, 1973), 31.
3 Artist's statement for the retrospective exhibition *Darby Bannard* (Coral Gables, FL: Lowe Art Museum, University of Miami, 1999).

Jack Bush

CANADIAN, 1909–1977 | Initially influenced by the Canadian modernist landscape tradition of the Group of Seven, Bush studied in Montreal in the 1920s and then at the Ontario College of Art in Toronto. Like many twentieth-century Canadian artists, he worked in advertising as an illustrator. Eventually, he became a principal at the Toronto commercial art firm of Wookey, Bush and Winter. In 1952, he visited New York to see the most current contemporary art, which until then he had seen only in reproduction. The same year he participated in the First Canadian Art Abstract Exhibition in Oshawa, Ontario, which led to his involvement with the important Toronto-based Painters Eleven—one of the first abstract artists' groups in the country. Bush was almost a generation older than most of the artists in the informal group who joined forces to garner attention from the public and art dealers.

By 1955, Bush had completely embraced abstraction and demonstrated a strong familiarity with Abstract Expressionism. In 1957, Clement Greenberg visited the Toronto studios of the Painters Eleven and took a fancy to a small group of watercolors by Bush. Encouraged by Greenberg, Bush continued his experiments with fluid color and began working on highly personal abstract compositions. As a result of one Manhattan bus ride, Bush created his 1962–65 Sash series, which was inspired by the glimpses of window displays as he sped past.

Bush was included in Greenberg's 1964 exhibition *Post Painterly Abstraction* and represented Canada at the ninth São

Paulo Bienal three years later. Internationally admired, he continued to carve out a place for himself in the annals of modernist abstraction. He befriended and influenced a generation of young Canadian artists through his sophisticated palette and international profile. He, in turn, was influenced by a generation of American abstract painters, including Jules Olitski, Frank Stella, and Kenneth Noland, while acknowledging his debt to older modernists such as Henri Matisse, whose vivid cut-outs opened the

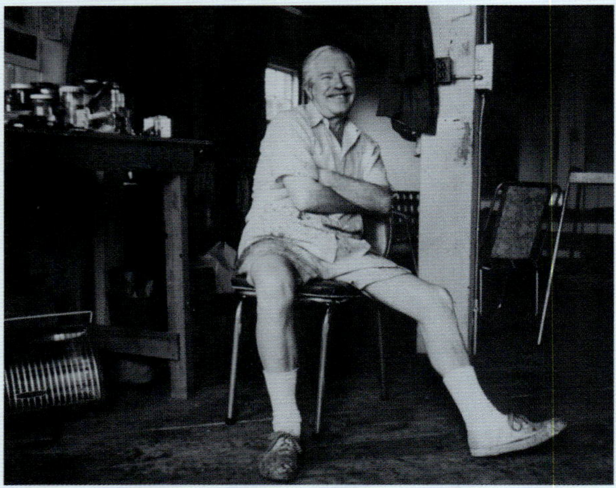

Jack Bush, 1975

Toronto artist's eyes to new possibilities during a European trip in the 1950s. Bush rejected Canadian provincialism. He admired the French Canadian painter Emile Borduas and the Montreal-based Automatistes, who were pioneers of Canadian abstraction.

Bush's stripped-down imagery of the 1960s became more textured and feathery a decade later. His paintings of the 1970s were distinguished by rich bursts of eccentric color shapes on textured surfaces. Often influenced by musical compositions, his late paintings were more poetic and controlled in their drawing and tonalities.

Reviewing a 1972 exhibition by the artist at the Museum of Fine Arts, Boston, New York Times critic Hilton Kramer wrote: "Bush has carried the development of color-field painting into a very personal realm of expression that is in some ways closer to Matisse himself than to some of the Americans who have obviously acted as an influence...he has taken a style that was often in danger of degeneration into an impersonal technical exercise and realigned it with the specifications of the experience."[1]

1 *New York Times* (reprinted in the Toronto *Globe and Mail*, Thursday, March 2, 1972).

Gene Davis

AMERICAN, 1920–1985 | Born in Washington, D.C., Davis was educated at the University of Maryland, College Park, and then at the Wilson Teachers' College in his hometown. He worked in journalism—as a White House Correspondent for the Transradio Press, a copy boy at the *New York Times*, a reporter for the United Press International in Jacksonville, Florida, and a sports writer for the *Washington Daily News*—before turning to painting full-time. He was often President Harry Truman's poker partner during his stint covering politics in the nation's capital.

Davis first exhibited drawings at a solo show at the Dupont Theater Gallery in 1952; the following year he showed paintings at a local college. He participated in the exhibition *Washington Color Painters* at the Washington Gallery of Modern Art in 1965 and became a leading figure among the Washington Color painters, who included Morris Louis and Kenneth Noland.

Davis's best-known paintings are acrylic on canvas, composed of vibrantly colored vertical stripes, a motif the artist initiated in the late 1950s. The titles often refer to music, which underscores the rhythmic impression of his art. Critic Ralph Pomeroy has said of Davis's work, "Davis has taken the stripe and stretched it to such a point that it can no longer clearly be defined as shape; it has become a line. By multiplying these non-forms into a mass, Davis compels the viewer to focus on color, color as separate and relational. Color has become the sole subject."[1]

In 1972, Davis created *Franklin's Footpath* in front of the Philadelphia Museum of Art. At the time, it was the world's largest artwork. Composed of stripes directly painted on the street, it was soon followed by a larger work titled *Niagara*, which was executed in the parking lot of Art Park, in Lewiston, New York. He

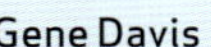

Gene Davis

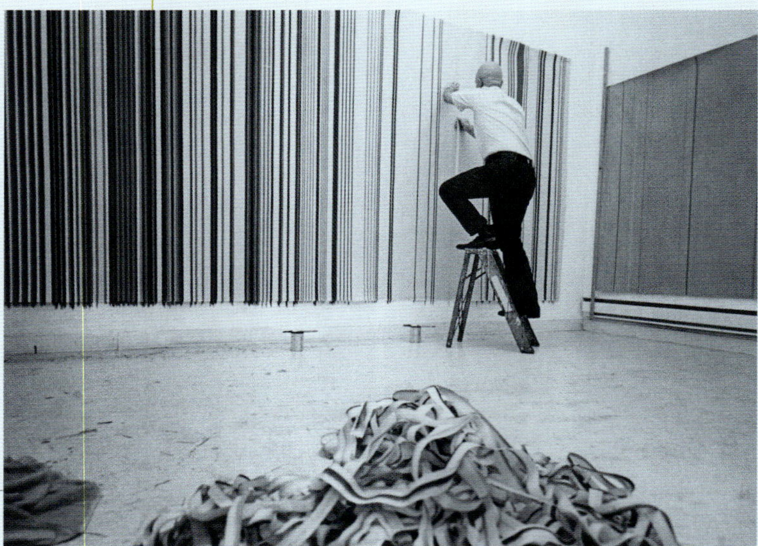

also experimented with "micro-paintings" as small as three eighths of an inch square. Beginning in 1966, Davis taught for many years at the Corcoran School of Art in Washington, D.C.

1 "Gene Davis," in *Contemporary Artists*, 2nd ed. (New York: St. Martin's Press, 1983), 228.

Ronald Davis

AMERICAN, B. 1937 | Born in Santa Monica, California, Davis was raised in Wyoming and attended the University of Wyoming. He became a painter at the age of twenty-two and studied at the San Francisco Art Institute in the early 1960s. Beginning in 1966, he taught at the University of California, Irvine. Early on, he was influenced by Abstract Expressionism, but in 1963 he began to paint hard-edge abstractions in response to Op art and such

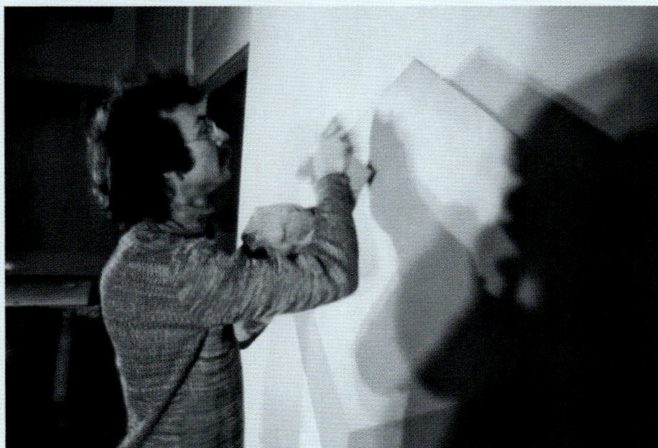

Ronald Davis in his studio, 1971

Color Field pioneers as Frank Stella. By the mid-1960s, Davis had relocated to Los Angeles and had his first one-man show there in 1965, at the Nicholas Wilder Gallery. At this time, he was making geometric-shaped paintings out of colored polyester resins and fiberglass. He continued to work in this vein until the early 1970s. For health and aesthetic reasons he discontinued the use of resin and fiberglass in 1972, but he often continued to shape his paintings eccentrically.

When Davis began to exhibit in New York in the 1960s, *Artforum* critic Michael Fried heralded his paintings as "among the most significant produced anywhere during the last few years."[1] Davis's works can be described as sculpture-as-painting or vice versa, as they play illusionistic form against real shapes. His uncanny illusions depend upon a resurrected Renaissance notion of two-point perspective. Toward the late 1970s, Davis experimented with extremes of scale and technique, producing works that often overwhelmed entire rooms and distorted viewers' perceptions of space. Over the next decade, Davis worked in series, producing a variety of paintings with titles such as Flatland Series (1980–81), Object Paintings (1982), Freeway and Freeline Series (1987), and Spiral Series (1988). In 1988, Davis began designing paintings on Macintosh computers; since the 1990s, his work has been dominated by computer-generated images.

Davis has also had a special connection with architecture. In 1972, he collaborated with Frank Gehry to produce a studio/residence for himself in Malibu, California. The innovative structure was crucial to the development of Gehry's ideas. In 1990, Davis collaborated with architect Dennis Holloway and anthropologist Charley Cambridge to build a complex of six living and studio buildings in Taos, New Mexico. Davis moved permanently to Arroyo Hondo, New Mexico, in 1993.

1 "Ron Davis," in *Contemporary Artists*, 2nd ed. (New York: St. Martin's Press, 1983), 230.

Friedel Dzubas

AMERICAN, 1915–1994 | Born in Berlin, Dzubas studied at the Berlin Gymnasium and from 1931 until 1933 attended the Prussian Academy of Fine Art and Kunstgewerbeschule. Beginning in 1933, he studied for three years with the Swiss modernist artist Paul Klee in Düsseldorf. Dzubas immigrated to the United States in 1939 and later met Clement Greenberg and many of the Abstract Expressionists, including Jackson Pollock. He was a member of the Société Anonyme, which was formed by Marcel Duchamp and his close friend Katherine S. Dreier to disseminate modern art in America.

Dzubas shared a studio with Helen Frankenthaler from 1952 to 1953. His work during that period was highly influenced by the Abstract Expressionist idiom, but by the 1960s, his canvases were characterized by bright, flat, pregnant colliding forms that emphasize the surface of the canvas. During the 1960s, Dzubas taught at Dartmouth College, the University of Pennsylvania, and Cornell University.

In the 1970s, Dzubas began to compose his pictures with stacks of large rectangular forms, in moody colors, often with soft edges that diffuse into the background, creating a sense of activity and drama. Dzubas's forms jostle one another, resulting in a palpable surface tension. The art historian Kenworth Moffett saw Dzubas's paintings of the 1970s as an alternative vision to Olitski's painting: "Dzubas' pictures dramatize the return, one might say the reclaiming, of a whole painting culture that recent modernist developments had appeared to render obsolete. They do this essentially by demonstrating that a wide range of light and dark accentuation—of value—is now made possible within a color-dominant picture."[1]

In 1976, Dzubas moved to Boston and until 1982 taught at the School of the Museum of Fine Arts. He was the subject of a 1983 retrospective at the Hirshhorn Museum and Sculpture Garden.

Increasingly, Dzubas emphasized brushstrokes and

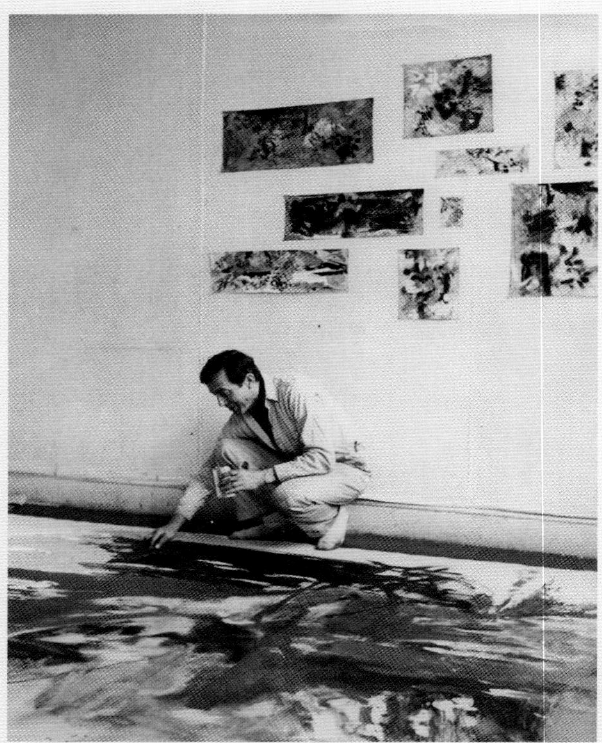

Friedel Dzubas in his studio, 1960s

touch, until by the 1980s his work resembled a brooding storm of colors and ambiguous shapes. During the last decade of his life he began to make very large monotypes that rivaled his canvases in scale and richness. Dzubas's work is often compared to that of the German Romantics and Venetian Renaissance painters, particularly in their baroque palette and grand manner. His paintings present a "somber, heavy, smoldering warmth," giving the impression that some grand, cosmic event is taking place. His forms tend to be impressionistic and nuanced, and his canvases often appear to glow, illuminated by some ethereal light.

1 Kenworth Moffett, *Friedel Dzubas* (Boston: Museum of Fine Arts, 1975), 3.
2 Ibid., 11.

Sam Francis

AMERICAN, 1923–1994 | Francis was born in San Mateo, California, and studied botany, medicine, and psychology at the University of California, Berkeley, before serving in the United States Air Force during World War II. His injuries in a plane crash and resulting spinal tuberculosis hospitalized Francis for several years, and it was during his rehabilitation that he began to paint. Fully recovered, he returned to Berkeley to study art and became greatly influenced by the work of the Abstract Expressionists, including Mark Rothko, Arshile Gorky, and fellow Bay Area painter Clyfford Still.

In the 1950s, Francis moved to Paris and began exhibiting works visibly influenced by Tachists such as the expatriate French Canadian Jean-Paul Riopelle, who constructed their abstract paintings with large patches ("taches") of liberally applied pigment. Francis's early work was often monochromatic, but his large mature pieces are dominated by splatters of bright contrasting color. He preferred to paint his canvases white and often left areas pristine and untouched; in later works, paint is sometimes confined to the edges of the canvas, which seems to reflect an East Asian respect for the powerful effect of negative space.

Clement Greenberg described Francis's unique ability to allow his canvas to breathe: "Sam Francis' liquefying touch is of a kind familiar to Abstract Expressionism at large, but even in his closed and solidly filled painting of the early 1950s that touch somehow conveys light and air."[1]

In a 1962 article in *Art Journal*, Priscilla Colt wrote that Francis was a lyrical painter in "the Watteau to Matisse tradition of French hedonism."[2] Yet, there is a darker dimension to his painting that Irving Sandler aptly draws attention to in his study of the New York School: "...the cellular abstractions, despite the beauty of their soaring, incorporeal, glowing colors, are also unnerving, calling to mind magnified human corpuscles, and in the red pictures particularly, bleeding tissue—an expression perhaps of the prolonged illnesses from which Francis suffered during much of his adult life."[3] The new emphasis on white in his canvases was prompted by his trips in 1957 and 1958 to Japan, where he came into contact with East Asian calligraphy and Zen Buddhism.

Francis participated in the New York scene from 1958 to 1960, and his work was well known among its artists. His Archipelagos, mural-scaled images from 1957 to 1960, which

Sam Francis in his studio, 1960s

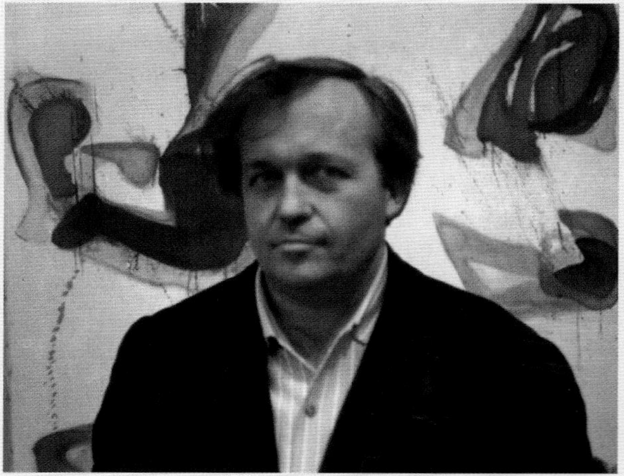

instill a state of weightlessness in an infinite, iridescent space, are his best-known works.

Francis settled in Santa Monica, California, in 1962, and his work for the next three decades continued to explore similar colorist and compositional issues. One of the few abstract painters to create prints as early as the 1950s, Francis continued to expand his graphic vocabulary with monotypes and other printmaking processes. He also produced a number of sculptural works later in his life and in the late 1970s began a series of large-scale mural projects.

1 *Post Painterly Abstraction*, exhib. cat. (Los Angeles: Los Angeles County Museum of Art, 1964).
2 Priscilla Colt, "The Paintings of Sam Francis," *Art Journal*, Fall 1962, 1.
3 Irving Sandler, *The New York School: The Painters and Sculptors of the Fifties* (New York: Harper & Row, 1978), 82–85.

Helen Frankenthaler

AMERICAN, B. 1928 | A native New Yorker, Frankenthaler studied with Mexican painter Rufino Tamayo at the Dalton School in Manhattan and went on to Bennington College in Vermont, where she encountered the instructor and abstract artist Paul Feeley. She briefly received private instruction from Hans Hofmann, an important figure for many artists of her generation.

In 1950, Frankenthaler organized an exhibition of fellow Bennington alumnae at the Seligman Gallery in New York, where she fortuitously met critic Clement Greenberg, who introduced her to the most progressive art of the period.

A precocious talent, she started to produce her first mature paintings in her late twenties. Her work draws from the mysterious calligraphy of the most provocative artist of the period. "...I looked at and was influenced by both Pollock and de Kooning and eventually felt there were more possibilities for me out of the Pollock vocabulary. De Kooning made enclosed linear shapes and 'applied' the brush. Pollock used shoulder and ropes and ignored the edges and corners. I felt I could stretch more in the Pollock framework...You could become a de Kooning disciple or satellite or mirror, but you could depart from Pollock,"[1] she says about the springboard for her artistic evolution.

A major breakthrough in her work occurred in 1952 when she concocted a mixture of house paint, enamel, turpentine, and oil, which she spilled onto unsized raw canvas. In her first major work in this manner, gestured lines in charcoal were used to suggest an abstracted memory of landscape. Eventually these lines disappeared in her work, notably in *Mountains and Sea* (1952), which inspired both Louis and Noland when they visited her studio in 1953. Virtually unknown, Frankenthaler's work provided guidance to the two Washington, D.C.–based artists who discovered a new world of possibilities in her experimentation.

Frankenthaler shared a studio with Friedel Dzubas in the early 1950s, and there is a superficial resemblance between both artists' paintings during the period.

Soon she abandoned even covert allusions to subject matter in her paintings for purely abstract formations. Unlike Noland, Stella, Louis, and others, she never chose systems to organize her color but preferred a more fluid drawing to guide her art making. After the mid-1970s, Frankenthaler's paintings became more dense and lush. The textures, density, and movement of her paint play a more central role and the sensuous richness of her color reached new heights.

A skilled printmaker, Frankenthaler has worked with many international graphic studios to produce an impressive oeuvre of luminously colored prints including etchings, lithographs, serigraphs, and Japanese-style woodblocks, the last made in collaboration with Japanese masters.

Helen Frankenthaler in her studio in front of *Small's Paradise*, 1964

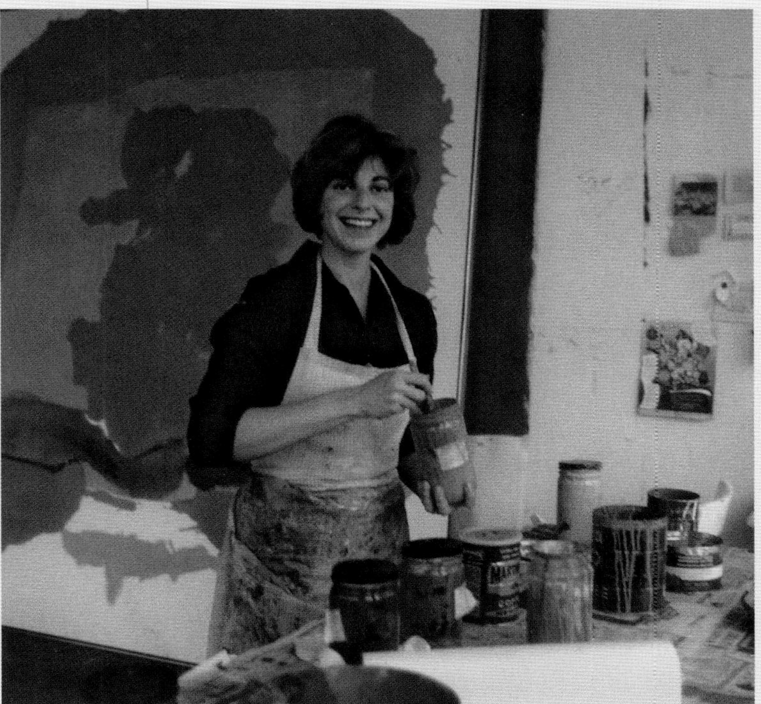

Alexander Liberman Photographic Collection & Archive Research Library, The Getty Research Institute, Los Angeles, California (2000.R.19)v

1 Henry Geldzahler, "An Interview with Helen Frankenthaler," *Artforum*, October 1965, 37.

Sam Gilliam

AMERICAN, B. 1933 | A leading African-American artistic voice associated with the Washington Color painters, Gilliam is recognized for creating rich fields of color and melding sculpture and painting. His artworks have always strained against their boundaries, their edges, and their surfaces.

A native of Mississippi, Gilliam grew up in Louisville, Kentucky, where he studied painting at the University of Louisville. He has taught in Washington, D.C., public schools in addition to universities in Washington, D.C., Maryland, and Pennsylvania.

Since the early 1960s, Gilliam has advanced the inventions associated with the Washington Color school, producing canvases rich in color and texture. Throughout the 1960s and 1970s, his paintings evolved from stretched to "draped" to "wrapped" canvases. By the 1980s, in addition to allowing the support to exist independently of the traditional stretcher, Gilliam began to add sculptural elements as extensions of his surface, thereby making uniquely shaped works. His three-dimensional works integrate the shapes found in his paintings with inventive ways of applying color, including pouring it directly onto the surface.

Gilliam often rakes huge quantities of acrylic paint and gel across a large canvas, then cuts the canvas into geometric shapes that he stitches together like a quilt. While the resulting compositions can be quite flat, their surfaces can appear pulsating and vibrant. He has also created multimedia installations, incorporating everything from polypropylene to computer graphics.

Since the 1990s, Gilliam, who lives in Washington, D.C., has continued to combine sculpture and painting. He has been commissioned to create various public works, including wall sculptures in the Davis Square Subway Station in Boston and a suspended sculpture for the University of Louisville's library.

Adolph Gottlieb

AMERICAN, 1903–1974 | Gottlieb was born in New York. In 1920 he enrolled in a life drawing class at the Parsons School of Design and also took a design course at Cooper Union in New York. In the winter and spring of 1921, he attended the painter Robert Henri's lectures at the Art Students League of New York and left with an understanding of the veteran artist's nonacademic approach to painting. He was particularly affected by Henri's advice to paint directly on the canvas instead of from a preliminary sketch. That same year, Gottlieb enrolled in an illustration course with realist painter John Sloan, who encouraged his students to pursue individual directions in their art but only after careful study of the great masters.

Taking Sloan's advice to heart, Gottlieb traveled throughout France and Germany for a year. He attended life drawing classes at the Académie de la Grande Chaumière and studied the masters and modern art in the city's galleries and museums.

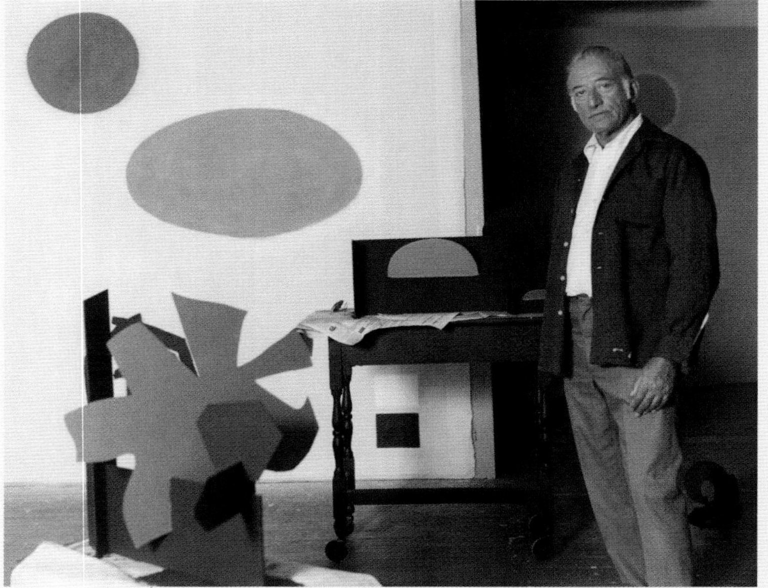

Courtesy the Adolph and Esther Gottlieb Foundation

Adolph Gottlieb in his Bowery Street studio, ca. 1968

When Gottlieb returned to America in 1922, he was one of the most well-traveled New York artists and one of the only ones to have firsthand knowledge of modern art in Europe.

He was a close friend of Barnett Newman, and the two spent hours visiting museums and galleries throughout the city. In 1923, Gottlieb studied with Sloan again at the Art Students League. He assimilated his teacher's somber tonalities and ability to fashion sculptural volumes in paint.

Beginning in the 1930s, Gottlieb's art demonstrated the influence of Milton Avery and Henri Matisse and their tendency toward pared-down drawing and rich fields of color.

Between 1935 and 1940, Gottlieb and nine other artists known as "The Ten"—among them, Ilya Bolotowsky and Mark Rothko—exhibited their works together and would come to be known as Abstract Expressionists. From 1937 to 1938, Gottlieb moved to the Arizona desert to improve his wife's health. There he painted barren, symbolic scenes that became increasingly abstract. The symbolic imagery of his work of this period revealed the influence of his friend John Graham—a painter, theorist, and mystic—along with his own interest in psychoanalysis and tribal art, which he collected all his life.

Gottlieb and his wife returned to New York in the fall of 1938 whereupon Gottlieb encountered the newly exiled Surrealists who reaffirmed his belief in the subconscious as a well of ideas. Gottlieb's experiments of this period resulted in his Pictographs, which he painted from 1941 to 1950. In this famous series, Gottlieb arranged abstracted, personal versions of Freudian, Jungian, and other mythological symbols in compartmentalized and ambiguous spaces. These were increasingly simplified until 1957, when he exhibited his first Burst paintings at New York's Martha Jackson Gallery. The Bursts make masterful use of color and distill Gottlieb's pictorial vocabulary to two iconic elements: a contained disc and a knot of winding calligraphy. He produced variations on this theme, known as the Imaginary Landscapes, most of his life, from the 1950s to the 1970s.

Gottlieb was awarded the grand prize of the seventh Bienal de São Paolo in 1963. During the last decades of his life, he taught at Pratt Institute in Brooklyn and at the University of California in Los Angeles. Tragedy plagued the end of his life, beginning with a catastrophic fire in 1966, which destroyed the contents of his studio, followed by his suffering a debilitating stroke in 1970, although he continued to paint with full intensity until his death in 1974.

Hans Hofmann

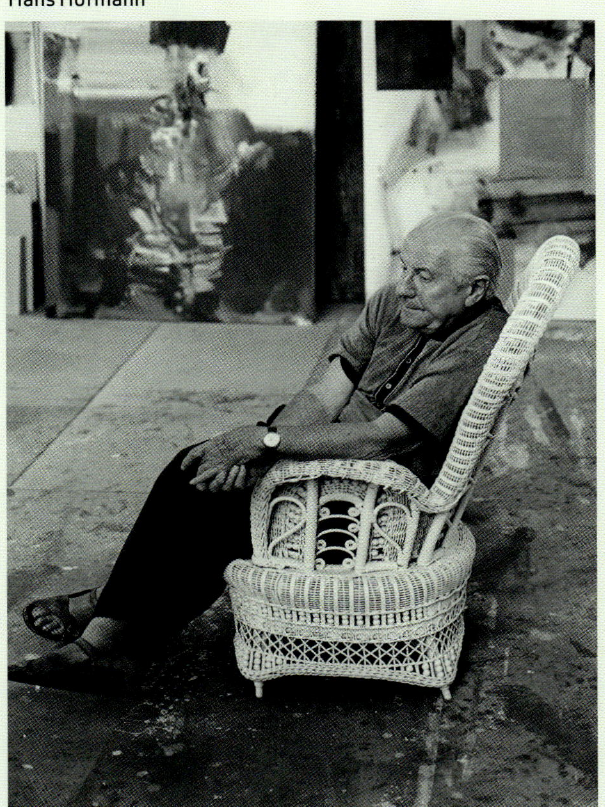

Photo Vytas Valaitis

Hans Hofmann

AMERICAN, 1880–1966 | A leading teacher and painter in New York, in the years following World War II, Hofmann was a crucial link between European and American Modernism.

Born in Weissenburg, Bavaria, he was raised in Munich. At sixteen, he obtained a job, in science, with the Bavarian government but soon gravitated toward the arts, beginning formal art training after the death of his father in the late 1800s. In 1898, Hofmann studied at Moritz Heymann's art school in Munich, where he was introduced to the dominant styles of the era, including Impressionism. Hofmann showed great promise and was encouraged to continue his studies in France. In 1904, he relocated to Paris, supported by a German patron. As a student of the Académie de la Grand Chaumière and the Académie Colarossi, Hofmann befriended Matisse, Picasso, and Braque and also became close to Robert Delaunay. Delaunay's emphasis on color deeply impressed Hofmann, who was beginning to form his own theories of color and composition.

In 1908 and 1909, Hofmann exhibited with the New Secession group in Berlin. Soon after, he left Paris for Corsica, to recover from a bout of tuberculosis, followed by what was to be a brief visit to Germany. The outbreak of World War I made a return to Paris impossible and deprived him of his patronage. To support himself, he opened the Hans Hofmann School of Fine Arts in the spring of 1915. The school quickly acquired an international reputation, attracting, after the war, many foreign students, including the American artists Louise Nevelson and Alfred Jensen.

In 1930, a former student invited Hofmann to teach a summer session at the University of California, Berkeley, an invitation that would be repeated in subsequent years. Hofmann was in the United States when Hitler and the National Socialist Party seized power in Germany, and the artist decided to stay in America. Settling in New York, he first taught at the Art Students League and then opened the Hans Hofmann School of Fine Arts in the fall of 1933. Hofmann opened a summer school in Provincetown, Massachusetts, in 1934, and for the next three decades divided his time between New York and Cape Cod. Many leading American painters studied with Hofmann, including Burgoyne Diller, Robert Goodnough, Wolf Kahn, Lee Krasner, Paul Resika, Robert De Niro Sr., and, briefly, Helen Frankenthaler. During the 1930s, 1940s, and 1950s, Hofmann was better known and more highly regarded as a teacher than as an artist, although his first New York exhibition, in 1944, was held at Peggy Guggenheim's acclaimed Art of This Century gallery. Throughout his career he produced powerful works that celebrated the material and expressive qualities of the fundamental elements of painting: shape, color, placement, scale, and touch. His theories of the "push-pull" of color and of activating the picture plane are still influential.

Only in 1958 did Hofmann stop teaching to devote himself to painting, turning his Eighth Street school premises into his studio and, in the last years of his life, producing a large body of inventive canvases. Late in his career, Hofmann's reputation as an artist finally began to equal his renown as a teacher.

In 1955, the critic Clement Greenberg organized a Hofmann retrospective at Bennington College. A longtime admirer of Hofmann's work, Greenberg believed Hofmann's art from the early 1940s was crucial to the development of Abstract Expressionism because of his seemingly automatist compositions and dripped paint, which predate the later innovations of the first generation of the New York school. In his introduction to Hofmann's Bennington show, Greenberg wrote: "Over the past fifteen years a body of painting has emerged in this country that deserves to be called major. Hans Hofmann's art and teaching have been one of its main fountainheads of style...If art critics and art bureaucrats in general have tended to overlook this, it is because their taste cannot solve Hofmann's difficult originality."[1] Greenberg attributed Hofmann's "difficulty" to his plethora of styles and his dissonant color contrasts, which according to the critic, "goes against a rule of painting so implicitly that we become aware of it as a rule only when it is violated."[2]

In 1963, the Museum of Modern Art mounted a retrospective exhibition of Hofmann's work that traveled throughout the United States and to South America and Europe.

Morris Louis

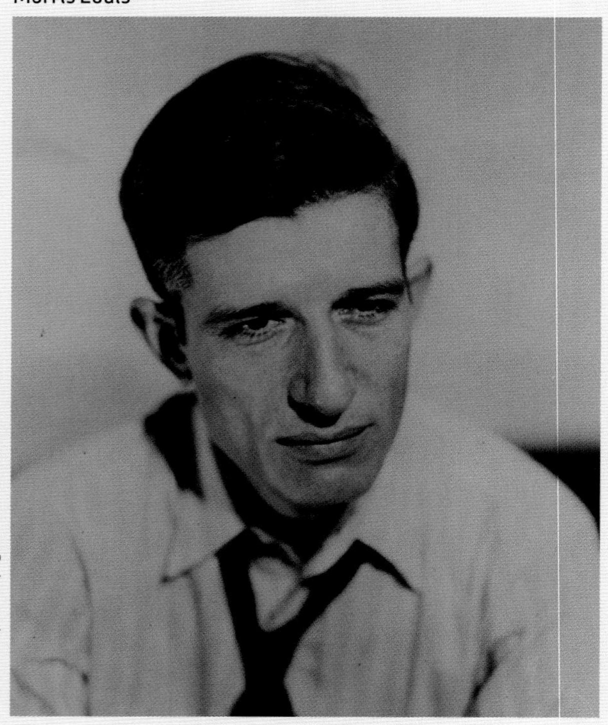

Photo courtesy Diane Upright Fine Arts, New York

1 "Introduction to an Exhibition of Hans Hofmann," in *A Retrospective Exhibition of the Paintings of Hans Hofmann*, exhib. cat. (Bennington, VT: Bennington College, 1955) in *Clement Greenberg: The Collected Essays and Criticism*, vol. 3, *Affirmations and Refusals, 1950–1956*, ed. John O'Brian (Chicago: University of Chicago Press), 240–41.

2 Ibid., 241.

Morris Louis

AMERICAN, 1912–1962 | One of the leading American colorists, Louis was born Morris Louis Bernstein in Baltimore. From 1929 to 1933, he studied at the Maryland Institute of Fine and Applied Arts. He worked at various odd jobs to support himself while painting and in 1935 served as president of the Baltimore Artists' Association. From 1936 to 1940, Louis lived in New York, where he met Arshille Gorky, David Alfaro Siqueiros, and Jack Tworkov.

In 1940, Louis returned to Baltimore and taught there privately. In 1952, he moved to Washington, D.C., where he taught at the Washington Workshop Center of the Arts and met fellow instructor Kenneth Noland, who became a close friend. Louis's first solo exhibition took place at the Workshop Center Art Gallery in 1953. Also that year, Louis and Noland visited Helen Frankenthaler's New York studio, where they were greatly impressed by her new "stain" paintings, including *Mountains and Sea* (1952). Upon their return to Washington, Louis and Noland experimented with various techniques of paint application.

The following year, Louis produced his Veil paintings, which were characterized by layers of transparent color stained into canvas— his first mature works. The first Veil was exhibited at *The International Art of a New Era: U.S.A., Japan, Europe* in Osaka, and later in Philadelphia. More were shown in his 1959 solo exhibition at French & Co., New York, which Clement Greenberg was instrumental in organizing. Louis's first solo show in New York (not of the Veils) had been held in 1957 at the Martha Jackson Gallery. He destroyed many of the paintings in this exhibition but resumed work on the Veils in 1958. Louis did not title his Veils either individually or as a group, and it is not clear when the term *veil* first came into general use. In his catalogue for the Louis memorial exhibition in 1963, critic Lawrence Alloway suggests that the term *veil* was at the time applied to Louis's painting in general: "The words most often used, both by art critics and by journalists, about Louis's art, are 'veils' and 'drapes.' The terms are apt, obvious even, not only because of the preservation of the canvas as part of the paint...but also because of the configuration of the paint trails. These are continuous and undulating. Like veils, the thin washes of color are continually overlaid, which produces a shifting density and a subtle, reserved, internal color relationship."[1]

The Veils were followed by Florals and Columns (1960), Unfurleds (1960–61)—consisting of rich veins of color flowing from both sides of large white fields—and the Stripe paintings (1961–62)—composed of vivid lines that careen down the canvas. Louis's work forms a bridge between Abstract Expressionism and post-painterly Abstraction, and he was posthumously included in the exhibition *Post Painterly Abstraction*, which Clement Greenberg was involved in organizing at the Los Angeles County Museum of Art in 1964. In 1967, critic Michael Fried presented Louis's first comprehensive American retrospective.

1 Quoted in *Morris Louis 1912–1962, Memorial Exhibition: Paintings from 1954–1960*, exhib. cat. (New York: Solomon R. Guggenheim Museum, 1963), unpaginated.

Robert Motherwell

AMERICAN, 1915–1991 | One of the youngest members of the New York school, Motherwell was born in Aberdeen, Washington, and studied philosophy at Stanford and Harvard universities before transferring to Columbia University to study art history with Meyer Schapiro. It was Schapiro, renowned both for his scholarship and his friendships with artists, who later encouraged the young man to concentrate on making art.

In addition to his renown as an artist, Motherwell was a prolific writer, lecturer, and teacher. His rigorous academic background made him a natural spokesperson for the Abstract Expressionists, and he often toured the country speaking about the latest art developments in New York and popularizing the ideas of the New York school. His essays offer insight into the ideas and thinking of his art milieu. He also served as general editor of the series *The Documents of 20th Century Art* published by Viking Press.

Motherwell began painting seriously after a trip to Europe in 1938; and after a sojourn in Mexico three years later with Chilean painter Matta Echaurren, he began to paint full-time. During the 1940s, he was introduced to and influenced by the European Surrealists, including Max Ernst and André Masson, who had found refuge in New York during the war. Motherwell served on the board of the short-lived journal *VVV* (1942–44), which sought to disseminate the ideas of Surrealism in America. Through William Baziotes, whom he met in 1942, Motherwell gained access to the group of artists later known as the Abstract Expressionists. In 1944, he had his first one-man show at Peggy Guggenheim's Art of This Century gallery in Manhattan.

Motherwell's work in the 1940s and 1950s evolved from abstracted Surrealism to a more gestural, nonobjective art that documented the engagement of the artist with the canvas. He began his first Elegy to the Spanish Republic painting in 1948, the first in a series that eventually totaled more than two hundred works. The defining motif of the Elegies—black, vertical elements alternating with ovoid forms—first appeared in a pen-and-ink drawing intended to illustrate a poem by writer and critic Harold Rosenberg. The title alludes to the Spanish Civil War (1936–1940), which witnessed the defeat of leftist forces by the fascist dictator Francisco Franco, a major political crisis that galvanized liberal Western artists and writers. The image derives, in part, from Henri Matisse's *Bathers by a River* (Art Institute of Chicago), which Motherwell was able to see often, when it was offered for sale by a New York dealer.

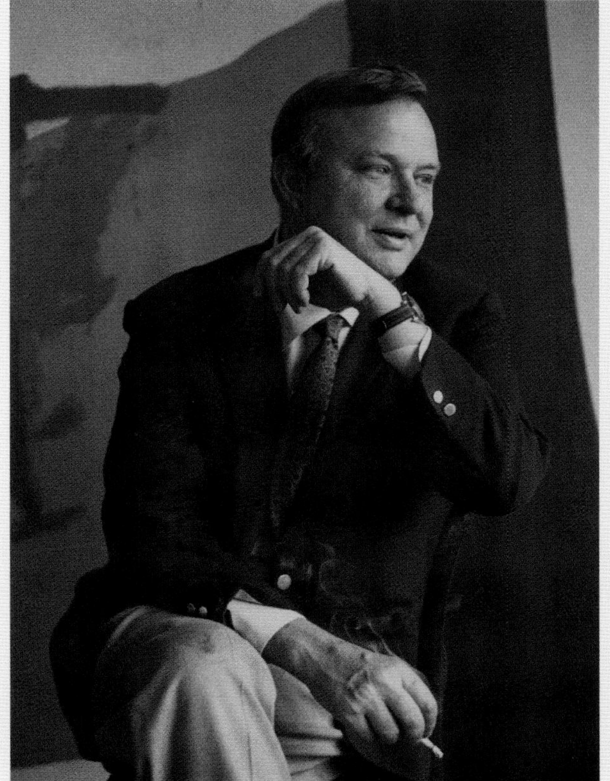

Robert Motherwell, ca. 1960s

Alexander Liberman Photographic Collection & Archive Research Library, The Getty Research Institute, Los Angeles, California (2000.R.19). Photo courtesy the Dedalus Foundation, Inc.

In the spring of 1958, Motherwell married Helen Frankenthaler. The couple vacationed that summer in Spain and France, which led to an important body of work known as the Iberia series. Motherwell wrote about the Iberia works: "I almost never start with an image. I start with a painting idea, an impulse, usually derived from my own world. Though images may sometimes emerge from some chord in my unconscious, the way a dream might. In Iberia, for example, you would have to know that a Spanish bull ring is made of sand of an ocher color, and that Spanish bulls are very small, quick and coal black."[1]

Throughout the 1940s and 1950s, Motherwell experimented with collage, as well as thinned paint and Magna—an early precursor of acrylic paint—and found a rich language of texture and form with which he worked for decades on both paper and canvas. In 1967, he began his Open series, which emerged from his observation of his small canvases leaning against larger works in his studio. He created large almost monochromatic works that communicate a strong sense of emotion and space through a very sparse artistic vocabulary. After the early 1970s, Motherwell lived and worked in Connecticut, continuing to explore color, form, and light and becoming a prolific printmaker.

1 Undated document by Robert Motherwell, Tate Gallery Archive, <http://www.tate.org.uk/modern/> (accessed August 1, 2006).

Barnett Newman

AMERICAN, 1905–1970 | A writer, teacher, activist, and artist, Newman is best remembered for his economical abstract paintings of pure color interrupted by "zips" or thin stripes. A first-generation Abstract Expressionist and native New Yorker, Newman relied on teaching for most of his life to support himself. Although the critics Clement Greenberg and Harold Rosenberg were early admirers of his painting, it was not until the 1960s that Newman began to receive critical recognition and commercial success.

The son of Russian Jewish immigrants, Newman studied philosophy at the City College of New York and took drawing classes at the Art Students League, where he met Adolph Gottlieb, in the 1920s. Through Gottlieb, who would become a lifelong friend, Newman met Milton Avery who became the nucleus of a group of gifted artists who met at Avery's home to study his work and discuss artistic matters.

Newman's earliest works were heavily influenced by Surrealism. He abandoned painting during the early 1940s, preferring to write about art and pursue his interest in natural science. He resumed painting in 1944 but continued to write avidly about art. In 1946, Newman, along with Mark Rothko and Clyfford Still, signed with Betty Parsons Gallery. Newman curated a show at the gallery in 1947 titled *The Ideographic Picture*, featuring eight artists from the Parsons stable, including himself. In 1948, he established a cooperative art school in Greenwich Village with several fellow Abstract Expressionists. Newman suggested the name, Subjects of the Artist, which he says, emphasized the importance of subject matter in abstract art. He organized a Friday-night lecture series, which included such visionaries as composer John Cage and sculptor Jean Arp. The school closed in 1949.

The critical response to Newman's first solo exhibition at Betty Parsons in 1950 was negative, and one of his paintings was vandalized. His second one-man show, in 1951, was installed with the help of his friends Lee Krasner, Jackson Pollock, and Tony Smith. Critical hostility continued and none of the work sold. A small retrospective of Newman's work was organized in 1955 at Bennington College in Vermont, with a catalogue essay by Clement Greenberg. The critic wrote: "There is no program, no polemic, in these paintings. They do not intend to make a point, let alone shock or startle. Newman is not interested in straight lines, right angles, or empty spaces as such, or in bareness or purity. He pursues his vision. The vertical stripes enter as a result, not as part of a layout. The color comes first and does the controlling. The stained surface spreads, ascends and descends, and in certain places it pauses. The line that marks the pause does not demarcate or limit; it simply inflects a continuity, and all it needs in order to do this is to proceed as directly as possible from one point to another. This has to do with economy, not geometry."[1] In contrast, Harold Rosenberg interpreted Newman's works as "a short cut to the unattainable."[2]

Barnett Newman in his studio, early 1950s

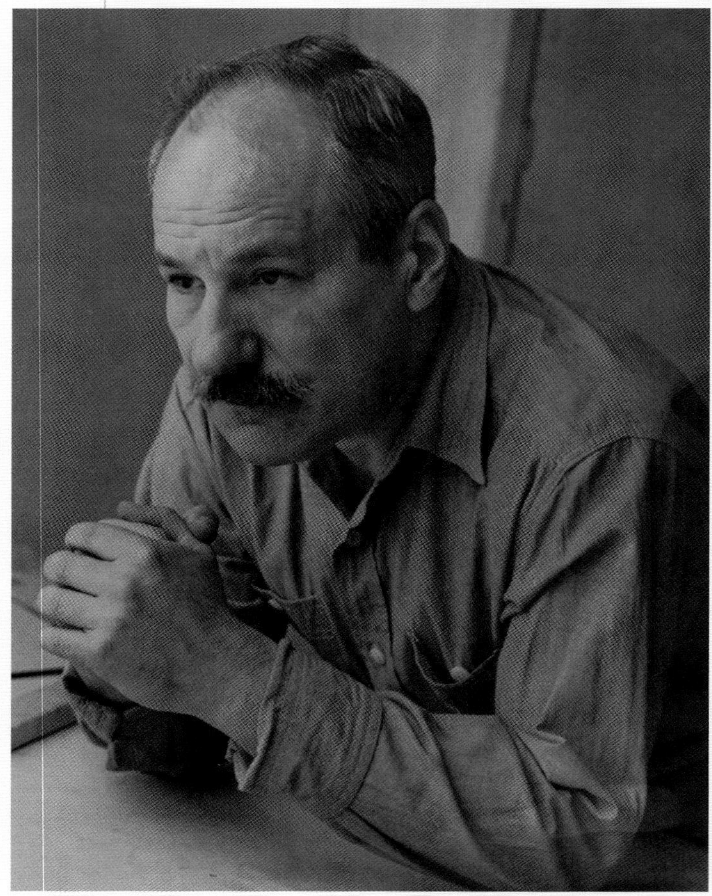

In 1959, Newman traveled to Emma Lake in Saskatchewan, Canada, to lead a summer workshop for Canadian artists. He proved influential to an upcoming generation of abstract artists in central Canada. In 1966, the Solomon R. Guggenheim Museum exhibited the Stations of the Cross, a series of black-and-white paintings (1958–64), begun shortly after Newman had recovered from a heart attack. This exhibition, Newman's first solo museum show, helped establish his reputation and notoriety as an avant-garde artist.

In the 1960s, Newman became an outspoken Zionist, publishing several letters challenging anti-Semitism in the Soviet Union and calling for the safeguarding of Israel.

1 "Introduction to an Exhibition of Barnett Newman," in *Barnett Newman: First Retrospective Exhibition*, exh. cat. (Bennington, VT: Bennington College, 1955), in *Clement Greenberg, The Collected Essays and Criticism*, vol. 4. *Modernism with a Vengeance, 1957–1969*, ed. John O'Brian (Chicago: University of Chicago Press, 1993), 54.

2 "Barnett Newman: The Living Rectangle," in Harold Rosenberg, *The Anxious Object: Art Today and Its Audience* (New York: Collier, 1966), 174.

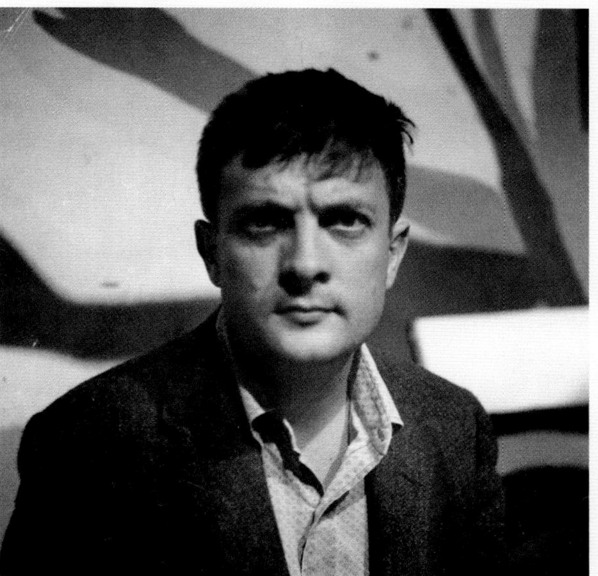

Photo Harry Noland

Kenneth Noland, ca. 1960s

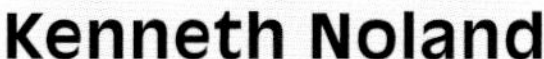

Kenneth Noland

AMERICAN, B. 1924 | Noland was born in Asheville, North Carolina, and attended the experimental Black Mountain College. In the late 1940s he worked with sculptor Ossip Zadkine in Paris, and in the early fifties he settled in Washington, D.C., where he met Morris Louis. The early influence of Abstract Expressionism proved decisive for Noland. He wrote: "Until Abstract Expressionism you had to have something to paint about, some kind of subject matter. Even though Kandinsky and Arthur Dove were improvising earlier, it didn't take. They had to have symbols, suggested naturally images or geometry, which was something real structurally. That gave them something to paint about. What was new was the idea that something you looked at could be like something you heard."[1]

After a fortuitous visit to Helen Frankenthaler's studio in 1953, Noland adopted her "stain" technique and allowed acrylic paint to soak into unprimed canvases. His preoccupation with the relationship of the image to the edge of the picture led him to make a series of studies of concentric rings using vibrant color combinations. Noland was one of the pioneers of the "shaped" canvas, initially with a series of symmetrical and asymmetrical diamonds or chevrons. His later shaped canvases are often irregular and asymmetrical.

Both Clement Greenberg and Michael Fried were early admirers of Noland, who represented America in the thirty-third Venice Biennale in 1963 and was included the following year in the exhibition *Post Painterly Abstraction*, which Greenberg largely curated. In the early 1960s, Noland established a studio near Bennington College in Vermont and briefly joined the art faculty. From 1963 to 1965, he and fellow Bennington faculty members Jules Olitski and Anthony Caro frequented each other's studios.

Noland often used predetermined, serial layout armatures for the placement of his colors. Beginning with his Target series, he also completed the Chevron, Stripe, Diamond, and Plaid series, among others, that allowed him to explore the limits of his love for color.

Faithful to the process of art making, Noland believes in the craft and skill of his daily practice. Early in his career, he was struck by his friend David Smith's workmanlike habits and "factory-studio" and resolved to adopt a similar methodical approach.

In contrast to his earlier work, which could appear disembodied as a result of his often industrial-seeming paint application, in the early 1980s, Noland began to investigate media that relied on tactile exploration: clay and handmade paper. This marks a period during which he returned to the imprint of the hand in the process of art making. He created new Chevrons in the 1980s but added transparency and layering in his revisiting of the form—testing the limits of acrylic paint. He was also experimenting with transparent gels that allow fluidity of motion. Always true to the materiality of his paint, he believed such exploration was required for new developments in abstraction.

Between 1979 and 1985, Noland completed an enormous mural in the atrium of I. M. Pei's Wiesner Art Gallery at MIT in Cambridge, Massachusetts.

About his work, Noland says, "Being an artist is about discovering things after you've done them. Like Cézanne—after twenty years of that mountain he found out what he was doing. If it isn't a process of discovery, it shows. I'm in it for the long haul."[2]

Noland divides his time between Maine and New York.

1 Quoted in Karen Wilkin, *Kenneth Noland* (New York: Rizzoli International Publications, 1990), 8.
2 Quoted in Wilkin, *Kenneth Noland*, 24.

Jules Olitski

AMERICAN, 1922–2007 | Olitski and his family came to New York from Snovsky, Russia (now Ukraine), in 1923. After a traditional art education at the National Academy of Design and the Beaux-Arts Institute in New York, Olitski spent 1949 to 1951 in Paris, working in the studio of the sculptor Ossip Zadkine. Olitski first came to Clement Greenberg's attention in March 1958, when the critic saw the painter's crusty French-inspired paintings in a New York gallery and signed the guest book. Olitski contacted Greenberg, initiating a friendship that lasted more than thirty-five years.

Olitski's work changed rapidly, with the knowledge of Frankenthaler and Louis's color-based abstractions. His Core canvases of the early 1960s achieved a sophisticated equilibrium between spreading color zones and tautly balanced organic shapes. His work changed dramatically after he joined the faculty of Bennington College in 1963, in part because of his friendships with Kenneth Noland, who lived nearby, and Anthony Caro, who soon arrived to teach at the college. The three frequented one another's studios and engaged in passionate discussions about art, a conversation often joined by Greenberg, a frequent visitor.

In 1965, Olitski began to apply paint with a spray gun, dispensing with linear drawing to concentrate on intense color sensations. Each canvas was a haze of atmospheric hues, its limits asserted by superimposed edge-drawing. In his catalogue essay for Olitski's exhibition at the 1966 Venice Biennale, Greenberg declared the centrality of these pictures to his conception of modernist painting: "The grainy surface Olitski creates with his way of spraying is a new kind of paint surface. It offers tactile associations hitherto foreign, more or less, to picture-making; and it does new things with color. Together with color, it contrives an illusion of depth that somehow extrudes all suggestions of depth back to the picture's surface; it is as if that surface, in all its literalness, were enlarged to contain a world of color and light differentiations impossible to flatness but which yet manage not to violate flatness."[1]

Michael Fried argued that Olitski's painting of the 1960s directly confronted questions of taste brought about by the importance of color in his work: "Olitski seems rather to be concerned with finding out how much of what he does on the strength of what he feels can come out looking acceptable, not to say ravishing, to eyes which, like his own, have been educated largely by the best modernist painting of the past twenty years."[2]

In the 1970s, Olitski's paintings became thickly textured but subdued in hue; over the next two decades, they grew relief-like and then brilliantly chromatic as he experimented with new pigments and additives. Never losing interest in figuration, Olitski always drew from the model, producing nudes notable for precise contours and economy of line. In the 1990s, Olitski began a series of landscapes on paper that wed the sublime to abstract color; these, in turn, influenced his later abstract paintings.

1 O'Brian, *Clement Greenberg*, vol. 4, p. 230.
2 Michael Friend, *Three American Painters: Kenneth Noland, Jules Olitski, Frank Stella* (Cambridge, MA: Fogg Art Museum, 1965).

Larry Poons

AMERICAN, B. 1937 | Born in Ogibuko, Japan, to American parents, Poons studied at Boston's New England Conservatory of Music and School of the Museum of Fine Arts. He received national acclaim when he was included in the Museum of Modern Art's 1965 exhibition *The Responsive Eye*, which included his iconic paintings of elliptical dots of intense color arranged along grids.

These paintings take the visual experiments of Kenneth

Larry Poons with *Untitled*, 1973

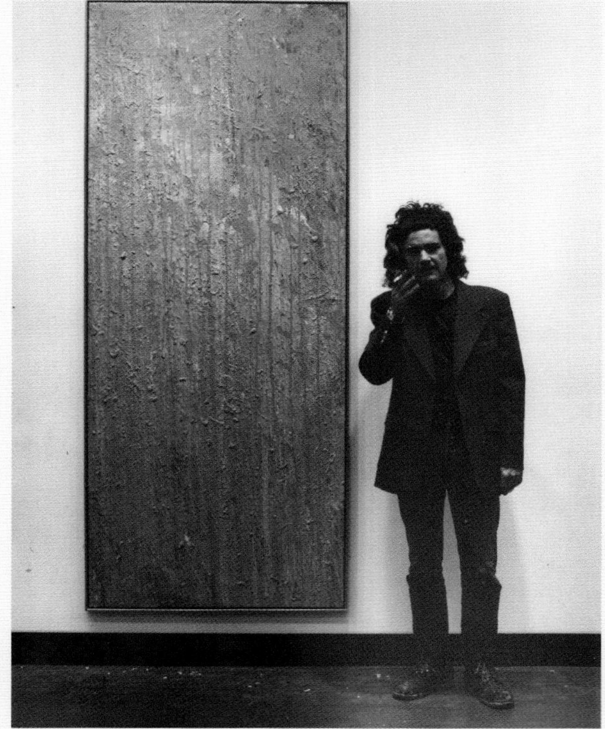

Noland and Bridget Riley to the extreme. By creating a kind of optical flickering with colored dots on colored fields (often the complementary color of the dots), his compositions elicit retinal afterimages and display a thoroughly modern approach to compositional structure. Influenced by Mondrian's experiments with color and composition, Poons's highly graphic style was a strong influence on the Op Art that followed. By 1966, however, his palette softened and he was experimenting with subtle variations in harmonious color.

In the 1970s, Poons began his "thrown" paintings. These dense waterfalls of color and paint were influenced by the work of Pollock and Morris Louis while offering another wholly fresh vision of how paintings could be structured with color. Poons's paintings often espouse a world of contradictions. In the early 1970s, critic Michael Fried wrote: "But while the paint substance tends for the most part toward separateness, stratification, and the suggestion of temporal sequence, the paint color tends on the contrary toward unity, immediacy, simultaneity. The result is a contest between the heightened, or deepened, tactility of the picture surface and the warm, mostly intense color that seems everywhere to lie beneath that surface and to erupt through it into visibility. And the result of that is an unprecedented, because multiples, declaration of surface: as if the different layers, brought forward by color and comprising the total material contents of the painting, themselves compete for presentness across its entire expanse."[1]

Recently, Poons has returned to the use of the brush, without diminishing his interest in texture and color. In his most recent work, he creates maelstroms of line and color on canvases that allude to representation without offering wholly recognizable forms. His exuberant paintings abound in explosive, broken color, applied in staccato, allover rhythms. Poons has become an influential teacher at the Art Students League and the New York Studio School of Drawing, Painting & Sculpture.

1 Michael Fried, "Larry Poons's New Paintings," *Artforum* 10 (March 1972): 50–52.

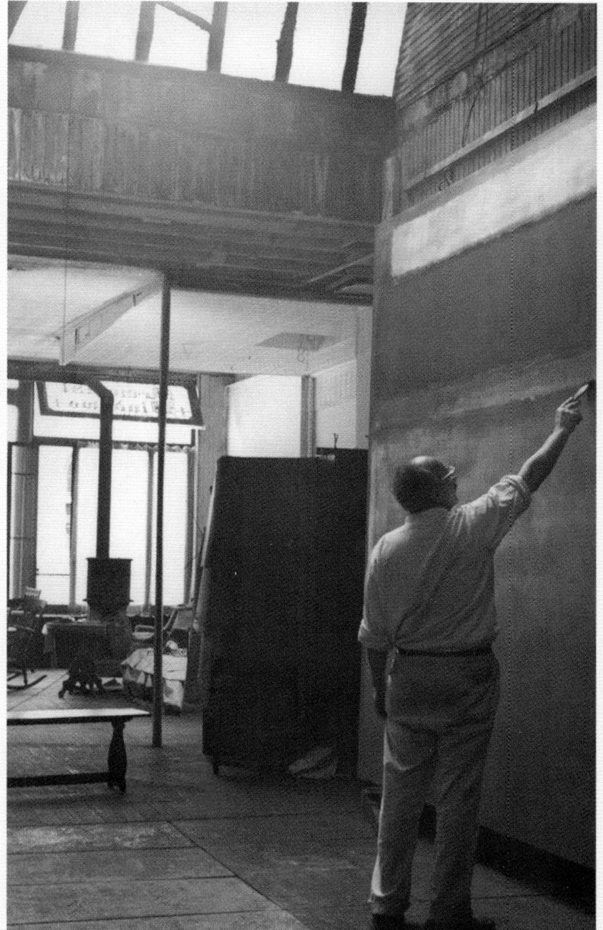

Mark Rothko in his 53rd Street studio, ca. 1953

Mark Rothko

AMERICAN, 1903–1970 | Born in Dvinsk, Russia (now Daugavpils, Latvia), Mark Rothko (born Marcus Rothkowitz) was sent to study the Talmud at the age of five. He immigrated with his family to Portland, Oregon, in 1913. A decade later, after a short period at Yale University, he left college to move to New York. One day, while visiting a friend at the Art Students League, he witnessed students sketching a nude model and began to consider becoming an artist. He studied with Arshile Gorky at the New School of Design and with Max Weber at the Art Students League. Rothko's earliest work reveals a strong Weberian influence, and it was from Weber that he seems to have gained an understanding of color as an emotional tool. At this time, Rothko's paintings were often moody and expressionistic.

In the 1920s, Rothko began giving art classes at the Center Academy, where he continued to teach until 1952. During this period he became one of a small group of artists, including Adolph Gottlieb, John Graham, and Barnett Newman, who gathered around the painter Milton Avery. The group socialized and vacationed together and enjoyed animated conversations about every aspect of art.

Rothko had his first one-man show at the Contemporary Arts Gallery. His portraits, which demonstrated a sophisticated treatment of color, received critical attention. His next works were more Surrealist in tone, inhabited by mythological and archetypical subjects that often utilized psychoanalytic imagery. During the Depression, Rothko, like other artists of his generation, found employment at various government programs, including the Works Progress Administration (WPA).

Soon after, Rothko discovered the writings of Friedrich

Nietzsche. Nietzsche's observations about the loss of myth in Western culture interested Rothko, and with these ideas in mind, in the early 1940s, he and his artist colleagues, especially Adolph Gottlieb, began to explore mythological subjects in ways dominated by their growing interest in form, space, and color.

About this time, Rothko suffered a long depression, after divorcing his wife. He returned to Portland and later traveled to Berkeley, where he met and became friends with Clyfford Still. In the fall of 1943 he returned to New York and exhibited at Peggy Guggenheim's Art of This Century gallery. He married Mary Alice Beistle (Mell) in 1945.

In 1946, Rothko began to create his Multiform paintings. Highly abstract works with an organic structure, these paintings demonstrate an important transition to the artist's mature style.

Rothko's 1949 show at Betty Parsons Gallery marked the beginning of his mature style. The vertical oil paintings shown were composed of symmetrical rectangular blocks of two or three colors. He chose not to title the works individually but rather to number each one. Rothko shied away from the abstractionist and colorist labels, preferring to emphasize his art's ability to communicate human emotions. He emphasized the spiritual aspect of his paintings, a sentiment that culminated in his ability to convince art patrons John and Dominique de Menil to construct the ecumenical Rothko Chapel in Houston, which opened in 1971.

Despite his growing artistic and financial success, Rothko's personal life was far from perfect. He became estranged from Newman and Still and seems to have felt a growing sense of alienation from family and friends. Slowly his palette began to shift from bright reds and yellows to darker hues, particularly black.

In 1958, Rothko was asked to create wall paintings for the Four Seasons restaurant on New York's Park Avenue. It was his first site-specific commission, but eventually, dismayed by the commercial setting, he refused to finish the project, returning the advance and dispersing the completed canvases to museums in London, Washington, D.C., and Chiba, Japan. During the 1960s, Rothko battled the alcoholism that contributed to the disintegration of his second marriage and eventual divorce. In the spring of 1968, Rothko suffered an aneurysm of the aorta. Ignoring doctor's orders, he continued to drink and smoke heavily. He committed suicide on February 25, 1970, at the age of sixty-six. Many of his late works are considered poetic expressions of the tragic sublime.

Frank Stella

AMERICAN, B. 1936 | Stella was born in Malden, Massachusetts, and studied at Phillips Academy, Andover, Massachusetts, an academic institution known for its superb museum, the Addison Gallery of American Art. Stella took some of his first art classes at Andover but concentrated on history at Princeton University, although he also took William Seitz's and Stephen Greene's art classes. Greene, in particular, had a powerful influence on Stella, and they remained close friends until Greene's death in 1999.

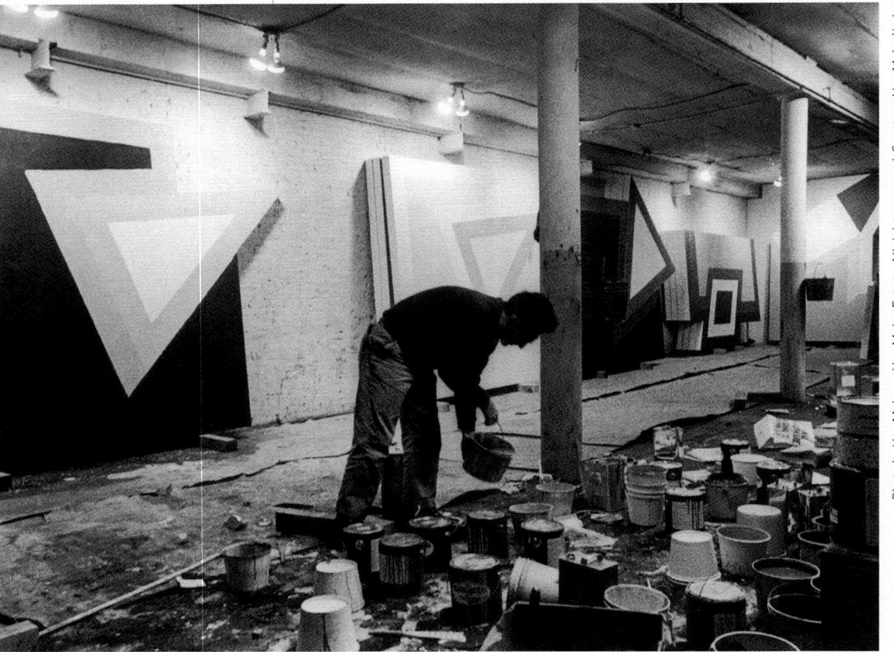

Frank Stella in his Walker Street studio, ca. 1965

Stella's first influence was the Abstract Expressionism of Jackson Pollock and Franz Kline, but after moving to New York in 1958, he found himself drawn to the work of Barnett Newman and Jasper Johns. He began to produce works that emphasized the picture-as-object and rejected the notion that a picture had to be a physical or visceral representation. He famously declared that painting was "a flat surface with paint on it—nothing more." This new aesthetic found expression in a series of Black Paintings that were composed of broad bands of black paint interrupted by thin pinstripes of unpainted canvas. Many of these works had coded references to Nazi Germany, including *Die Fahne Hoch!* (1959), which derives its name from a Hitler Youth anthem and uses the same proportions as banners used by that organization. The title also alludes to Jasper Johns's paintings of flags and has been interpreted as Stella's "throwing down of the gauntlet" regarding the role of painting and its representational possibilities. These Black Paintings opened new paths for abstraction and influenced the future development of Color Field painting and Minimalism.

In an essay for a 1965 exhibition titled *Three American Painters*, critic Michael Fried explained that Stella's art flowered from those pioneering Black Paintings: "In subsequent series of paintings executed in aluminum, copper, and purple metallic paint...Stella's grasp of deductive structure grew more and more tough-minded, until the paintings came to be generated in toto, as it were, by the different shapes of the framing edge, and variations occurred only within the series as a whole rather than within a particular shape of canvas."[1]

Throughout the 1960s, Stella made paintings that used a wider range of colors and shapes —he was an innovator of the shaped canvas—adopting extremely eccentric configurations generated by rows of folded or nested stripes. These explorations developed into the more elaborate structures of the series Irregular Polygons, beginning in 1966, and the rainbow-like Protractors, of 1967, which depend on complex arrangements of arcs, circles, and interlocking rings of intense color. Stella began exploring the possibilities of printmaking beginning in the late 1960s and was a pioneer of the offset lithography technique.

Since the 1970s, Stella has been increasingly fascinated by what he sees as the continuing struggle between real and fictive illusion in Western painting, a theme thoroughly dissected in the Charles Eliot Norton lectures he delivered at Harvard University in 1983–84 (published in 1986 as *Working Space*). He introduced collage, graffiti, and three-dimensional forms into his paintings, eventually utilizing an array of industrial materials to create relief-like works that projected so far from the wall as to resemble sculpture more than painting. By the 1980s, Stella's forms were rougher and more aggressive than in his previous work and often painted in strong color combinations that challenged the viewer. In 1993, Stella was commissioned to produce murals and decorations for the proscenium, dome, and boxes of the Princess of Wales Theatre in Toronto, Canada. Following this project, he opened a Toronto studio for the purpose of building large-scale projects. He has also been commissioned to produce architecture, including a bandshell for the city of Miami.

In recent years, Stella has investigated the possibilities of fully three-dimensional metal sculptures, exhibiting them since 2003 at Paul Kasmin Gallery in Manhattan. Composed of aluminum, tubing, and stainless steel, Stella's recent work is focused on sculptural issues of volume, profiles, and textures, in contrast to the coloristic and painterly concerns that once preoccupied him. Stella lives and works in New York.

1 "Three American Painters: Kenneth Noland, Jules Olitski, Frank Stella" (1965), in Michael Fried, *Art and Objecthood: Essays and Reviews* (Chicago: University of Chicago Press, 1998), 251–52.

Clyfford Still

AMERICAN, 1904–1980 | A first-generation Abstract Expressionist, Still was a precursor to the Color Field painters and their experiments with bolts of rich vertical color. Born in Grandin, North Dakota, Still attended Spokane University in Washington. After graduation, he taught at Washington State College in Pullman, Washington. He spent the summers of 1934 and 1935 at the Trask Foundation (now Yaddo) in Saratoga Springs, New York. In 1943, his first solo exhibition was held at the San Francisco Museum of Art; during the same period, he met Mark Rothko in Berkeley, California.

Still's early works are influenced by Surrealism but also begin to explore pure abstraction. After World War II, the artist entered what has been termed his "breakthrough period" of high abstraction in a large format. He was a pioneer of mural-sized canvases that concentrated on sensations of pure color. Still's mature work is characterized by vast fields of color with jagged edges.

When Still was in New York in 1945, he met Peggy Guggenheim and had a solo exhibition at her Art of This Century gallery the following year. When he returned to San Francisco, he began teaching at the California School of Fine Arts. Solo exhibitions of his work were held at the Betty Parsons Gallery, New York, in 1947, 1950, and 1951 and at the California Palace of the Legion of Honor, San Francisco, in 1947. In 1948, Still returned to New York and worked with Rothko, Robert Motherwell, William Baziotes, and others to develop the school known as Subjects of the Artist. In 1959, a Still retrospective was held at the Albright-Knox Art Gallery, Buffalo. The artist spent time in New York and San Francisco before finally settling in Maryland in 1961.

Still did not like his pictures to be separated from one another or exhibited with work by other artists. He felt his paintings could only be understood as part of a whole. His obsession with maintaining total control resulted in his rejecting offers to buy his paintings and declining invitations to exhibit. The Clyfford Still Museum, slated to open in Denver in 2009, will house more than 2,150 works from the Clyfford Still Estate.

Exhibition Checklist

WALTER DARBY BANNARD

Yellow Rose #4, 1965
Acrylic on canvas
68 x 62 inches
Private Collection; courtesy Jacobson Howard Gallery, New York
Plate 35

China Spring #3, 1969
Alkyd resin on canvas
66 ⅛ x 99 ¼ inches
The Baltimore Museum of Art; National Endowment for the Arts and Matching Trustee Funds (BMA 1972.11)
Plate 36

JACK BUSH

Orange Centre, 1964
Oil on canvas
81 x 68 ½ inches
Art Gallery of Alberta Collection, Edmonton (79.22)
Plate 37

Burgundy, 1968
Acrylic on canvas
84 x 68 inches
Collection Cam Allard, Edmonton
Plate 38

Red Pink Cross, 1973
Acrylic on canvas
66 ¼ x 89 inches
Private collection; courtesy Foley Hoag LLP, Boston
Plate 39

GENE DAVIS

Sun Ball, 1960
Magna on canvas
88 x 93 ⅝ inches
Courtesy Charles Cowles Gallery, New York
Plate 34

RONALD DAVIS

Double Pink Slab, 1969
Polyester resin
58 x 129 inches
Collection Mr. and Mrs. David Mirvish, Toronto
Plate 41

FRIEDEL DZUBAS

Lotus, 1962
Oil on canvas
80 ½ x 68 ½ inches
Estate of Friedel Dzubas; courtesy Jacobson Howard Gallery, New York
Plate 32

Trough, 1972
Synthetic polymer on canvas
96 ¼ x 98 ⅜ inches
Hirshhorn Museum and Sculpture Garden, Smithsonian Institution, Washington, D.C.; museum purchase with funds donated by the Smithsonian Resident Associates Program, 1975
Plate 33

SAM FRANCIS

Blue Balls, 1960
Oil on canvas
90 ⅝ x 79 ⅛ inches
Smithsonian American Art Museum; gift of S. C. Johnson & Son, Inc. (1968.52.17)
Plate 14

HELEN FRANKENTHALER

Seven Types of Ambiguity, 1957
Oil on canvas
95 ½ x 70 ⅛ inches
Private collection
Plate 8

Interior Landscape, 1964
Acrylic on canvas
104 ⅞ x 92 ⅞ inches
San Francisco Museum of Modern Art; gift of the Women's Board (68.52)
Plate 9

Flood, 1967
Synthetic polymer on canvas
124 x 140 inches
Whitney Museum of American Art, New York; purchase, with funds from the Friends of the Whitney Museum of American Art (68.12)
Plate 10

Off White Square, 1973
Acrylic on canvas
79½ x 235 inches
Greenberg Van Doren Gallery, New York; Bernard Jacobson Gallery, London; Leslie Feely Fine Art, New York
Plate 11

SAM GILLIAM
Green Web, 1967
Acrylic on canvas
90½ x 39¾ inches
Smithsonian American Art Museum; gift of the Woodward Foundation (1977.48.3)
Plate 40

ADOLPH GOTTLIEB
Sentinel, 1951
Oil on linen
60 x 48 inches
Adolph and Esther Gottlieb Foundation, New York
Plate 12

One, Two, Three, 1964
Oil on canvas
132 x 78 inches
Adolph and Esther Gottlieb Foundation, New York
Plate 13

HANS HOFMANN
Yellow Hymn, 1954
Oil on canvas
50 x 40 inches
The Renate, Hans and Maria Hofmann Trust; courtesy Ameringer & Yohe Fine Art, New York
Plate 4

Gray Monolith, 1963
Oil on canvas
72 x 60 inches
The Renate, Hans and Maria Hofmann Trust; courtesy Ameringer & Yohe Fine Art, New York
Plate 5

MORRIS LOUIS
Loam, 1958
Acrylic on canvas
90¾ x 148 inches
The Museum of Fine Arts, Houston; museum purchase with funds provided by the Brown Foundation Accessions Endowment Fund (76.319)
Plate 15

Mem, 1959
Acrylic on canvas
97 x 140 inches
Collection Virginia and Bagley Wright, Seattle
Plate 16

Floral V, 1959–60
Acrylic and magna on canvas
98⅜ x 137¹³⁄₁₆ inches
Private collection, Denver
Plate 17

Theta, 1961
Acrylic resin (Magna) on canvas
102 x 168 inches
Museum of Fine Arts, Boston; anonymous gift (67.623)
Plate 18

ROBERT MOTHERWELL
Chi Ama, Crede, 1962
Oil on canvas
82 x 141 inches
The Phillips Collection, Washington, D.C.; purchased by The Phillips Collection through funds donated by The Judith Rothschild Foundation, Mr. and Mrs. Gifford Phillips, The Chisholm Foundation, The Whitehead Foundation, Mr. and Mrs. Laughlin Phillips, Mr. and Mrs. Marc E. Leland, and the Honorable Ann Winkelman Brown and Donald Brown, 1998
Plate 6

Open 165, 1970
Acrylic on canvas
53½ x 108 inches
Collection Mr. and Mrs. David Mirvish, Toronto
Plate 7

BARNETT NEWMAN
Horizon Light, 1949
Oil on canvas
30½ x 72½ inches
Sheldon Memorial Art Gallery, University of Nebraska-Lincoln, UNL; Gift of Mr. and Mrs. Thomas Sills (1974.U-1184)
Plate 2

KENNETH NOLAND
Earthen Bound, 1960
Acrylic on canvas
103 ½ x 103 ½ inches
Courtesy the artist
Plate 19

Dark Sweet Cherry, 1966
Acrylic on canvas, diamond
56 x 70 inches (point to point)
Collection Mr. and Mrs. David Mirvish, Toronto
Plate 20

Space Jog, 1970
Acrylic on canvas
74 ⅜ x 126 inches
Collection Mr. and Mrs. David Mirvish, Toronto
Plate 21

Following Sea, 1974
Acrylic on canvas, diamond
98 ¼ x 98 ¼ inches (point to point)
Collection Mr. and Mrs. David Mirvish, Toronto
Plate 22

JULES OLITSKI
Cleopatra Flesh, 1962
Synthetic polymer paint on canvas
104 x 90 inches
The Museum of Modern Art, New York; gift of G. David Thompson, 1964 (262.1964)
Plate 23

Tin Lizzie Green, 1964
Alkyd and oil/wax crayon on canvas
130 x 82 inches
Museum of Fine Arts, Boston; purchased with the aid of funds from the National Endowment for the Arts (1977.617)
Plate 24

Julius and Friends, 1967
Acrylic on canvas
71 ½ x 149 ¾ inches
Private collection; courtesy Foley Hoag LLP, Boston
Plate 25

Greek Princess—8, 1976
Acrylic on canvas
102 ⅛ x 132 ¼ inches
Hirshhorn Museum and Sculpture Garden, Smithsonian Institution, Washington, D.C.; museum purchase, 1976
Plate 26

LARRY POONS
Han-San Cadence, 1963
Acrylic and fabric dye on canvas
72 x 144 inches
Des Moines Art Center; purchased with funds from the Coffin Fine Arts Trust; Nathan Emory Coffin Collection of the Des Moines Art Center (1970.19)
Plate 29

Untitled, 1969
Acrylic on canvas
153 x 101 inches
The Museum of Contemporary Art, Los Angeles; gift of Ronald Davis (83.35)
Plate 30

Yellow and Brown Womb, 1972
Acrylic on canvas
118 x 73 ½ inches
Collection Mr. and Mrs. David Mirvish, Toronto
Plate 31

MARK ROTHKO
Number 18, 1951
Oil on canvas
81 ½ x 69 ⅞ inches
Munson-Williams-Proctor Arts Institute, Museum of Art, Utica, NY (53.216)
Plate 1

FRANK STELLA
Moultonville II, 1966
Fluorescent alkyd and epoxy paint on canvas
124 x 86 inches
Collection Mr. and Mrs. David Mirvish, Toronto
Plate 27

Flin Flon IV, 1969
Polymer and fluorescent polymer paint on canvas
96 ½ x 96 ½ inches
National Gallery of Art, Washington, D.C.; Robert and Jane Meyerhoff Collection (1994.82.1)
Plate 28

CLYFFORD STILL
Untitled, 1965
Oil on canvas
111 ¾ x 89 inches
Private collection, Denver
Plate 3

Selected Bibliography

Agee, William C. *Sam Francis: Paintings, 1947–1990*. Exhib. cat. Los Angeles: Museum of Contemporary Art, 1999.

Ashton, Dore. *Twentieth Century Artists on Art*. New York: Pantheon Books, 1985.

Ashton, Dore, and Jack D. Flam. *Robert Motherwell*. Exhib. cat. New York: Albright-Knox Art Gallery and Abbeville Press, 1983.

Brown, Julia, and Susan Cross. *After "Mountains and Sea": Frankenthaler 1956–1959*. Exhib. cat. New York: Solomon R. Guggenheim Museum, 1998.

Doty, Robert, and Diane Waldman. *Adolph Gottlieb*. Exhib. cat. New York: Whitney Museum of American Art and Solomon R. Guggenheim Museum, 1968.

Elderfield, John. *Morris Louis*. Exhib. cat. New York: Museum of Modern Art, 1986.

——. *Helen Frankenthaler*. New York: Harry N. Abrams, 1989.

Fried, Michael. *Morris Louis*. New York: Harry N. Abrams, 1979.

——. *Art and Objecthood: Essays and Reviews*. Chicago: University of Chicago Press, 1998.

Geldzahler, Henry. "An Interview with Helen Frankenthaler." *Artforum*, October 1965, 36–38.

Greenberg, Clement. *Clement Greenberg: The Collected Essays and Criticism*. Edited by John O'Brian. Chicago: University of Chicago Press, Vols. 1 and 2, 1986, Vols. 3 and 4, 1993.

Lippard, Lucy R. (ed.). "Questions to Stella and Judd." *Art News*, September 1966, 55–61.

Moffett, Kenworth. *Kenneth Noland*. New York: Harry N. Abrams, 1977.

——. *Jules Olitski*. New York: Harry N. Abrams, 1981.

——. *Larry Poons: Paintings, 1971–81*. Exhib. cat. Boston: Museum of Fine Arts, 1981.

O'Neill, John P. (ed.). *Clyfford Still*. Exhib. cat. New York: The Metropolitan Museum of Art, 1979.

Rose, Barbara. *Frankenthaler*. New York: Harry N. Abrams, 1971.

Rubin, William S. *Frank Stella*. Exhib. cat. New York: Museum of Modern Art, 1970.

Temkin, Ann (ed.). *Barnett Newman*. Exhib. cat. Philadelphia: Philadelphia Museum of Art, 2002.

Upright, Diane. *Morris Louis: The Complete Paintings*. New York: Harry N. Abrams, 1985.

Waldman, Diane. *Kenneth Noland: A Retrospective*. Exhib. cat. New York: Solomon R. Guggenheim Museum, 1977.

——. *Mark Rothko 1903–1970: A Retrospective*. Exhib. cat. New York: Solomon R. Guggenheim Museum, 1979.

Wilkin, Karen. *Frankenthaler: Works on Paper 1949–1984*. Exhib. cat. New York and Washington, D.C.: George Braziller and International Exhibitions Foundation, 1984.

——. *Kenneth Noland*. New York: Rizzoli International Publications, 1990.

——. *Hans Hofmann*. New York: George Braziller, 2003.

——. *Jules Olitski: Six Decades*. Exhib. cat. Miami: The Goldman Warehouse, 2005.

Wilkin, Karen (ed.). *Jack Bush*. Toronto: McClelland and Stewart, 1984.

Index

Photography Credits

PLATE 1: © 2006 Kate Rothko Prizel & Christopher Rothko/ Artists Rights Society (ARS), New York

PLATE 2: © 2006 Barnett Newman Foundation / Artists Rights Society (ARS), New York

PLATE 3: Photograph Denver Art Museum, 2006, © The Clyfford Still Estate

PLATES 4 & 5: © 2006 Estate of Hans Hofmann/Artists Rights Society (ARS), New York

PLATE 6: Photograph Steven Sloman, Art © Dedalus Foundation, Inc./Licensed by VAGA, New York, NY

PLATE 7: Photograph Sean Weaver, Art © Dedalus Foundation, Inc./Licensed by VAGA, New York, NY

PLATE 8: © 2007 Helen Frankenthaler

PLATE 9: Photograph Don Meyer, © 2007 Helen Frankenthaler

PLATE 10: Photograph Geoffrey Clements, © 2007 Helen Frankenthaler

PLATE 11: © 2007 Helen Frankenthaler

PLATE 12: Photograph Jordan Tinker, Art © The Adolph and Esther Gottlieb Foundation/Licensed by VAGA, New York, NY

PLATE 13: Photograph Ellen Page Wilson; courtesy PaceWildenstein, New York, Art © The Adolph and Esther Gottlieb Foundation/Licensed by VAGA, New York, NY

PLATE 14: © 2006 Samuel L. Francis Foundation, California / Artists Rights Society (ARS), NY

PLATE 15: © 1958 Morris Louis

PLATE 16: © 1959 Morris Louis

PLATE 17: © 1993 Marcella Louis Brenner

PLATE 18: Photograph © 2007 Museum of Fine Arts, Boston, © 1961 Morris Louis

PLATE 19: Art © Ken Noland/Licensed by VAGA, New York, NY

PLATES 20–22: Photograph Sean Weaver, Art © Ken Noland/ Licensed by VAGA, New York, NY

PLATE 23: Digital Image © The Museum of Modern Art/ Licensed by SCALA/Art Resource, NY, Art © Jules Olitski/ Licensed by VAGA, New York, NY

PLATE 24: Photograph © 2007 Museum of Fine Arts, Boston, Art © Jules Olitski/Licensed by VAGA, New York, NY

PLATE 25: Photograph Dennis Griggs, Art © Jules Olitski/ Licensed by VAGA, New York, NY

PLATE 26: Photograph Lee Stalsworth, Art © Jules Olitski/ Licensed by VAGA, New York, NY

PLATE 27: Photograph Sean Weaver, © 2006 Frank Stella/ Artists Rights Society (ARS), New York

PLATE 28: © 2006 Frank Stella / Artists Rights Society (ARS), New York

PLATE 29: Photograph Michael Tropea, Art © Larry Poons/ Licensed by VAGA, New York, NY

PLATE 30: Photograph Squidds & Nunns, Art © Larry Poons/ Licensed by VAGA, New York, NY

PLATE 31: Photograph Sean Weaver, Art © Larry Poons/ Licensed by VAGA, New York, NY

PLATE 32: © 2007 Estate of Friedel Dzubas

PLATE 33: Photograph Lee Stalsworth, © 2007 Estate of Friedel Dzubas

PLATE 35 & 36: Art © Walter Darby Bannard/Licensed by VAGA, New York, NY

PLATE 37: © 2006 Artists Rights Society (ARS), New York/ SODRAC, Montreal

PLATE 38: Photograph Eric Haug, © 2006 Artists Rights Society (ARS), New York/SODRAC, Montreal

PLATE 39: Photograph Dennis Griggs, © 2006 Artists Rights Society (ARS), New York/SODRAC, Montreal

PLATE 41: Photograph Sean Weaver

American Federation of Arts Board of Trustees